The Political and Economic Transition in East Asia

The Political and Economic Transition in East Asia

Strong Market, Weakening State

Edited by

Xiaoming Huang

Routledge
Taylor & Francis Group
LONDON AND NEW YORK

First published in 2001
by Curzon Press

This edition published 2011
by Routledge
2 Park Square, Milton Park, Abingdon, Oxon OX14 4RN

Simultaneously published in the USA and Canada
by Routledge
711 Third Avenue, New York, NY 10017

Routledge is an imprint of the Taylor & Francis Group, an informa business

First issued in paperback 2011

Typeset in Garamond by LaserScript Ltd, Mitcham, Surrey

British Library Cataloguing in Publication Data
A catalogue record for this book is available from the British Library

ISBN: 978-0-700-71221-2 (hbk)

ISBN: 978-0-415-51523-8 (pbk)

To Tina

Contents

List of Tables

List of Figures

List of Abbreviations

ABC	Agricultural Bank of China, China
ADB	Asian Development Bank
AFP	Agency France Press, France
AMCs	Asian Model Countries
AMEs	Asian Model Economies
AMF	Asian Monetary Fund
APE	Asia Pacific Entrepôt
APEC	Asian-Pacific Economic Cooperation
ARF	ASEAN Regional Forum
ASEAN	Association of Southeast Asian Nations
BIS	Bank of International Settlements
CASS	Chinese Academy of Social Sciences, China
CBC	Construction Bank of China, China
CBN	*China Business News*, China
CCP	Chinese Communist Party, China
CD	*China Daily*, China
CDBW	*China Daily Business Weekly*, China
CEPD	Council on Economic Planning and Development, Taiwan
CET	*China Economic Times*, China
CMEI	*China Monthly Exports & Imports*, China
CPI	Consumer Price Index
CQ	*China Quarterly*
CT	*Zhongguo shibao [China Times]*, Taiwan
CTEN	*Zhongshi wanbao [China Times Evening News]*, Taiwan
DGB	*Da Gong Bao*, Hong Kong
DJN	*The Dow Jones News*, New York.
DJP	*Dow Jones Press*, New York
DPP	Democratic Progressive Party, Taiwan
EAEC	East Asian Economic Caucus

EPZs	Export Processing Zones
ETDZs	Economic and Technological Development Zones, China
EU	European Union
FCJ	*Free China Journal*
FCR	*Free China Review*
FDI	Foreign Direct Investment
FEER	*Far Eastern Economic Review*
FIEs	Foreign-Invested Enterprises
FSA	Financial Supervisory Agency, Japan
FSC	Financial Supervisory Committee, South Korea
FTZs	Free Trade Zones
G7	Group of Seven Industrialised Nations
GATT	General Agreement on Tariffs and Trade
GDP	Gross Domestic Product
GITIC	Guangdong International Trust and Investment Corp, China
GNP	Gross National Product
HKS	*Hong Kong Standard*, Hong Kong
HSIP	Hsinchu Science Industrial Park, Taiwan
ICBC	Industrial and Commercial Bank of China, China
IFC	*Industry of Free China*, Taiwan
IMF	International Monetary Fund
IT	Information and Technology
ITICs	International Trust and Investment Corporations, China
JSP	Japanese Socialist Party, Japan
KEIA	Korea Economic Institute of America, Korea
KMT	Nationalist Party, Taiwan
KNI	*Kyoto News International*, Korea
KT	*Korea Times*, Korea
LDP	Liberal Democratic Party, Japan
MAC	Mainland Affairs Council, Taiwan
MCA	Ministry of Civil Affairs, China
MITI	Ministry of International Trade and Industry, Japan
MOEA	Ministry of Economic Affairs, Taiwan
MOF	Ministry of Finance, various countries
MOFA	Ministry of Foreign Affairs, various countries
MOFE	Ministry of Finance and Economy, South Korea
MOFTEC	Ministry of Foreign Trade and Economic Cooperation, China
MPs	Members of Parliament
MSF	Market Stabilisation Fund, Taiwan
NATO	North Atlantic Treaty Organisation
NIEs	Newly Industrialising Economies

NPC	National People's Congress, China
NSC	National Science Council, Taiwan
NT	New Taiwanese Dollar (Currency of Taiwan)
NYT	*New York Times,* United States
ODA	Official Development Assistance, Japan
OECD	Organisation of Economic Cooperation and Development
PBOC	People's Bank of China, China
PRC	People's Republic of China
R&D	Research and Development
RMB	*Renminbi* (Currency of China)
SAFE	State Administration of Foreign Exchanges, China
SCMP	*South China Morning Post,* Hong Kong
SEF	Straits Exchange Foundation, Taiwan
SETC	State Economic and Trade Commission, China
SEZs	Special Economic Zones
SMEs	Small and Medium-sized Enterprises
SOEs	State-Owned Enterprises
SSB	State Statistical Bureau, China
SSN	*The Shanghai Securities News,* China
TVEs	Township and Village Enterprises
USCBC	United States-China Business Council
VAT	Value Added Tax
WJ	*Shijie Ribao* [World Journal], United States
WP	*Washington Post,* United States
WTO	World Trade Organization
Xinhua	New China News Agency, China

List of Contributors

Seiji Endo is Associate Professor of International Relations, Seikei University, Tokyo, Japan. He received his LLM in international relations from the University of Tokyo, before joining the Faculty of Law at Seikei University. He has also held academic positions at St. Antony's College, Oxford and Wellesley College in Massachusetts, USA. His teaching and research interests are in the areas of international political economy, globalisation and the changing structure of world politics, and the political economy of conflicts in the post-Cold War era. Professor Endo publishes widely in these areas, both in English and Japanese, a recent article being 'East Asian Security: Issues in the Post-Cold War Era' in *East Asian Economies in Transformation: Experiences and Issues* (1995).

Stephen P. Green is a PhD candidate in Government at the London School of Economics and Political Science, London, UK. He is also an Associate Fellow of the Asia Programme at the Royal Institute of International Affairs in London. His PhD research is in the politics of equity market development in the People's Republic of China. Forthcoming publications include 'Negotiating with the Future: the Culture of Modern Risk in Global Financial Markets' in *Society and Space*, and a book chapter on financial market policy reactions to the Asia crisis.

Peter Harris is Associate Professor of Asian Studies and Director of the Asian Studies Institute at Victoria University of Wellington, Wellington, New Zealand. He received his BA in Oriental Studies and MPhil in International Relations from Oxford University. Before taking up his current position, he was the founding Director of the Asia 2000 Foundation of New Zealand and Representative of the Ford Foundation in China. His research interests include the social consequences of reform in China, rights and governance issues in developing states, and the history of modern Chinese political thought. Recent publications include review articles on the development of Chinese nationalism in *The China Journal* and *Asia Pacific Viewpoint*, and an essay on the impact of the reform process in China on rights, law and governance, published in Stockholm as part of a book-length study of reform in Asia by the Swedish Foreign Ministry.

Xiaoming Huang is Lecturer in East Asian Politics, School of Political Science and International Relations, Victoria University of Wellington, Wellington, New Zealand. He received his LLB and LLM from Peking University, Beijing, and PhD from the University of Southern California, Los Angeles. Before joining Victoria University he had held various teaching and research positions at the East-West Center, Honolulu; the United Nations University, Tokyo; the Wilson International Center for Scholars, Washington, DC; the Center for International Studies/Pacific Council on International Policy, Los Angeles; the University of Tampere, Finland; the University of Trondheim, Norway; and the University of Pittsburgh. Dr Huang teaches East Asian politics, comparative political economy of Pacific Asia, and the institutional and cultural foundation of governance in East Asia. His current research projects include a book-length manuscript on the conditions and consequences of the Asian model. Dr Huang's recent publications include an article in *International Studies Quarterly* (1997) and a book, *Taiwan Revisited: Politics, Society, Economy and Cross-strait Relations* (1996).

Kwan S. Kim is Professor of Economics, University of Notre Dame, Indiana, USA. He is a development economist, occasionally serving as an economic consultant for governments of developing countries and for international agencies. His career includes four years as a Rockefeller Foundation scholar in Kenya and Tanzania; two years as a senior economist with the US Agency for International Development; a semester at the Universidad Autonoma de Nuevo León in Mexico, the Maastricht School of Management, and the American Graduate School of Business in Arizona; a year as a Monbusho scholar at Hitotsubashi Institute of Economic Research in Tokyo; and short stints as a researcher and consultant at East-West Center in Hawaii, the Hudson Institute, UNIDO in Vienna, the National Productivity Center in Singapore, and National Finance in Mexico. He has published extensively in over fifty professional journals in the areas of development studies, international economics, and quantitative analysis. His publications include *The State, Markets and Development* (1994), *Economic Cooperation and Integration: East Asian Experience* (1997), and *Growth, Distribution and Political Change: Asia and the Wider World* (1999).

Christopher Lingle is Visiting Associate Professor of Economics, Case West Reserve University, Cleveland, USA. He earned his doctorate in economics from the University of Georgia and has held various teaching and research positions since then at Emory University, Georgia State University, the National University of Singapore, the European Center of Miami University in Luxembourg, Centre Universitaire de Luxembourg, the University of Natal in South Africa and the Shanghai University of Finance and Economics. Dr Lingle's research focuses on the processes of marketisation and democratisation in authoritarian regimes as well as the relationship between democracy and economic development. His work has appeared widely as chapters in books, in the international press, and in numerous scholarly journals, including *Singapore's Authoritarian Capitalism: Asian Values, Free Market Illusions, and Political Dependency* (1996) and *The Rise and Decline of the Asian Century: False Starts on the Road to the Global Millennium* (1998).

Harry D. Shutt is an independent consultant based in London, UK. Mr Shutt received his BA from Oxford University and MA from the University of Warwick. Formerly with The Economist Intelligence Unit, Mr Shutt has been an independent economic consultant since 1979 with a particular interest in the developing world. He has worked extensively in South East Asia, Sub-Saharan Africa, the Middle East, the Caribbean, and more recently, China and the former Soviet Union. He is the author of *The Myth of Free Trade. Patterns of protectionism since 1945* (1985), and *The Trouble with Capitalism: An Enquiry into the Causes of Global Economic Failure* (1998).

Shiping Zheng is Associate Professor of Political Science, The University of Vermont, USA. He received his MA from Fudan University in China and PhD from Yale University. He was a visiting scholar at the Harvard-Yenching Institute and has taught at Fudan, Northeastern, and McGill University. His research interests include Chinese politics, US-China relations, and East Asian political economy. His recent publication is *Party vs. State in Post-1949 China* (1997).

Preface

The initial idea for this book came from a panel at the International Convention of Asian Scholars, organised by the International Institute of Asian Studies, Leiden University and held in the summer of 1998 in the coastal town of Noordwijk, the Netherlands. With encouragement from the participants, it was decided to expand the panel papers and publish them as an edited volume. While I bear primary responsibility for organising the project and editing the book itself, this publication is the result of hard work and firm commitment by the contributors and the publisher. I therefore thank all my fellow contributors for their enthusiasm, patience and encouragement especially when, at times, things did not appear to be going well. I would also like to thank Jonathan Price at Curzon Press for his unfailing interest and support for the project, and Helga Lasschuijt of the IIAS for facilitating the original panel.

As with any other academic project, many have been involved who do not feature in the book's final form but without whose support and advice, or initial participation, this book could never have eventuated. On behalf of the contributors, I therefore thank Dr. Mark T. Berger of Murdoch University, Professor Mitchell Bernard of York University, Dr. David Bourchier of the University of Western Australia, Professor Alasdair Bowie of George Washington University, Professor Edward Friedman of the University of Wisconsin-Madison, Dr. Sheng Hong of Unirule Institute of Economics, Dr. David Martin Jones of the University of Tasmania, Dr. Douglas Kammen of the University of Canterbury, Professor Jacob Kovalio of Carleton University, Professor Andrew MacIntyre of UC San Diego, Professor Anthony Milner of Australian National University, Professor Ralph Pettman of Victoria University of Wellington, Professor Pasuk Phongpaichit of Chulalongkorn University, Dr. Steve Tsang of Oxford University, and Yoke Leng N. Thomas of Wel International.

On the administrative side, I thank the Faculty of Humanities and Social Sciences of Victoria University for the research grant and the conference leave grant which made it possible for me to travel to Leiden and Perth for conferences, and to work on the project itself. In particular, I thank Joy Aitken, Toni Geoghegan, Alison Munro, Patricia Stratton and Maureen West of the FHSS for their administrative support.

For research assistance, I thank Hannah Schmidt for her enthusiastic role. Needless to say, exchanges with my students in class also provided me with a tremendous source of ideas and inspiration. The final finishing touch to the book was elegantly provided by Adrienne Nolan. For her, this is only one small fraction of the administrative jungle she helps us survive on a daily basis.

I want to use this opportunity also to record my sincere gratitude to Associate Professor Stephen Levine and all my other colleagues at the School whose wise decision in late 1996 changed my life, for good. I want to thank Dr Gerald Chan for his advice and unfailing support that goes beyond the making of this book.

Finally, with the blessing of my fellow contributors, I dedicate this book to my daughter, Tina.

XMH
Kelburn, Wellington

PART 1

Introduction

CHAPTER ONE

Xiaoming Huang

Between the State and the Market: The Problem of Transition in East Asia

There used to be the strong state and the governed market in Asian Model countries, or AMCs.[1] The political and economic transition of the past 10 years or so, however, seems to have turned the tide around. Various forms of institutional restructuring, particularly the process of democratisation, have brought the state to its knees. On the other hand, renewed faith in the market as *the* solution to the problems of modern political and economic life, and the post-Cold War liberal movement, have lifted the market to a position formerly occupied by the state under the Asian Model. Thus, after 10 years of intensive and large-scale political and economic transition, we expect to see a reversal of the relationship between the state and market as the primary organiser of economic, and perhaps also political and social, activities.

This book is an assessment of such a transition. It is about the political and economic transition over the past decade in Korea, Taiwan, Japan and China, a region often referred to as East Asia, and the new political economy it has generated. The problem of transition in these countries had different sources. When China began the reform process in the late 1970s and early 1980s, it was an issue of 'deconstructing' the socialist system, whereas for both Korea and Taiwan in the 1980s, it was more an issue of transforming the political environment for a sustainable economic growth. Into the 1990s, Japan seemed to have reached a turning point in the evolution of the Asian Model of development.

Differing internal dynamics aside, the early years of the post-Cold War seemed to envisage a universal cure for the organising of economic and political life in the East Asian countries. This sense of universal cure was generated not only by the changing global balance of power and ideas at the end of the 1980s, but also by an apparent conversion of development strategies and institutional arrangements in these countries as a consequence of the reform, restructuring and democratic movements in

Korea, Taiwan and China during the 1980s. By the early 1990s, people felt sufficiently confident in referring to the particular system of development organisation and its related institutional arrangements as the Asian Model. Sharing the same model indicates the same method used by these AMEs to achieve the growth results. More importantly, it identifies the same problems and therefore demands the same universal cure.

The cure, put in the simplest way, sees as the root of the problems in these transitional economies and polities, the over-stretched state and the marginalised market. In IMF's terms, the problems in AMEs were the over-expansion of the public sector, budget deficit, central bank-driven inflation, and a weak currency. The immediate aims of the economic reform and institutional restructuring, therefore, were fiscal discipline, capital flow accountability, and the transforming of the state from the chief economic organiser and participant to a minimum provider of the regulatory environment in support of the function of the market. It began with a set of target institutions (a minimum state, an unrestricted market, a property-rights centred legal system, etc.) and the adaptation of the existing conditions for the working of these institutions (Sachs 1997).

Now, after a decade of political change, economic reform, and various experiments of institutional restructuring, dramatised by visionary expectations, obdurate resistances, continual tensions and alarming crises, the transition deserves an assessment. How much has the transition achieved of its original aims along the lines of the 'evil state' diagnosis? Have the AMEs moved from the state-dominated to the market-disciplined arrangements? What has the decade-long transition taught us about the conditions and consequences of East Asian development? What has been the pattern of political economy in the transition and how should we interpret the new institutional arrangements emerging from the transition?

The Case for An Assessment

The transition in East Asia has been widely seen as a key testing ground for the post-Cold War liberal movement. After the failures of fascism early this century, and those more recently of Communism, Asian development, along with all its eye-catching performance and unconventional ways of achieving it, has been an unusual challenge. For many observers, Asian development has been a successful mistake. The AMEs were able to 'manufacture' (Gertti and Wyman 1990) rapid economic growth and social development under the umbrella structure that challenges our long-held theories about economic dynamism, political change, modernisation and development. The transition in many ways has been seen as the termination of the Asian Model development. An examination of the transition and the emergent arrangements will help assess to what extent this is true.

This assessment is also important since any cursory survey of what happened in the region over the past decade would provide conflicting evidence in relation to some of the basic questions raised earlier. What we have witnessed in the AMEs was a mixture of two sets of dynamics. On the one hand, the problem of the state has been the primary target of transition in all these countries, irrespective of their being socialist, military-authoritarian, or a one-party state in the past. In Korea and Taiwan, for example, democratic transition took place in an anticipated fashion of dramatic institutional replacement: restoration of constitutionalism; withdrawal of the military from politics; establishment of a multi-party system and open and competitive elections; and invigoration of local politics and local government, within a relatively short period of time. In China, similar attempts were also seen in the early years – stalled only after the tragedy of 1989. In Japan, in a relatively moderate fashion, the one-party dominance began to weaken and political reform has gradually picked up.

In the reorganisation of economic activities, market economy became the guiding principle. China was the first to tackle the problem of the state and its statist economic model, as decades of the socialist experience had left an all-purpose and omnipresent state that suppressed almost all the possibilities of normal economic growth. Removal of the Party from dominating the state, and the state from dominating society and the economy, was clearly the aim of the institutional restructuring in China – at least in the early 1980s. Such an urgency to separate the state from the economy did not come to the other East Asian countries until a decade later when the economy in Japan ran into serious trouble, and again, when the financial crisis spread across the region in the late 1990s.

On the other hand, there was growing suspicion among policy elites and the general public in the region about the consequences of dramatic institutional restructuring driven by target institutions of market economy and democratic political order. This was partly because of the contrasting developments in Russia and China, and partly because the deepening of reform was seen as an undermining of the underlying social structure and political establishment. Concerns were growing over the survival of dominant interests, balance of contending social forces, and governability of the existing and emerging arrangements.

With these conflicting trends, it is tempting for people to think that the transition is perhaps making a case for a model of social change where instead of a wholesale dismantling of the existing political, corporate and social arrangements, one would more likely see an ambivalence in the attitudes of leading societal forces, a tendency for them to compromise in the process of restructuring, and ambiguity in the emerging arrangements concerning key target values such as the state and the market. The assessment intends to investigate these attitudes, the pattern of public behaviour and the nature of the new arrangements so that the transition and the new political economy it generates can be better understood.

The need and urgency for such an assessment was dramatically highlighted by the recent financial crisis in the region. Different interpretations of the causes of the crisis and attempts to relate it to the Asian Model raised serious questions about the exact nature of the Model, the ongoing transition and the global economy, and how they relate to one other. Answers to these questions would provide the necessary basis for an accurate interpretation of the crisis and the 'Asian problem' in general, as well as the dynamics of the Asian Model development beyond its national boundaries.

In an attempt to make such an assessment, eight contributors from areas of political science, economics, international relations and Asian studies, were invited to consider the conditions and consequences of the reshaping of the state's relations with forces and institutions in the AMEs both at home and abroad. Questions to be addressed included: what are the new market conditions which forced the state into its new role and what is this new role; what are the new conditions of the state that redefined the boundaries of its authority and functions and what are these boundaries; how do the state and market interact under the new market and state conditions and has market dominance really replaced state dominance; and finally, what are the new global conditions in which the AMEs survive and are these conditions incompatible with the global dynamics?

This volume is clearly more than a narrow examination of either the 'miraculous' performance by the AMEs in the past several decades or the financial crisis of 1997–98, and it is therefore not about the miracle or the end of Asian capitalism (World Bank 1993, ASRC 1998). It is about the conditions under which the AMEs were required to go beyond the institutional arrangements they had accumulated through the decades of their aggressive growth and how they have proceeded with the project. It is more than a narrow assessment of either the political system or the economic institutions, and is therefore not about the process of democratisation or the trend of marketisation (Friedman 1994a). It is about the interactions between the existing arrangements and changing conditions, and how the dynamism of the interactions has effected the emergent order. Finally, it is more than an investigation of the individual experiences of the AMCs concerned, and therefore is not about Japan or China. It is about forces and problems common among them and essential to their emerging political economy.

To examine these issues, one needs to go back to the initial conditions under which the Asian Model development originated and subsequent developments in terms of institutional arrangements (keiretsu, chaebol, etc.), growth strategy (export-oriented), operational regimes (tax code, interest rate, exchange rate, tariffs, etc) which constitute the core elements of the Asian Model. In other words, one needs to understand why the transition was necessary and what was to be reformed or restructured in the first place. On the other hand, a discussion of these conditions and core elements of the Asian Model will help the reader understand the issues and problems addressed in each individual chapter.

The remainder of this introduction, therefore, will make a case about the Asian Model: the initial conditions that demanded *and* made possible a particular set of responses from the AMEs, the institutional consequences of the responses (strong state, autonomous bureaucracy, incorporated society, internal capital market, etc.); and new conditions that challenged the existing arrangements. This interpretation of the Asian Model, drawn upon what this author calls the theory of institutional selection,[2] sees the transition being necessitated by the inability of the Asian Model arrangements to either further contain the tensions building up within the system over the decades, or reduce them through incremental adjustments. The analysis built on the interpretation provides a theoretical foundation for the thematic arguments throughout this volume. First, institutional changes in the transition could not be a clear-cut replacement. Rather, there was a mixture of old and new arrangements which accommodated both new conditions and existing interests. Second, it was the interplay of human interests, surrounding conditions, and existing arrangements that determined the direction of the transition and the structure of the new arrangements.

The Asian Model

What is the Asian Model? The question is necessary because there are too many conflicting, if not confusing, 'theories' about why the AMEs succeeded, how they did, and consequently what kind of problems they presumably have. In addition, many of the models developed in these "theories" fail to provide a systemic depiction of the variables and their causal relationship in the making of Asian development. More often than not, we confuse the Asian model with Asian values, Asian development, Asian traditional society, and most of all, with the Asian state, so it seems logical to look first at these theories.

Theories about the Asian Model can be divided into four groups. Those of the first group, which constitute the mainstream of Asian Model interpretations, focus on unique institutions as independent variables. For them, it is the particular type of state structure and capacity, corporatist business management, and mutually dependent state-society relations that were instrumental in producing the dramatic economic performance (for example, Johnson 1982).

The second group stresses the importance of the growth strategy and related operational regimes. It is the growth strategy and an effective and efficient execution of that strategy that were at the core of Asian development. This view is particularly popular among specialists in professional areas such as banking, export, capital management, human resources, social policy, industrial management, and macroeconomics, all in the general category of what the World Bank report refers to as 'public policy' (World Bank 1994).

The third group locates the independent variables outside the AMEs. They see as indispensable the international trade system, Cold War security environment, and the unique relationship in market access and capital supply between the United States and the AMEs (Haggard 1996). Finally, there is a sizeable group of scholars who consider the unique qualities of the people and their culture as the primary factor effecting the growth and development (Tai 1989). Culture for this group is not just a secondary factor supporting the function of the main structure and institutions, rather, culture itself became the basis for economic organisation and promotion, and the social and political arrangements it required.

Admittedly, each one of these theories identifies a particular set of forces that shaped the formation of the Asian Model: institutional arrangements, operational regimes, global conditions, and cultural qualities. But in each of these 'models,' one cannot really see at first glance how one condition led to another, along the lines of the historical evolution of the Model. For example, when did the cultural qualities start to function in such a positive and dramatic way and why, given that they were permanent qualities of these peoples well before the new 'Asian Renaissance' (Godement 1997)? Also, for example, why did the growth strategy and operational regimes come to exist and for what purpose? As far as the institutional arrangements are concerned, one can similarly question whether these institutions were either the conditions for the development or its consequences – why, for example, did the growth alliance form and in response to what?

Furthermore, from these models, one cannot obtain a clear picture of how these sets of forces/variables related to each other. How were the institutional arrangements, for example, affected by the international conditions? How, if ever, did the international conditions lead to the operational regimes? And how did the cultural qualities determine the growth strategy?

The interpretation of the Asian Model advanced here addresses these problems. The Asian Model is an export-oriented growth strategy in response to the initial economic conditions faced by the AMEs. This strategy was necessitated and sustained by the international trade, financial, security regimes and global market structure; the state-dominated growth alliance; and operational regimes aimed at industry-specific export promotion. The growth alliance and operational regimes were further supported by the political culture and social structure in these AMEs. The working of this Model has brought not only rapid economic growth and social development, but also a strong, and in many cases, authoritarian state; an autonomous, and in many cases, corrupt bureaucracy; an incorporated society, often with an 'illiberal' middle class; an internal capital market incorporating interests and resources beyond single corporations and simple business calculations,; and a controlled, privileged and often underdeveloped domestic market. Now, how did all these come to form the Model?

The Path To Growth

From Japan to China, from Taiwan to Korea, the AMEs faced a similar set of conditions which, to a great extent, determined the path of their initial economic take-off and subsequent mode of development. There was, for example, total economic and social devastation in these countries. Japan was completely destroyed during World War II. Similar destruction took place in Taiwan and Korea during the same war, but the Korean War and prolonged enmity between China and Taiwan prevented Korea and Taiwan from immediately embarking on a programme of normal economic development after the War, as had happened in Japan. China was a different story. Although it too was devastated after almost a century of internal fighting and external intrusions, the experiment of the modified

Soviet model allowed the Chinese to respond to the post-War conditions in a dramatically different way. After some initial positive results in the early 1950s, the experiment soon proved to be making conditions worse, thus prompting an urgent demand for an alternative response. The Chinese took up that challenge in the late 1970s.

The total economic and social devastation had significant consequences. First, a primary national purpose, designed for a quick economic recovery, fast growth and 'catching up', served as a principal mechanism for prioritisation and mobilisation in society. Second, the War-related devastation had not only destroyed the industrial infrastructure and resource base and weakened the production capacity of the AMEs, but also severely limited the purchasing power of the population. Elements necessary for the national economy to operate were insufficient either on the supply or demand side.

Third, the total destruction forced the AMEs to rely on external support for their early recovery. A patron-client relationship formed between the AMEs, on the one hand, and either the United States-dominated West, or the Soviet-dominated East on the other. The initial emergence of AMEs took place mainly in those countries in junior partnership with the United States. In economic terms, the patronage made available to the AMEs the much needed 'supplies' in the form of financial aid, and 'demands' in the form of open markets. These open markets were particularly important because they served as a substitute for domestic demands in the short-term, as well as a facilitator for capital accumulation in the initial take-off and further development in the AMEs.

The responses of the AMCs were essentially the same, though their timing was historically conditioned. With their limited domestic markets and an urgent need of hard currency to finance development programmes, the main focus of their economy was on the hard-currency markets abroad which, in turn, shaped the export-orientation of the economies. The export-oriented growth strategy, however, also required an ability on the part of the AMEs to target their economic activities. Th mere comparative advantage in labour and resources was not sufficient to be cost-effective or to make products competitive on the international markets. The AMCs, when compared with industrialised countries, were disadvantaged in terms of infrastructure, resources, capital, technologies, market access and trade facilities, not to mention their inexperience of global expansion.

To be competitive, therefore, elements in the national economy needed to be reorganised, with more effective and efficient use of resources. Consequently, different forms of institutional manipulations (Pei 1998) were developed which turned the national economy into a giant internal capital market (Chowdhury and Islam 1993). This capital market reduced internal transactional costs, evened out business risks, eased burdens on individual firms for capital accumulation and market share, and provided mutual preferential treatment. These arrangements resulted in the shared competitiveness of individual firms on the global market.

In addition to these corporatist arrangements, there was also the manipulation of policy and regulations on the part of the government. The design and implementation of a fiscal policy, monetary policy, industrial policy, tax code, interest rate, exchange rate, tariffs, etc., was targeted at the concentration of national resources on key industries and the strengthening of the competitiveness of national products. These manipulations effectively separated the national economy from the global one, with the former being a coherent and corporative operation and the latter a battlefield of competing transnational interests.

The responses were the result of a pure capitalist calculation and led to a unique type of growth strategy that focused primarily on the international market, and a particular set of institutional arrangements and operational regimes which made the working of that strategy possible. Similar conditions had existed elsewhere immediately after World War II. For example, in the aftermath of Europe's 'total' devastation, a United States-dominated patron-client relationship was established in Western Europe and a Soviet Union-dominated patronage in Eastern Europe. Nor was the situation in Latin America much different from that in East Asia. Indeed there was a similar attempt in Latin America after the War for rapid economic growth (Gerffi and Wyman 1990).

But it was the prevailing cultural and social conditions in the AMCs which made their response much more effective, and the necessary institutional arrangements not only desirable but also possible. The growth strategy and its associated growth alliance and operational regimes required an environment of strong and effective public authority which would focus on the programme of national development, allocate resources, set priorities among competing social and sectoral interests, and suppress 'disturbing' social and political demands.

The Model also demanded a social structure that would support the function of the nation-wide internal capital market, and provide mutual discipline and benefits to the parties involved – corporate management, labour unions, social groups and the state itself. Finally, for the Model to work, the domestic and international arenas needed to be separated so that manipulation and suppression of the domestic demands would be possible and the export-oriented strategy and operational regimes would make sense. The AMCs were known for their paternalistic social structure; strong, effective and authoritarian state; well-developed and autonomous bureaucratic elite; and a history of a closed, centralised, self-sustainable political and economic system (Pye 1985). These conditions perfectly satisfied the requirements for a strong public authority, a corporatist social structure, and the separation of domestic and international arenas, and provided an ideal foundation for the Model to work.

Growing Pains

The rest of the story is well known. A rapid and sustained economic growth and profound economic and social development took place. Often overlooked, however, are the institutional consequences of the Model which lie at the heart of the debate about the nature and direction of the ongoing transition. Let us now look at some of these consequences.

First, the working of the Model resulted in a very strong state in these countries – one party dominated for a long period of time. In China, the strong state took the form of the Communist Party-state. Taiwan and Korea for many years were under the party-military regimes. In Japan, the LDP dominated national politics and state institutions until very recently. Second, the Model also nurtured a unique professional group of bureaucratic elites. In each of these countries, behind the strong state, the bureaucrats provided the daily management of the state's functions.

Third, the Model led to the emergence of a growth alliance between the government, the business community and the labour force. Such an alliance subjected the interests of corporate elites and wage-earners to the greater national or industrial interests. This alliance was further strengthened with the rise of the middle class who benefited from the process of economic growth. Fourth, the Model promoted an internal capital market incorporating interests and resources beyond single corporations. Within this 'market,' economic calculations could hardly be seen as purely 'economic.' Finally, there was a controlled, privileged, and, often underdeveloped, domestic market as a result of the concentration of national resources on the international market. This domestic market was usually under the protection of the state and competition was controlled.

It is these consequences which have caused the 'growing pains' of the AMCs. They intensified tensions within the Model, to the extent that further growth proved impossible without changes in the Model. There are certain areas in which tensions became particularly intense. The first concerns the state itself. On the one hand, the state was required, by nature of the Model to avoid political, economic and social influences, either in the form of rent-seeking activities or general public inputs, in order to be able to exercise its organising, prioritising and manipulative functions effectively (Weiss and Hobson 1995, Skocpol and Evans 1985). Bureaucrats were not subject to openly competitive processes of check and balance, and enjoyed freedom in policy-making and implementation. For that reason, the state was strong, arbitrary, and often authoritarian.

On the other hand, also by nature of the Model, the state was deeply involved in society in general and the economy in particular. Because of the corporatist connections with the business community and other social forces, and their role as the chief operator of the nation-wide 'internal capitalist market,' these bureaucrats became easy targets for corporate influence. The state, whilst becoming closely intertwined with dominant social forces and maintaining mutually beneficial relations with them, tended to be weak, corrupt and ineffective, and was therefore ultimately a contradictory institution in the Model.

The second area of tension lies in the relationship between the state and society. There is generally an under-development of civil society in the AMCs. A substantial part of the society, particularly those of the elites and rising new middle class, were actively involved in the process of development, and therefore deeply connected with the state through the process. The business community depended on the state for protection, subsidies, contract deals, and favourable manipulation of the economic conditions and perhaps a bail-out should things turn sour. The general public depended on the government for, among other things, the provision of services such as social welfare.

The close 'incorporation' between the state and society left little room for 'intermediate organisations' to have a meaningful or effective function. Consequently, even there were signs of a middle class emerging with the prolonged economic growth, the overall political attitude of society did not seem to be necessarily 'democratic' (Jones 1997, particularly chapter 3). The nature of the new society raised questions about the very founding assumption of civil society: separation of the society from the state (Migdal, Kohli and Shue 1994).

On the other hand, the underdevelopment of civil society was effected partly through a variety of disciplinary and punitive mechanisms – social and economic as well as political – and open acts of repression by the state. These mechanisms and acts of state repression suppressed forces not in line with the overall direction of national programmes and inhibited the growth of an independent and assertive public, particularly that of credible and effective oppositions. Consequently, however passive and deferential it might choose to be, the political society, centred on key opposition forces, was ever present and the state faced a constant unspoken challenge. When the state itself became divided concerning the overall direction of the country, and therefore unable to justify the use of disciplinary mechanisms and repressive acts, or when the state was unable to deliver economic promises, the suppressed political society quickly became active and the tensions turned into political crises. This was witnessed in Taiwan and Korea in the 1980s and is seen in China even today. Like the state itself in the Asian Model, society also holds an ambivalent attitude towards the state and the relationship between them is not as simple and clear cut as agent-structure theories might have us believe.

Finally, there have always been tensions between the national economy and the international market in the Asian Model. The AMEs survived and flourished primarily on the international market. State capacity and manipulation, and corporatist social structure were targeted at their competitiveness on the international scene. For the AMEs to continue to grow, the AMCs wanted to ensure that the international market remain open to free flows of products, capital and resources. On the other hand, however, they wanted the inward flows of these elements tightly controlled as the Model required the separation of the domestic market from the international one. In a sense, the Asian Model was one with the state 'on the fence,' and the market in the Model had a dual structure. There were 'markets' on both sides of the national boundary and each functioned, or was pursued to function, according to a different set of principles. The state was the primary controller of the boundary and interactions between the two markets. This is perhaps why the AMCs were always suspicious of the global market.

Nevertheless, the global market has increasingly become too powerful to be ignored and the dual structure difficult to be sustained. Globalisation required the flows to be promoted in both directions. If all countries in the world were to take a selective approach to the global process, eventually no flows would be possible in either direction. Also, with the strengthening of the globalisation dynamics, it became increasingly difficult to clearly demarcate the 'national' economy from the global market. Added to that fundamental problem was the shrinking of the 'international' markets themselves, partly because of the over-production, over-competitiveness or over-protection of these markets. Together, these factors posted a significant challenge to the AMEs founded on the principle of dual markets and the primacy of the international one.

Many of the growing pains of the AMEs were caused by the building up of tensions in the Model. While these tensions may be inevitable in a growth and development of such magnitude, they were a clear indication of the alienation of these economies from the global system, underdevelopment of their domestic markets; and problems in the representation of emergent societal interests. The state became a self-interested complex against the many forces at home and abroad. The AMCs reached a point in the 1980s where various methods of confining, defusing or suppressing the tensions proved to be ineffective. More importantly, efforts to continue this confinement and suppression would seriously damage the prospects of sustainable development.

Finally, the AMEs found themselves increasingly at odds with the liberal principles successfully practised in the industrialised countries and enthusiastically embraced as an ideal model for the 'post-ideological' (Fukuyama 1989) world. With the 'genetic' problems of the Model itself, changing internal and external conditions, and the dynamism of global forces, the AMCs reached a point where the Model, that is, the growth strategy and its related institutional arrangements and operational regimes, needed an overhaul.

Expectations of the Transition

Adding to the difficulties and complexity of the transition were the interpretations and expectations of the policy elites, academics, and the general public in the AMCs, as well as those attentive observers outside the AMCs. Different interpretations led to different expectations of the transition in terms of its purpose, strategy and tactics, methods of social and political mobilisation, and key institutional targets.

The transition in the AMCs, for example, was seen as a restructuring of the Soviet model and the socialist system in general, featuring party-state dominance, military-style economic management, and concentrations of resources on heavy industries. The restructuring demanded the Party to withdraw from the state, the state to withdraw from owning and managing the economy; and the introduction of market mechanisms. China was a primary example of a transition of this nature. There was argument, however, to expand this interpretation to include other non-Communist AMCs. Key components of the transition in Taiwan, for example, included the dismantling of the Leninist party-state system (Dickson 1997) and withdrawal of the state's heavy hand in the economy (Wade 1990). It is not difficult to find substantial similarities between Taiwan and South Korea during the Cold War in terms of the dominance of the party-military-state complex. In the case of Japan, the long domination of the ruling LDP was a form, however 'soft,' of the party-state system. Even in purely technical terms, their economic model was compared directly to that of the Soviet Union – both of them were driven primarily by increase in inputs rather than in productivity (Krugman 1994), and both heavily relied on government planning, guidance, support, protection, and even direct ownership.

The transition was also seen as part of the modernisation process where the traditional society is transformed. The modernisation interpretation sees the problems in the AMCs in broad historical, rather than narrow ideological, terms. It proposes a different set of target institutions based on a different set of rationales. This modernisation interpretation includes in its explanatory framework a wider range of countries in the region. It focuses on the desirability and feasibility of some target institutions which would provide fairness, transparency, effectiveness and efficiency in the management of the public sector. Unlike the proven case of the necessity and urgency for post-socialist transition, the reform to *modernise* involves some major human experiences whose constant contention precludes an easy agreement on the essential elements and standards for a modern society (Huntington 1996, Yamazaki 1996).

The modernisation interpretation is built upon the belief in the stages of human evolution, inadequacy of the traditional society and its inevitable decline under modern conditions. It naturally depicts a world of societies at different historical stages. There is an invisible line that separates those pre-modern, developing, or traditional countries from the industrialised, developed and, thus, modern ones. While indicators vary for different definitions of a modern society, two primary ones are considered the minimum – the extent of its economic growth and social development, and the nature of its core institutions. There seems to be little disagreement among people from either the East or West concerning the first indicator. Contemporary forms of material and technology, as well ways and means of living have been accepted world-wide as essential to being modern. In fact, the Asian Model has been uniquely successful in raising the living standards in the AMCs to the 'modern' level.

The problems the modernisation interpretation encounters in the Asian Model and therefore its belief in the necessity for the reform of the Model, concern primarily the second indicator. It is a widely held view that modern society is defined by a set of core institutions that regulate the relationships within it, as well as the processes and procedures of their change. These institutions and procedures can be summarised as the principles of humanism, egalitarianism and utilitarianism. The modernist interpretation considers the core institutions themselves as the principal purpose rather than means with which other values are to be achieved as many in the AMCs believe. For modernists, the core institutions are not only instrumental in bringing about economic growth and social development, but also the defining elements of any modern society. For this reason, modernisation in the AMCs is considered 'incomplete' (Borthwick 1992: 542). This incompleteness is not only found in China, Taiwan and Korea, but also in Japan in terms of its political culture, social structure, and policy process. The transition in the region was therefore very much envisaged as a movement towards the installation (or restoration if interrupted) and consolidation of these core institutions, or a restructuring of the existing arrangements to meet modern standards.

There is a particular version of the modernisation interpretation based on the strict liberal principles of political economy and the successful experiences of the industrialised countries. At the core of the global movement of institutional idealism after the Cold War was a specific model of political economy – (global) market economy, (liberal) democratic politics, and (individualistic) civil society. This movement faces particularly serious problems in the AMCs where the market is managed, politics controlled and society incorporated. If modernisation in the AMCs is 'incomplete' for many modernists, it is simply a build-up of an institutional malfunction for the institutional idealists, which would eventually lead to the collapse of the system. The institutional idealists had great expectations of the transition in the AMCs, circumstanced by the ending of the Cold War, hoping as they did that a fundamental institutional restructuring would solve the Asian problem at its institutional roots.

It is not difficult to see the various theoretical arguments, human experiences and even ideological beliefs upon which these interpretations are based. At the same time, problems are just equally visible. First, the post-socialist interpretation applies mainly to China and perhaps even more narrowly to its early stage of reform. When applied to other AMCs the post-socialist interpretation becomes strained. More controversies are found in the modernisation interpretation. For example, there are significantly different views not merely about what constitutes the core institutions, but whether they are, in fact, a necessary component of modern society. Citing recent exemplars, many commentators claimed that a combination of capitalist and democratic institutions best served human interests, ensured fairness, provided effectiveness and efficiency, and were consequently necessary in a modern society. Others, particularly those in the AMCs, see these issues differently. For them, substantial progress has been made in relation to the first indicator, without necessarily incorporating these core institutions. The view was widely held among many East Asian elites that core institutions, rather than being an end in themselves, were more the means to an end in terms of the first indicator, and therefore substitutable depending on their effectiveness in a particular context.

A deeper problem perhaps lies in the overall approach of these interpretations towards social change: the target-institution-based approach gives a set of clear targets in the form of ideal institutions, but often overlooks the process and conditions that determine whether and how these institutions will operate. A comparison of two recent works by Francis Fukuyama (1992 and 1995) provides a good illustration of this point. Without an accurate assessment of the conditions in a particular social environment, and the use of it to justify the strategy and tactics in bringing about desired social change, one is likely to finish up with either an idealistic illusion or violent ideological confrontation. What one has witnessed in the AMCs over the past decade is that the interplay of major forces in the transition seems to have generated a delicate balance between local reality and idealistic pressures.

The interpretation of the transition as the restructuring of the Asian Model discussed earlier reflects such a balancing act. Unlike the target-institution-based interpretations, the Asian Model interpretation sees the transition as a process less driven by target institutions, and more by specific functional problems. It was a transition in the sense of moving away from something (the problem of the omnipotent state), rather than marching towards something (target institutions). Chinese reform began in this way twenty years ago. Reform in Japan also seemed to be undergoing a 'muddling through' experience. In Taiwan, during the recent financial crisis, there was quite an ambivalent attitude toward the state and its role in managing the economy. Restructuring of the corporate structure, such as the chaebol or the keiretsu, could not really proceed unless it became an indisputable fact that they hindered further economic growth. It is not that the target-institutions were undesirable. In fact, one could find many examples of the successful installation of new institutions, for example, in Taiwan and Korea. But there was always a gap between ideal institutions and their actual implementation and function, and between the interests the target institutions represented and those that the existing arrangements involved. The transition, in a sense, was an interaction between the two sets of institutional dynamics and the interests they represented or were dictated by, rather than a simple changeover from one to the other.

The Book's Structure

Along the lines laid out above, the chapters are organised in four parts, each dealing with one aspect of the changing conditions facing the AMCs and how they affect the on-going transition and emergent new arrangements. The two chapters in the first part focus on the conditions of the new market economy and how the state responded. Professor Kim in his chapter on South Korea examines, from an historical perspective, the state's changing methods and tactics in governing and regulating the market economy. After surveying the scope and nature of state interventions in markets in the earlier periods of Korean industrialisation, the chapter addresses the problems and challenges facing the government under the new market conditions, especially in the context of trade liberalisation, globalisation, and the economic crisis in 1997–98. The chapter investigates the impact of these conditions on the governance and restructuring of the Korean state.

Professor Zheng's chapter considers the Chinese government's responses to the problems arising from the new market conditions. In four separate but related areas, currency stabilisation, export competitiveness, state-owned enterprise restructuring, and banking system reform, the chapter offers a detailed account of the government's adaptation to changing, and even unpredictable, market conditions and assesses the strengths and weakness of the Chinese state in meeting the challenges. It depicts the fundamental dilemma facing the Chinese state, still centred on the surviving political and financial institutions, in managing the increasingly sophisticated and 'unruly' market because of the expansion of global capital and the process of globalisation. In both chapters evidence is ample for an increasingly aggressive and powerful market that the state has to respond to.

The second part deals with the new political conditions emerging in the AMCs, particularly the problem of the changing nature of the state itself. The chapter by Professor Harris traces the long tradition of the Chinese state where both a clear purpose and effective means were at the core of the its institutions and practices, and how that tradition was challenged during Deng's economic reform and institutional restructuring, and is now completely lost in the emergent political and social environment in China.

Professor Harris argues that in the early decades of the People's Republic, the state was strongly teleocratic, having evolved from teleological conceptions of the state in China's own political history, as well as from the purposeful quality of Marxism and Maoism. In recent decades, however, the state in China has gradually lost, or been deprived of, its sense of purpose. Whether this means that it will eventually evolve towards a condition similar to that of Oakeshott's state as societas is unclear, though the possibility cannot be discounted. Because of the critical importance of having a purposeful and effective state for the Asian Model to work, this fundamental change in the Chinese state would have a profound impact on its emergent political economic order.

Professor Endo, on the other hand, sees the weakening of the Japanese developmental state as an effect of the globalisation of neoliberal political economy, particularly in East Asia. In an attempt to explain why Japan's seemingly powerful economy lost its competitiveness during the 1990s, the chapter focuses on the changes in the structure of regional political economy in East Asia since the 1980s, and the dysfunction of Japan's development model in the new structure. The chapter sets to examine the impact of the neoliberal political economy on the surviving developmental state of Japan.

Professor Endo believes that the problems of the Japanese state and the regional political economic order in East Asia are strongly interrelated. Those relating to the restructuring of the Japanese state can be clearly traced to the emergent structure of the regional political economy. While the developmental state is undergoing fundamental changes, the emergent model may not be a happy choice after all. Caught in such a dilemma, the Japanese state has became a 'feeble' institution. In both China and Japan, a relatively weak and ineffectual state seems to have emerged as a result of the political and economic changes of the past decade or so.

The third section of the book, with its two chapters providing a case study on Taiwan, relates the changing political institutions to the new economic conditions and examines the emerging pattern of the state's engagement with the market. Professor Huang's chapter examines whether the reformed, and presumably weakened, state is still willing and capable of performing the governing role as it did in the more controlled political environment of the past. It is argued that through the process of democratisation the monolithic and autonomous state has become a contested political arena, so that it is much more difficult for the state to act as it has in the past: either the collective will of the state becomes difficult to form, or the state is incapable of enforcing it in the more open and transparent political environment.

The chapter, focusing on post-Cold War Taiwan, investigates the new state of Taiwan and, at the same time, the persistent manipulation of the market by the government. It argues that the state is still a preferred and capable institution in an environment of democratic politics and market economy – even more so in Taiwan – and that the new state activism should be understood in terms of not only the legacy of the Asian Model development, but also the fundamental logic of human collective action itself.

Mr. Green's chapter examines a complicated shifting relationship between government and business and argues that the state has become more sophisticated in facing the growing challenges of the market, rather than being weakened by them. In fact, the chapter identifies two models of the emergent state. The 'intelligent state' is one that has drawn back from the direct style of the 'developmental' era but still actively and effectively pursues comparative advantage. The other model is the 'kidnapped state', since this state is controlled and debilitated by internal and exterior interests and is characterised by a lack of clear policy and a failure to support development. Taiwan's political economy is defined by the relationship between these competitive and potentially conflicting models. Negotiation between the two is examined through various macroeconomic issues and areas in this chapter and Taiwan's resilience during the Asian crisis is explained in light of this dual paradigm.

The fourth part addresses the problem of the global market, how the AMEs have tried to adapt to the new global conditions, and what kind of relations the AMEs can and should build upon. The two chapters, in a rather interesting debate, offer two different views of the cause of unsatisfactory interaction between the AMEs and the global system. Dr Lingle, in his chapter, draws a rather gloomy picture of how the AMCs might survive the challenges of global dynamics. Dr Lingle argues that the inhibitions of capitalist markets were consistent with the political culture of these countries. Shared aspects of their political culture reproduced flaws in the institutional infrastructure of their economies and, consequently, they were ill-prepared to sustain external shocks generated by inevitable global capital flows. As such, the rigidity of conservative political institutions led to policies that interfered with the self-adjusting mechanisms in their economies. While restoration of stability in the AMEs will be a difficult path to follow, the slow pace of institutional change will make recovery an even longer one. Dr Lingle is convinced that it may require a generation before some AMEs can replicate the institutional infrastructure required for sustainable economic growth in the increasingly efficient global capital market.

In the following chapter, however, Mr. Shutt believes the problem lies in the global economic system itself. He argues that neither vulnerability to the effects of global economic liberalisation nor the failure of established institutions of political and economic governance, are confined to the AMCs. It would thus be quite wrong to draw any simplistic conclusion linking the fragility of their economic success with their authoritarian political systems, in contrast to the robustness of Western market economies under a liberal democracy. Such a theory cannot, in any case, explain the two greatest success stories of sustained East Asian development over the last 30 years – Japan and South Korea (one a relatively liberal democracy, the other a military dictatorship). After considering a growing cause for concern at the effects of 'rolling back the frontiers of the state' in Western countries and the associated loss of democratic accountability, as well as the disastrous experiment in extreme economic liberalisation in the former Soviet Union while seeking to replace totalitarianism with democracy, the chapter concludes that durable economic prosperity can only be built on the basis of far more genuinely democratic institutions than have so far been established anywhere.

The concluding chapter finds that the studies in this collection, with their diverse and sometimes even opposing views, form a consensus that the transition has been a process in which neither the market has taken over nor has the state merely held onto itself. Rather it has been a process of their constant interaction and mutual adjustment, driven by more fundamental forces. The conceptualisation of political economy as determined primarily by the state-market relationship therefore seems to limit our ability to understand the innovative, entrepreneurial and pragmatic nature of the efforts in the AMCs to develop an effective new political economy, and the consequent ambiguity in the emerging relationship between the state and the market.

This final chapter sees the need for going beyond the state-market dichotomy taken for granted in the Asian Model debate, and explores explanations of the Asian phenomenon in a broader context of human experience. In the constant interaction between institutions (state-centric arrangements, for example) and dynamics (such as market forces), or in other words, when state meets market, it is the relentless pursuit of human interests that ultimately determines how the state and market will interact and what arrangements will emerge from their interaction. It is this historical logic that underlies the state-market ambiguity in the emergent political economy in East Asia.

Notes

1 An Asian Model country (or in its narrower use, an Asian Model economy) can be defined as one which has upheld basic principles essential to the economic success in the region for the past 50 years: growth-centered market calculations at all levels; state-activism in producing and maintaining

economic order and priorities; and strategic planning and manipulation at the national level against internal pressures and external disadvantage. While those AMCs we discuss here are all in Pacific Asia, it is not necessarily a geographic concept.

2 The theory of institutional selection sees the dominance of a particular form of human organisation (tribe, family, multinational empire, factory, the nation-state, etc) as a consequence of successive institutional selections either through violence and revolutions or reforms and evolution, as human beings respond to their ever-changing environment for an assured satisfaction of their material, social and emotional interests. The theory explains, for example, why the nation-state became the primary form of human collectivity in its competition with others such as the city-state in Athens or the grand empire of Rome (Spruyt 1994). It also helps us understand why marriage, family, or the nation-state itself are increasingly facing the challenges of alternative forms of human associations such as domestic partnership or unions of states.

PART 1

The New Market Conditions

CHAPTER TWO

Kwan S. Kim

Market Liberalisation and the Problem of Governance in South Korea*

Introduction

The financial crisis that erupted in Thailand in mid-1997 led in no time to the sharp decline in value of currencies, stocks, and other assets in a number of AMCs, including South Korea (hereafter referred to as Korea), disrupting the financial systems and real economies of these countries. For Korea, large contractions in economic activity have been accompanied by soaring numbers of unemployed and homeless. The current crisis unfolded against the backdrop of the miraculous performance that had registered an outstanding average annual GDP growth of 8.6 per cent over the preceding three decades. While Korea's success has in the past been acclaimed as a model of the 'developmental state,' neoliberal economists today see the current crisis as reflecting the legacy of state governance. It is now argued that in the context of the contemporary global economy, the state should do less where markets work and focus only on improving the climate for enterprise and competition, in opening the economy to global markets.

This chapter takes a look at the dynamics of the new market economy in Korea and how they affected the Korean state's efforts to overcome its past legacy of statist development while at the same time maintaining continual economic growth. It will argue that market liberalisation is a powerful force that redefines the nature of the state's functions and redirects its involvement and activities. However, market liberalisation does not necessarily force the state out of the game. Rather it pushes the state into its proper position for safer and effective management of reform and development.

* Research for this chapter was supported by a grant from the Institute for Scholarship in Liberal Arts and a seed grant from the Kellogg Institute for International Studies, University of Notre Dame. The author wishes to acknowledge Meric Mekik Gunseli for research assistance.

To make its case, this chapter will first briefly recount the condition of the market under the developmental state in the recent history of Korean industrialisation. It will then focus on the new market conditions brought about by the reform programme of the government and global economic changes, dramatically showcased in the recent economic crisis of 1997–98. It will further examine policy adjustments and the deepening of the reform programme by the government in response to these new conditions. The chapter will conclude by looking at the new relations the market demands to have with the Korean state.

The Market Under the Developmental State

Korea, well into the 1960s, represented a truly backward economy based on a subsistence agriculture. Its per capita income in 1961 was $82 (in 1960 prices), which then placed the country below those of Haiti, Ethiopia, Peru, Honduras, Yemen, and about 40 per cent below India's. The country in the immediate post-Korean war period was an economic 'basket case'. It relied on foreign aid for sheer survival. Undisciplined capitalism during this period had done very little for development.

Beginning with the military coup in 1961, the country's economy began to make a dramatic turnaround. In two decades, the country's real per capita income more than tripled, placing Korea in the top third of all middle income countries. By 1996 Korea, with its 42 million population and per capita income of over US$10,000, emerged as the world's eleventh largest trading nation. In 1992 a civilian president was elected, for the first time after three decades of authoritarian regimes. Externally, Korea began to play an active role in global affairs by joining the World Trade Organization (WTO) and the Organization of Economic Cooperation and Development(OECD) in 1996.

Behind this transition to a modern economy has been the complex and subtle evolution of a state-managed economy. Guided by the belief that a well-managed, state-led economy would function better than one based on unfettered market forces, the state's active role in development evolved in the early stage of industrialisation. Korea had what Myrdal referred to as a 'hard state', whose interventions focused on the development of areas of the economy perceived to have a longer-term potential. Korea's authoritarian state pursued pragmatic approaches to industrialisation, accommodating market forces only when they were seen to work. The market system did not serve as an organising principle of the economy but as an instrument in attaining the national goal of industrialisation. Korea's rapid industrialisation owed itself to the developmental state role played by its government and has been extensively documented (Amsden 1989; Chang 1993; Wade 1995; Kim 1997a).

Over the longer term, nonetheless, the developmental state strategy paved the way to structural imbalances and distortions and sowed the seeds, eventually, for the financial turmoil in 1997. The centrepiece of the strategy was industrialisation via export promotion. An extensive system of industrial targeting was introduced in which a set of promising export industries was chosen for government support. The most important means of supporting the targeted firms was the allocation of financial resources by the state. While high-leveraged financing for targeted firms relied heavily on the state-guaranteed external borrowing, the domestic banks were restricted in credit decisions by government regulations, and were required to hold large amounts of monetary stabilisation bonds which paid below-market rates. This practically inhibited the development and growth of interbank money markets and established a centralised banking system.

As all the support and incentives were to be given to those firms in the targeted sectors, the large conglomerates in Korea, known as 'the chaebol,' received the lion's share in subsidised loans. Large-scale enterprises, able to capitalise on scale economies in production, were in a better position to outbid smaller firms in government-financed projects. This practice of 'policy loans' not only led to a rapid rise in industrial concentration but also rendered Korea's corporate sector and the economy, vulnerable to external shocks and financial instability.

As bankers complied with government guidance in credit allocation, they placed a trust in the state's unspoken guarantee of bank loans. They became lax in examining loan applications, particularly from large conglomerates, and extended loans indiscriminately for profitable but risky ventures. While bankers did not take very seriously the risk factor in lending, the centralised economic systems in Korea created patron-client relations between the state and the corporate sector – a kind of crony capitalism. The chaebols cultivated a symbiotic relationship with the government, which could help them out if something went wrong with their investment. The Korean state's intervention in the financial sector resulted in the problem of moral hazard (Radelet and Sachs, 1998). The outcome was over-borrowing by the chaebols with their consequently unstable debt-equity position, and the rise in external debt for the economy.

By the late 1970s it was not uncommon to find the chaebols having liabilities five to ten times as high as their own net worth. Burdened with excessive interest payments in relation to their equity, they became increasingly vulnerable to changes in economic conditions and external shocks. Their operations were rendered precarious, particularly in bad times when the economy was in a downturn, as was the case in the early 1980s. By the end of 1996, the average debt-equity ratio of the top 30 chaebols reached 400 per cent, which was twice the international banking norm of 200 per cent. When Korea joined the OECD in 1996, it further encouraged capital inflows by opening its financial market. The domestic banks, mainly merchant banks, heavily imported foreign capital, mostly of short-term maturity. The cumulative external debt rose from $42 billion in 1992 to $157 billion in November 1997, the eve of the crisis. Significantly, almost 90 per cent of the debt originated from the private sources of merchant and commercial banks.

The debt issues aside, it is worth further noting that the industrial targeting policy of the past three decades has led to serious structural imbalances and distortions in the Korean economy. The past targeting approach specified only which sectors of the economy should be promoted for expansion. Loans tended to be approved on the basis of superficial compliance with the administrative guidelines and not on the merits of individual projects. Many worthwhile projects failed to be undertaken.

These weaknesses were manifest as early as in the late 1970s. when a number of government-supported projects had to be discarded. Too many production units were crowded into a few sectors, resulting in overcapacity of these industries. On the other hand, the borrowed money was all too often lavishly invested in speculative real estate markets and other unproductive non-tradable activities. Korea's developmental state also rewarded successful exporters by basing support on the quantitative results of their exports. This policy not only resulted in an economy-wide inefficiency in resource allocation, but also created a structural imbalance biased against the development of domestic goods industries. Moreover, such a support system has favoured the production of assembly-type exports which rely heavily on foreign raw materials. This has led to the need for more imports through exports with a consequent chronic pressure on trade balance.

In summary, Korea's past strategy for growth maximisation led to serious structural distortions and imbalances, as reflected by the syndromes of business concentration, stagnant productivity, fragile corporate financial structure, corporate bankruptcies, and tenuous inter-industry linkage. The market was simply marginalised and subordinated to the state's developmental rationale. The Korean state's failure to reform the flawed industrial and financial systems, in preparation for global economic integration, turned out to be the major, structural cause of the current crisis.

The New Market Conditions as Crystallised in the Financial Crisis

Korea entered the current crisis under a reasonably healthy macroeconomic with a balanced budget, high savings, and low inflation rate. Few scholars expected that the financial turmoil which erupted in Thailand would so quickly spread to a country like Korea, whose economy, until the eve of the financial meltdown in November of 1997, had been perceived by international creditors to be 'fundamentally sound' (according to then IMF Managing Director, Michel Camdessus). Indeed, well into late 1996 Korea's trade deficits, as shown in official statistics, had also been below the manageable level of 5 per cent of GDP, which did not seem to be of concern to policy-makers.

Beneath the seemingly placid surface, however, the Korean crisis had for some time been brewing and the country's external balance began to deteriorate beginning late in 1996. By mid-1997 Korea had a serious problem with its external debt which, as already noted, rapidly rose as a result of cumulative trade deficits. The total external debt, before the Korean government's request for the IMF bailout, was more than five times the country's useable foreign exchange reserves that shrank to $30 billion. Moreover, the financial structures of the Korean corporate sector were over-leveraged by relatively short-term debts.

With the breakout of the ASEAN turmoil that erupted in the summer of 1997, it was simply a matter of time before investors would lose confidence in the Korean financial market and begin withdrawing investment funds out of Korea. The country found itself unable to defend the value of the Korean *won* at the time of capital flight. It could not secure new funds from international markets nor could it have maturing loans rolled over. Foreign capital continued to be withdrawn. The domestic stock prices plunged and the exchange rate soared. Concern about the continued depreciation of the *won*, foreign as well as domestic investors panicked and fled the stock market, creating a vicious circle of plummeting stock prices and further devaluing the *won*. The nation plunged into a full-blown financial crisis involving real-sector adjustments. What started as a liquidity problem soon turned into a triple crisis involving balance-of-payments, financial and corporate governance.

In retrospect, the causes of the crisis can be attributed to the deep structural factors both internal and external in origin, which provided a fertile ground for the crisis to erupt. Chief among them is the legacy of structural distortions and weakness inherited from the past industrial policy. More direct external causes can be found in the unfavourable international developments after the mid-1990s when the health of the country's trade was severely eroded. More significantly, the poor governance of the economy under Young-Sam Kim's (YS Kim) civilian regime was another contributing factor.

As for the structural causes, unlike the debt crises elsewhere in the developing world, the snowballing rise in Korea's external debt after the mid-1990s resulted from the microeconomic problems of low performance and profitability of domestic firms – especially of the chaebols. As already noted, at the root of the problem was the clientelistic state-business relationship inherited from past industrial policy. The Korean government relied excessively on the chaebols for export success and the latter, in turn, had privileged access to government subsidised credit. The chaebols, on the other hand, accustomed to rapid growth and believing that they were too big to fail, became overly ambitious in their investment decisions. External borrowing undertaken during the boom years in the early 1990s alone caused the short-term debt to reach almost $100 billion or about one third of GDP.

Business clientelism was reinforced by Korea's deeply flawed financial systems which operated under the presumption of an implicit bailout policy by the state. This expectation led to imprudent lending by bankers to meet the chaebols' excessive demand for credit. Imprudent lending continued, despite the rise in the banks' non-performing assets, as the asset-market bubble introduced in the late 1980s began to burst in the 1990s with Korea's declining exports. Korea's highly centralised banking system lent it to frequent political interventions on behalf of the chaebols. Imprudent and undisciplined borrowing led to over-investment in the sense that too many investment projects were undertaken which turned out to be not very profitable. As profit margins at the enterprise level became increasingly narrower, the business sector was rendered potentially more vulnerable to any unanticipated shock (Graham 1999).

This explosive situation was exacerbated by unfavourable external developments after the mid-1990s when Korea's export expansion slowed down from the annual growth rate of 33 per cent in 1995 to that of 3 per cent in 1996. This resulted in the drastic rise in Korea's current-account deficits and external debt, as indicated in Table 2.1. Among the factors contributing to Korea's growing trade deficits were the collapse of Korean export prices and the loss of competitiveness resulting from the Chinese *yuan* depreciation in 1994 and the subsequent *Yen* depreciation against the US dollar to which the Korean *won* had been essentially pegged. While the nominal exchange rate of the *won* had remained stable until October of 1997, there is evidence to indicate that it actually appreciated substantially

Table 2.1 Macroeconomic Indicators in Korea 1994–98

	1994	*1995*	*1996*	*1997*	*1998*
Real GDP Growth Rate (%)	8.6	8.9	7.1	5.5	−5.8
Unemployment Rate (%)	2.4	2.0	2.0	2.0	7.0
CPI Inflation Rate (%)	6.2	4.5	4.9	4.5	7.5
Current Account (US$ in billions)	−4.5	−8.9	−23.7	−8.2	−40.0
Capital Account (US$ in billions)	–	–	23.3	1.3	−4.0
Foreign Debt (US$ in billions)	89.0	120.0	164.0	158.0	154.0
Won/Dollar Exchange Rate	789.0	775.0	844.0	1415.0	1215.0
(Appreciation rate, %)	2.4	1.8	−8.2	−40.3	16.5
Yield Rate on Corporate Bond (%)	12.9	13.8	11.9	13.4	9.0

Notes: Figures for foreign debt, exchange rate, and bond rates are for the end of the year.
Source: Korean Development Institute.

in real terms during the summer of 1997 when its regional trade competitors in Southeast Asia (Thailand, Malaysia, the Philippines and Indonesia) had large devaluations of their currencies vis-à-vis the US dollar (Corsetti, Pesenti and Roubini 1998).

Beginning in 1996 the collapse of export prices, particularly in Korea's major export items of semi-conductors, chemicals, shipbuilding and steel products was particularly drastic in eroding Korea's trade balance. The decline in Korea's terms of trade began in 1994 and continued until the eve of the crisis in late 1997. The relative export prices fell as much as 30 per cent over the period. The declining external demand for Korean exports coincided with a depressed Japanese economy and a cyclical downturn in the Asian region, and was associated with an oversupply of manufactured goods for export in the regional and global market. The results for Korean industry were the syndromes of over-investment, stockpiled inventory, and stagnant productivity associated with wage increases, which quickly dissipated the strong profit positions of Korean firms held in the preceding years.

Weakened profitability exerted pressures on the stock and currency markets, simultaneously slowing investment growth. Although political uncertainty ahead of the Presidential election for 1997 prevailed, the productive capacity of Korean industry was by then greatly under-utilised, thereby raising costs when sales were already weakening. Consequently, many enterprises began to incur losses and encounter cash flow problems and difficulties in servicing the debts that had accumulated during the boom years to finance large investments.

While the combination of these external and internal factors provided a fertile ground for the crisis to erupt, the primary contributing factor was the poor governance of YS Kim civilian state (1992–97). There had been high expectations that this legitimate regime would undertake political and economic reforms for a market-oriented democracy. In hindsight, there were two aspects of policy failure; first, the premature decision in 1966 to move toward financial liberalisation by joining the OECD, and second, the lack of political will or the inability of the government to undertake the long overdue, necessary structural change.

First of all, the YS Kim regime was complacent and unprepared to undertake the necessary structural changes, and to properly address the problems of its pronounced boom-bust cycle during the mid-l990s. Around this period, there had already been a series of threatened bankruptcies of major corporations which, at the same time, created significant bad loan problems for the financial sector. The lack of credit from the banking sector hammered stock and property markets. Big corporations such as Hanbo Steel and Kia Motors, once virtually guaranteed by the government, sought protection from creditors after banks were forced to cut them off.

The government was indecisive and, in some instances, continued with bailout efforts which caused non-performing loans to surge even higher. When chaebols such as Hanbo Steel, Jinro, Dianong, New Core Group, and KIA motors-which were considered as being too big to fail-went bankrupt as a result of low performance and consequent cash flow problems, this should have signalled to the government that something was going seriously wrong.

Perhaps the most significant policy blunder was the decision in 1966 for an abrupt financial liberalisation when Korea did not have a fully developed, market-disciplined financial system. With the blessing of a superb international credit rating, Korea was quickly inundated with unmonitored fresh credit. Many newly created financial institutions known as 'the merchant banks', procured foreign currency funds on a short term basis which were used for long-term investments in Southeast Asian countries such as Thailand and Indonesia.

By the time the region experienced its currency crisis in mid-1997, stiff lending competition was reflected in extremely low margins in Southeast Asia, which were often 0.2 percentage point above funding costs-the difference of only one-tenth of what they were in 1993 (Kim 1998: 521). Claessens, Ghosh, and Scott state, 'Following a long period of government control over the financial system, [Korea's] liberalisation measures in the late 1980s and the 1990s were mostly half-baked and often not backed up by improvements in the supervisory and disclosure framework.' (Claessens, Ghosh and Scott 1999: 83).

By borrowing directly from abroad or indirectly from the domestic merchant banks, which in turn borrowed from abroad, the chaebols acquired more than $30 billion of foreign assets since 1996. The merchant banks, with little prior experience of the global capital market, quickly piled up foreign currency liabilities. By the end of November 1997, Korea's total external debt rose to US$157 billion, of which short-term liabilities accounted for about 40 per cent of the total. The external liabilities of financial institutions, which consisted mostly of domestic merchant banks, reached US$112 billion, accounting for the lion's share of more than 70 per cent of the external debt. Unlike the case of Latin America's external debt, public sector liabilities were less important; they remained below 14 per cent of the total debt throughout 1997.[1] Many merchant banks had outstanding loans with the chaebols who had either gone bankrupt or sought protection from creditors. In addition, they had sizeable amounts of Russian Treasury bills, as well as Thai, Indonesian, and other ASEAN bonds, which became unredeemable or had to be resold at a huge discount.

At this point in time, foreign banks started to curtail their lending to Korean banks. Their major creditors were Japanese banks who themselves were experiencing problems and began to recall their loans from Korea. The merchant banks were forced to buy up dollars with the *won* reserves to pay their foreign-currency debts. This resulted in a drastic depreciation of the *won*. When the Korean Congress on 18 November 1997 failed to legislate the Bank Reform Bill – a Korean version of the Big Bang, investor confidence in the market fell to rock-bottom, precipitating a liquidity crunch for Korean banks.

These were the circumstantial factors which could have been mitigated by proper governance. Unlike in Taiwan, Singapore, or China, the Korean policy-makers were complacent about the economy being either ignorant of, or oblivious to, the potential consequences of inaction. The central government's monetary and bank supervisory authorities did not seem to even realise the magnitude of indebtedness incurred by the private sector. For example, the competitive strength of Korea's export sector in the mid-1990s continued to erode, with a large gap emerging between the real exchange rate and the total factor productivity for Korean exports. And yet, there was inaction on the part of the government to make any adjustments. An overvalued exchange-rate system continued. There was also the problem of lack of transparency in corporate data. Big businesses in Korea are embedded in a web of cross-shareholdings and debt guarantees with their affiliates. Sorting out their transactions separately would be an accounting challenge.

In this context, there is also some evidence to suggest that relations between the state and Korean businesses were so bad that the economy became practically ungovernable. The 'embedded bureaucracy,' as described by Peter Evan (1998) for Korea's developmental state, no longer functioned in the regime's transition to democracy. Despite the economic downturn and declining profits at the enterprise level, the chaebols continued with their expansionist plans. The civilian government also began to lose control over labour movements, although increases in labour costs began to exceed productivity gains, thus contributing to the decline in international competitiveness of Korean exports.

In summary, the latest economic crisis resulted not so much from macroeconomic imbalances[2] but from the weaknesses in Korea's corporate and financial systems and, to a greater extent, poor governance of the economy. The outbreak of the crisis in Southeast Asia served as a trigger to ignite a spark in the field of land mines waiting to be exploded. In retrospect, the complacency and misguided management of Korean policy-makers has much to do with the crisis in 1997. With properly cautious and preventive measures, the crisis could have been avoided, or at least the impact could have been lessened. In broader terms, the crisis amplified the new market conditions in the Korean economy and the government's habitual response proved to be seriously inadequate.

IMF Pressure and Policy Adjustment

The Korean government, realising that the nation was in serious financial difficulty, agreed in December 1997 to a $58 billion bailout by the International Monetary Fund (IMF). The IMF's bailout decision was based on the fear of possible default by Korea, which was the world's eleventh largest economy. The default of Korea would pose a grave threat to the international monetary system. The immediate purpose of the bailout was to provide bridging finance to reduce current-account deficits and keep inflation in check by restricting domestic demands. Specific adjustment measures called for austere fiscal and financial policies: the introduction of a floating exchange rate system; complete liberalisation of the capital market; and abolition of the import source diversification system. The agreement further stipulated macroeconomic targets that must be achieved for monetary, fiscal, and exchange-rate policies.

The IMF adjustment package in the case of Korea went well beyond its standard stabilisation programme. It added far-reaching institutional reforms across the board in an effort to make the entire system operate more like a Western model. These structural reform measures encompass the banking, corporate, trade and labour sectors, and are aimed at removing features of the economy that have been seen as impediments to growth (such as monopolies, trade barriers, and non-transparent corporate practices) and improving the efficiency of financial institutions and mediation.

Specific provisions for the financial sector reform included the establishment of an independent central bank with the primary function of controlling inflation; creation of a consolidated supervisory body with jurisdiction over all financial and corporate operations; and requirements of the firm to report audited and consolidated financial statements, the closing down or recapitalising of troubled financial institutions; elimination of government-initiated loans; enhancement of transparency in banking transactions; and removal of all restrictions on foreign borrowings by domestic firms.

As for corporate restructuring, the chaebols are required to focus on their own specialities and be subject to stricter disclosure rules and financial market discipline. Management must be shared widely by the public and be made accountable to shareholders. Although the structural adjustment programme centres on corporate governance and restructuring of the banking sector, it also calls for labour market reforms. They are seen as an integral part of the problem of corporate governance. The adjustment programme urges sweeping reforms to facilitate redeployment of labour to make Korea's labour market more flexible.

The key element in the IMF's stabilisation package was the raising of the interest rate. Interest was raised from the pre-crisis rate of 12 per cent to 27 per cent by the end of 1997, and up to 30 per cent in early 1998. The aim of this interest rate policy was to induce investors to keep their savings in domestic currency and, additionally, to attract foreign investment in the hope that this would stabilise the value of the Korean *won.* High interest rates would not only attract capital inflow but also crimp aggregate demand, which should improve the country's trade balance.

The interest rate policy, to a certain extent, succeeded in stabilising the currency market by preventing capital haemorrhage. Although high deposit rates offered by domestic banks seem to have suppressed the outflow of domestic capital, the social cost of doing this has been a widening income gap between the wealthy few and the remaining impoverished population. In the economic turmoil which has affected the whole of the working population only a few of the domestic capitalist class have reaped financial benefits.

Moreover, the increase in the country's foreign exchange reserves has largely been attributable to drastic reductions in domestic demand. In this

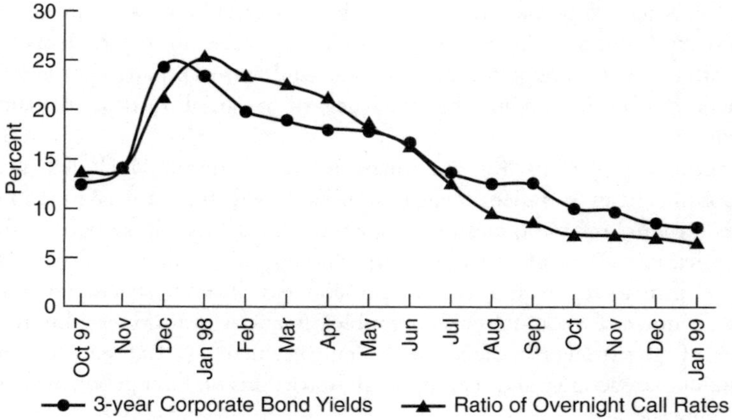

Figure 2.1 Corporate Bond and Overnight Call Rates

Source: Appendix I.

respect, the IMF prescription for high interest rates was an excessive austerity measure in a country where the macroeconomic conditions were basically healthy to begin with. Above all, the high interest rate policy failed to achieve its primary objective of inducing net capital inflows. On the contrary, it diminished investors' confidence in the economy as they were concerned that excessively high rates could push Korea's corporate sector into insolvency.[3] Figure 2.1 shows how interest rates changed with the IMF stewardship.

The IMF prescriptions for austerity, which centred on high interest rates and currency depreciation, had been in force during the first six months. Exports, which are the locomotive of Korea's economic growth, fell over the first seven months under the IMF regime; a decline by 13.9 per cent to $10.1 billion in July 1998 for the third consecutive month. Shipments dipped 3.5 per cent in May and 6.6 per cent in June of the same year.

On balance, the IMF programme had more of an adverse impact on Korea's macroeconomy; it triggered a stagflation in which consumer price inflation continued in an environment of rising unemployment.[4] Figure 2.2 shows movements of the consumer price index (CPI), industrial output, and retail sales. They are plotted on the basis of a year-on-year percentage change since the outbreak of the crisis. In the first half of 1998 under the IMF stewardship both industrial output and retail sales plunged rapidly while consumer prices continued to rise.

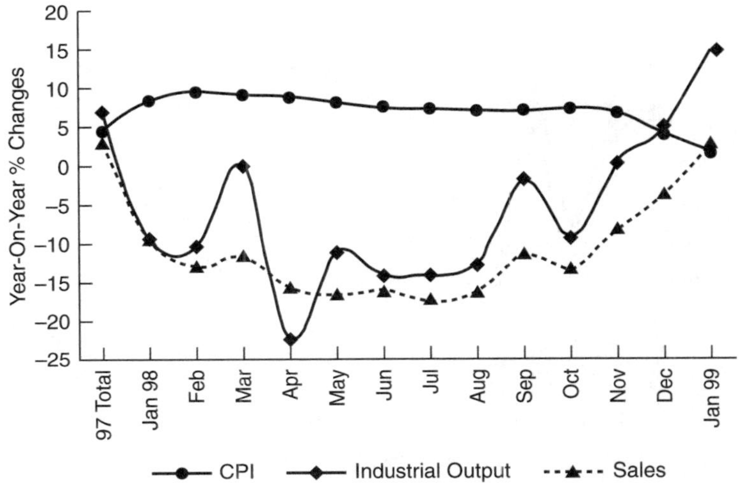

Figure 2.2 Trends in CPI, Industrial Output and Sales

Source: Appendix II.

In effect, during the first half of 1998 alone, consumer spending fell by 12 per cent, with investment dropping by 40 per cent. Korea's real GDP contracted by 5.3 per cent while the unemployment rate had soared to a 7 per cent high by mid-1998, in an economy where the average unemployment rate had hovered around the low 2 per cent before the crisis. Given the industry's heavy dependence on imports, the devaluation of the domestic currency raised production costs while the high interest rate policy crimped both investment and consumption.

At the enterprise level, the high interest rate policy exacerbated the firm's financial instability especially in the case of a number of the large chaebols who already had a high debt-equity ratio. High interest rates lent themselves to soaring debt-servicing costs, thus precipitating the possibility of bankruptcy (Kim and Koo 1998). Foreign investors continued to remain concerned that soaring interest rates could push the chaebols into insolvency, which would deter inflow of foreign capital.

More severely effected have been the smaller firms. The credit squeeze and excess capacity in industry especially hit small-scale establishments, most of whom heavily depend on the chaebols for business. With the economy contracting, and as their big business customers cut back on production and investment, small subsidiary firms are experiencing

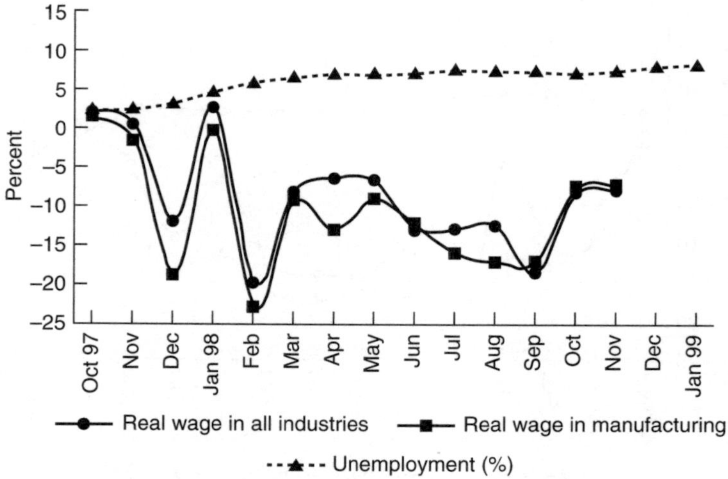

Figure 2.3 Trends in Unemployment Rate and Year-on-Year Real Wage Changes

Source: Appendix III

plummeting sales and bankruptcies. The figures for small business bankruptcy have been alarming: during the first five months of 1998 all but 18 of the 5,239 bankrupted corporations were small firms with fewer than 300 employees. In Korea, small firms employ three times the work force of large companies.

The 'whirlwind' layoffs and pay reductions of workers have been another effect of economic meltdown and corporate bankruptcies. In 1997, the jobless rate in Korea, having stabilised at around 2 per cent until November of that year, began steadily to increase and peaked at 7.6 per cent in July 1998 (Figure 2.3).

The July figure is more than three times the unemployment rate before the economic crisis. This rapid rise in the first half of 1998 was largely attributable to the bankruptcies of small and medium-sized firms which were hit disproportionately severely by the IMF's high interest rate policy (Park 1999). Moreover, the IMF crisis shattered the tradition of lifetime employment to which Korean workers had been accustomed, and aroused a constant fear of being laid off. The workers have succumbed to the pressure of huge pay cuts or freezes, which have resulted in a drop in their real income.

Figure 2.3 shows the year-on-year percentage changes in real wages for all industries and manufacturing. Monthly real wages are calculated as a ratio to those in each corresponding month of the preceding year. The comparison shows declines in all months during 1998 except in January of that year. In February 1998, for instance, the real income of the Korean worker was lower by more than 20 per cent.

Government statistics do not distinguish the part-time workers from the full-time ones. Nor do they count as 'jobless' those workers discouraged from searching for a job. If these potentially employable persons are included, the actual jobless rate could be much higher. According to a National Statistical Office estimate, the number of jobless may have surpassed the two million mark (*Korea Times* 22 February 1999: 8). Given that a jobless worker in Korea has, on average, three additional family members to support, nearly 8 million people – or about one-fifth of the total population – are having extreme difficulty in making ends meet. It is well to note that the jobless, as defined in government figures, include the homeless and daily workers without a fixed residence.

While corporate failures and restructuring gave rise to wage-cuts and mass layoffs, the high interest policy benefited the wealthy few who could continue living off their bank deposits now attracting a higher rate of interest. In Figure 2.4, the trends in incomes of the lower and middle groups during the 1990s, as represented by the bottom three and the next four deciles respectively, are plotted as a percentage of the high income group represented by the top three deciles. The trend shows how the wealth of the rich has increased under the strict terms of the IMF bailout package while the income gap between the rich and the remainder of the population has widened. The relative income of the poorer Koreans fell to 28.5 per cent in 1998 from the preceding seven-year period's 31.4 per cent average, while that of the middle Koreans dropped to 68 per cent in 1998 from 75 per cent over the corresponding preceding period. The gap is expected to grow throughout 1999, albeit at a slower pace, as the restructuring of the economy continues.[5]

A more worrisome feature of the crisis is social disturbance and violence. Joblessness and recession have driven many Korean workers into a desperate situation, triggering an explosion in the number of homeless and the desperate. As the unemployment rate and poverty incidence increase, and income distribution deteriorates, crime rates related to property, as well as the frequency of suicide, have risen sharply. Robberies and thefts in the first half of 1998 rose 60 per cent over the same period of the preceding year. The incarcerated population also increased by 20 per cent compared with the previous year (*Newsreview*, 6 June 1998: 34).

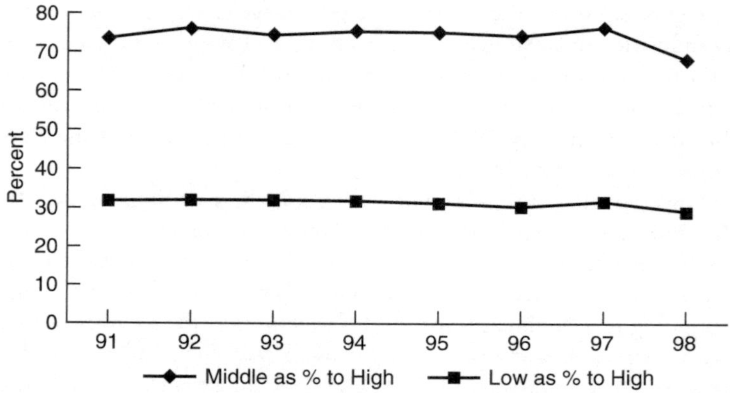

Figure 2.4 Income Gap By Classes

Source: Korea Institute of Public Finance

Reform and Restructuring

The IMF initially assumed that Korea, after swift financial and corporate restructuring, could survive its recession through a flexible interest rate policy under a stabilised foreign exchange rate regime. As its policy prescriptions led to a deeper recession than earlier anticipated, the IMF, after several months of stewardship, finally allowed the Korean state to increase its governance of the economy. The newly elected President Dae-jung Kim (hereafter DJ Kim), upon taking office in February 1998, began the task of leading the country out of the IMF 'trusteeship.'

DJ Kim's government took a Keynesian stance and formulated a new macroeconomic policy to stimulate domestic demand and ward off a worse economic collapse. High interest rates and retrenchment policies employed to tide over the currency crisis were seen as ineffective without lowering public expenditure, which would then inevitably cause severer deflation. An agreement was soon reached with the IMF in that the budget deficit for the remaining 1998 was to increase to 4 per cent of GDP from the 1.7 per cent initially stipulated by the Fund. To finance the deficit, the government would issue eight trillion won ($6.12 billion) in bonds.

The macroeconomic policy took a reverse turn: the central bank was allowed to increase its money supply at lower interest rates, and the IMF-mandated fiscal targets were progressively relaxed to accommodate the cyclical downturn in revenues. At the same time, the DJ Kim government took a swift and active role in financial-sector restructuring.[6] It took a risk by assuming responsibility for a portion of the bank debts, and used public funds to rescue financial institutions. The goal of the financial reform was to strengthen the regulatory framework in the financial sector so as to conform more closely to international norms, and to promote private efforts for bank recapitalisation within this context. Thus, the rehabilitation of the banks, which were to take responsibility for negotiating with troubled corporations, is a key element in the strategy for corporate financial restructuring.

To expedite financial reform, the DJ Kim government opted first to consolidate and enhance the supervisory authority of the Financial Supervisory Committee (FSC) formally established in April 1998 as an integrated financial supervisory body. Commercial and merchant banks, and all other financial institutions, have been continuously monitored for the attainment of rehabilitation or recapitalisation plans and capital adequacy targets at the 8 per cent rate recommended by the Bank of International Settlements (BIS). The government has, to a certain extent, succeeded in reducing insolvent institutions or recapitalising them.[7] Nevertheless, recapitalisation has, to date, led to a significant resource commitment and unintended ownership of financial assets by the government. By the end of the third quarter of 1998, the government had spent on financial sector restructuring, more than half the total budget of 64 trillion *won* (14 per cent of GDP) that was allocated for it. Privatisation of the banks has so far been held at bay, because of the lack of qualified domestic capital and the reluctance of foreign investors to commit resources.

Given the vital role of the chaebols in causing the crisis, the DJ Kim government gave a high priority for the reform of industrial structure. More than at any time before, the state was expected to work closely with the business community. The first phase of corporate reform, due to be completed in the fall of 1998, called for special measures from the government. The Ministry of Finance and Economy (MOFE) devised a complete corporate restructuring scheme, known as 'the big deals,' which was to be agreed for implementation among major business groups. The 'big deals' are an attempt to alleviate one of the main problems with the Korean economy, excess manufacturing capacity. The chaebols had invested heavily in industries such as semiconductors, which had suffered from oversupply and weak international prices in global markets. This excessive investment, and the debts amassed to complete the projects, are blamed as key causes of the debt crisis.

The DJ Kim administration has been pushing the chaebols into mergers and asset swaps in order to increase specialisation and reap the benefits of consolidation and scale economies.[8] While reducing debt/equity ratios, excess capacity, and corporate governance at the enterprise level, the goal is to ultimately improve the country's industrial efficiency and international competitiveness. In corporate restructuring, the government opted to deal separately and more urgently with the top-five chaebols (Hyundai, Samsung, LG, Daewoo, and SK) among more than sixty others. The top five are, in many respects, the leaders of Korean industry – more globalised in their operations, much bigger in size and with greater access to external financing and an easier cash flow position. For the non top-five firms – ranging from the small and medium-sized suppliers to the top firms, it was felt necessary for the government to adopt more lenient measures since, unlike the top five, they would be more severely affected by the credit crunch.

The top five were required to agree on the approaches to financial and operational restructuring to meet the government-imposed targets for debt/equity ratios and other international norms. By the end of 2000, their total production units are to be reduced from 271 to 136. Their average debt-to-equity ratio is to fall below the international norm of 200 per cent from the prevailing 400 per cent. They are further required to raise their capital base by selling off assets and subsidiaries and issuing stocks overseas.[9] By a recent accord among the five chaebols, they are committed to the raising of a total of some $30 billion in foreign funds as restructuring costs by 2000.

Sweeping structural reforms are expected to continue. In December 1998, the government announced its decision to sell a 51 per cent share in the first established major Korean bank (Korea First Bank) to a foreign consortium led by US-based Newbridge Capital. The government's move was strikingly bold as the chaebols and many civic groups who were keen to preserve the nation's economic sovereignty were openly hostile to this deal.

The DJ Kim government has made good progress in macroeconomic stabilisation, although much of the problem still remains in the real sector areas. Interest rates have been stabilised at a 10–12 per cent level, and consumer spending has been slowly rising throughout 1999. The useable foreign exchange reserves, which are the reserves available to the central bank after subtracting the country's emergency foreign loans and deposits at domestic banks' overseas branches, rose from a low $7 billion at the time of the IMF bailout to $48.5 billion a year later (Figure 2.5). This is clearly attributed to Korea's all-out efforts to acquire foreign exchange.

Given the contraction of global import demand and the deterioration of the domestic demand, however, both exports and imports initially suffered declines in the wake of the outbreak of the crisis. Imports –

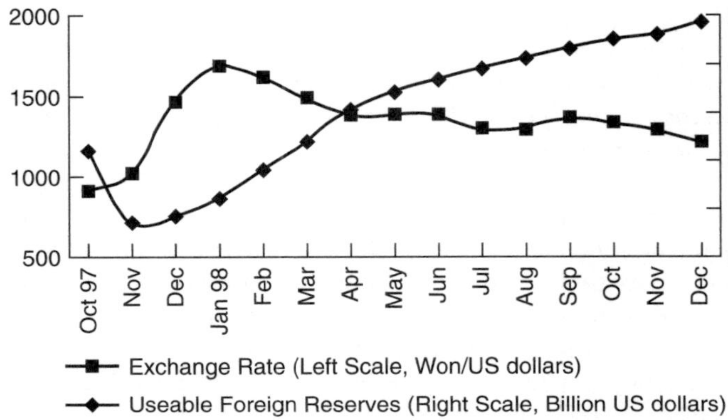

Figure 2.5 Foreign Exchange Rates and Useable Reserves

Source: Ministry of Finance and Economy, South Korea

mainly for domestic consumption – fell more rapidly than exports, which declined slightly throughout the first three-quarters of 1998. Nevertheless, thanks to the relentless export drive by a few chaebols and the government's moves for structural reform, the export of semiconductors, automobiles, ships and machinery, continued to exhibit upward trends, particularly to countries in Southeast Asia. Coupled with some success in inducing foreign direct investment, the country's trade surpluses since late 1998 have been accompanied by increased imports for the first time since the crisis. Increased imports accounted largely for the purchase of foreign plants and equipment by local companies. This should promote Korea's growth potential and export industry, and is thus viewed as a welcome sign of an economic turnaround.

Amid the continuing current account surpluses, the domestic banks have been able to repay foreign currency denominated debt to the central bank. This has increased useable foreign exchange reserves and stabilised the value of the domestic currency. Indeed, with the replenished foreign reserves, the value of the *won* has firmed up against the US dollar. It moved below 1200 *won* to the dollar at the end of 1998 – an appreciation of more than 40 per cent a year later. At the height of the currency crisis the domestic currency plunged to 1,960 won against the dollar.

By the end of October 1998, Korea's external debt stood at $153.5 billion, of which the short-term debt accounted for a little more than 20 per cent. With this level of short-term debt, domestic financial institutions should have little difficulty in repaying external loans in the next six months. The government is moving to further reduce external liabilities by more than $20 billion before the next millennium. If such a repayment plan succeeds, it will enable Korea to fully escape from the IMF retrenchment programme.

Towards the end of 1998, recovery of the rest of the economy had also picked up steam. Led by the expansion of exports and domestic consumption in automobiles, semiconductors and telecommunications, Korean industry began to regain much of its lost vigour. Buoyed by falling inventories and increased investment demand, foreign direct investment also gained lost impetus as it reached $8.9 billion in 1998, up 27 per cent from the previous year (*Newsreview*, 6 February 1999: 26). The latest IMF projection places Korea's economic growth rate for 1999 at a positive 2 per cent, a turnaround from a negative 6 per cent in the previous year.

Korea's success in stabilisation is attributable to a combination of pragmatic domestic policy and fortuitous external developments. Reasonable global interest rates, a strong Japanese yen, stable Chinese yuan, and low commodity prices throughout most of 1998 have certainly helped Korea in generating trade surpluses.[10] Also the fact that DJ Kim's government inherited a balanced budget with low inflation economy, eased its efforts for financial restructuring. Concurrently, with the efforts to stabilise the currency market, the DJ Kim regime has been able to launch, with marked success, a rehabilitation of the financial sector as an urgent reform task.

To clear up the non-performing loans and recapitalise the financial sector,[11] the government could spend 64 trillion won – an amount equal to 15 per cent of the annual GNP (Cho 1999).[12] Although the exact contribution of external factors to the stabilisation is difficult to ascertain, the determined political will and consistency of DJ Kim's policy had a vital role to play in restoring investor confidence and in mobilising collaboration from diverse domestic interest groups.

Finally, it must be understood that the Korean economy is still at the crossroads, as it has only just begun to deal with longer-term structural problems and faces uncertain prospects in the global market. First of all, the prospect for Korean exports in the next few years is still clouded with uncertainty.[13] The Asian market, which has so far provided one of the main markets for Korean exports, still suffers from its financial crisis. There are signs that the Japanese *yen* and the Chinese *yuan* may fluctuate.

Second, while the macroeconomic stabilisation policy is relatively easy to implement by a few centralised governing institutions, structural reform measures are much more complex and arduous as they involve conflicting interests of divergent socio-economic groups. One year after the collapse of the currency, the real-sector structural reform in Korea is still lagging behind. For instance, while the government assisted the restructuring of only the top five, each of the remaining chaebols has become bigger and more powerful, and excess capacity of the surviving businesses has yet to be rationalised. On the other hand, bankruptcy of small firms is still frequent. The banking system has not been fully recapitalised.

Third, as corporate restructuring and downsizing is expected to continue, there will be a further rise in unemployment. The modern-sector segment of the labour market is still rigid, and there is a strong possibility of labour agitation as the economy recovers. Workers in the modern sector, which includes mainly the regular employees in large-scale firms and some public enterprises, generally enjoy relatively high wages and protection of job security, often under militant unions.[14]

Although this segment of the labour market is small, with the unionised workers representing less than some 15 per cent of the total labour force, disruptions in the normal operation of their employers could critically affect progress in economic recovery because of the strategic importance of the modern-sector firms in the Korean economy. There is thus a need to improve flexibility in the modern-sector labour market to enhance international competitiveness for Korean exports.

Finally, the most urgent challenge in economic governance is rising poverty and inequality in the country. In contrast to the macroeconomic indicators that show the economy on a recovery path, there has been no clear indication, as yet, that human misery is being kept at bay. On the contrary, unemployment reached a record level of 8.5 per cent in January 1999 (Figure 2.3),[15] and is projected to peak at 10 per cent in 1999 – leaving 2 million people out of work.[16] Unskilled young people have been hit hard by employment contraction. The teenage group, consisting mostly of middle and high school graduates seeking unskilled jobs, constituted the highest jobless rate of 25 per cent of the total unemployed, followed by 12.3 per cent for the twenties' age group. In July 1999 farm employment numbers had increased to 2.65 million representing a 4.1 per cent increase from the previous year and reflecting a reverse migration from urban to rural areas.

In tandem with rising unemployment, the real income of an urban household during the third quarter of 1998 had plunged to its lowest level in 35 years.[17] The monthly household income of 1.76 million won ($1,300) reflected a drop of 20 per cent from the previous year.[18] Correspondingly, the monthly real income of the remaining urban worker fell to US$ 420. According to a recent survey,[19] 60 per cent of salaried persons saw their wages cut sharply, while only 10 per cent had a slight increase in their earnings. These figures for unemployment and wages are respectively the highest and lowest levels recorded in a country where layoffs and homelessness have been non-existent over the past four decades of development.

In this regard, the impact of the crisis on the distribution of income has by no means been inconsequential. While the recession induced by the austerity measures triggered an explosion in the number of jobless and homeless, the earlier high interest rate policy benefited the rich who could continue to live off their bank deposits. Most strikingly, incomes of a small group of domestic capitalists and CEOs in fact rose during the past year of economic contraction. Thus, amid the historically low trends in average income, the gap in income between rich and poor further widened in a country that has been proud of its heritage of growth with equity. Clearly, the unresolved problems of growing unemployment, depressed incomes for the working population, and a widening income gap, remain.

An Alternative Restructuring Strategy

In only a year, Korea has made remarkable progress in overcoming the crisis. In the absence of drastic changes in the global economy, economic recovery is expected to accelerate throughout 1999 and result in a positive GDP growth. The rapidity of Korea's economic rehabilitation reflects the fact that the crisis was a liquidity problem and, more significantly, is in large measure attributable to the good governance of the DJ Kim administration. The range of reforms and the speed at which they have been implemented are unparalleled in the recent experiences of other emerging markets.

Korea's reform process will, and should, by no means end with the current changes. In the long run, there remains the arduous task of transforming the entire society into one equipped to cope with the global economic reality. Without comprehensive structural and institutional reforms, Korea cannot be assured of making the recovery sustainable to avoid a recurrence of the present crisis. Until the country develops a competitive financial system; a flexible labour market; a diversified ownership structure in the chaebols; technology-oriented small businesses; and a democratic system founded on a viable civil society, it cannot be viewed as being on the path to sustained prosperity in the global economy.

Long-term institutional reforms are bound to involve conflicting interests of diverse social groups in a democracy. Most urgently, Korea has yet to develop social consensus among business, labour, and government.

The reform-oriented DJ Kim government has been encountering a daunting challenge from both the chaebols and the labour force – both of which are too big a contending force for the government to tame.

The main agendum in corporate restructuring is to reduce to a bare minimum the chaebols' overlapping businesses. The 'big deals' that led to the consolidation of the top five chaebols have reshaped the nation's industry, making the business structure more concentrated. Such consolidation, however, will not solve the basic oversupply problem in the industry unless the selected businesses are willing to make difficult choices regarding layoffs and investment. The newly installed government supervisory committee can have lending by banks to a firm halted, if it fails to comply with the committee's request for its merger with other firms. Over time, however, as the macroeconomic situation improved, many chaebols have acquired access to different sources of funding from increasingly liberalised capital markets. They have begun to rebuff the government. This new power of the chaebols throws into question the viability of the government's plan for swaps and mergers among the firms.

In the context of chaebol restructuring, the state must also come up with an alternative framework for a flexible labour market by breaking away from its past heritage of job security and rigid wage structure. While a flexible labour market would be necessary to make Korean exports more competitive and induce foreign investment, the recent rise in the unemployment rate poses a serious social problem, since the country does not have an adequate safety net for the unemployed. The difficulty in labour reform emanates from the divergently interrelated stakes involved in policy change among the three groups of government, business, and labour.[20] Business and labour have long maintained a symbiotic link, which has its historical origin tracing back to Korea's authoritarian past. In the past, the chaebols were frequently assured of being financed by government-subsidised credits when faced with a financial crisis. In return, they were able to maintain social stability by holding on to their employees and subcontract suppliers even during an economic downturn.

The DJ Kim government prefers to have some control over layoffs to protect the interests of the labour force since it needs to retain their political support. In restructuring the economy, the government must start by introducing a clear set of rules governing layoffs and establishing a national safety net for the laid-off. In the long run, the workers' cooperative participation in the production process will be essential for business success. To achieve this, for instance, a scheme for employee stock ownership could be introduced, which can replace part of direct cash payments. Worker's shareholding can be a first step in the search for a consensus. The Korean labour force has shown in the past a willingness to trade job security for management-sharing.

As regards external relations, since globalisation is no longer an option, Korea is destined to pursue its national strategy for global economic integration. As restructuring efforts are moving in the direction of neoliberal market reform, a new role of the state need to be articulated. There is a clear need, as a late-comer in the global market, to expedite the development of market forces internally to prepare for global challenges. Trade strategy must aim at reducing liabilities while maximising benefits from an integrated world. In a global environment, the conventional comparative advantage theory should be understood in the dynamic context where systemic development of high-value, technology-intensive products; speed and types of investments; economic management; and the strategic alliance with foreign partners, would be essential for success in export competition.

In the long run, sustainable international competitiveness for a resource-poor country such as Korea can be assured only by developing a knowledge-based industry. Paul Krugman (1994) argues that East Asian growth is driven by simple over-investment, and not by gains in productivity. This argument suffers from a methodological problem in estimating the sources of growth,[21] as it overlooks important points about East Asia. In East Asia – including Korea, productivity and investment are virtually inseparable.

Productivity gains in the region, aided by high savings and investment, have been made possible by extensive technology transfer, adaptation and development. The World Bank estimates that gains in total factor productivity account for as much as a third of East Asian growth (for Japan, Taiwan and South Korea) during the period 1950 to 1980.[22] Thus, rather than passively embrace the dictates of free trade, the state needs to take concrete action in creating an environment in which knowledge capital can accumulate. Specific measures should include support of R&D efforts; development of world class clusters to create knowledge networks; joint ventures for technology transfer; and human capital development through educational reform.

Moreover, the task of enhancing international competitiveness must be tackled in ways that reduce domestic poverty and economic inequality. As poverty and inequality in society are likely to rise with the deepening of globalisation (Kim 1997b), the state will be forced to play an increasingly active role in social welfare, and govern the market to deal with the rising human toll. The state must be prepared with comprehensive programmes to develop human capital, to manage the dislocations caused by external shocks, and to provide safeguards for the victims.

In summary, the challenge facing Korea is to articulate and implement an alternative restructuring strategy – one that will conform to the GATT rules of a multilateral, open trading system, while at the same time enhance the international competitiveness of the country's exports. The task of restructuring the economy in a democracy is further complicated by the fact that the democratic process of policy formulation must be learned in an environment where its culture and tradition have not been conducive to modernisation.[23]

The Korean Lessons

The last ten years or so have seen Korea experiencing dramatic economic reform and restructuring. Market liberalisation has brought into the system dynamic and powerful economic forces and turned the 'governed' market into something which is significantly challenging the assumptions of the government about how the market functions and the methods it used to make the market work. Instead of being a simple process of moving towards a set of ideal institutions, the transition itself turned out to be a source of problems as well as inspirations. What lessons then can be learned from the Korean case? There are three important lessons that are particularly relevant for other transitional economies: the importance of distinguishing financial liberalisation from trade liberalisation; good governance in the reform process; and the need for a comprehensive scope in market reform.

First of all, the Korean experience tells us that unfettered financial liberalisation implemented in a weak institutional setting makes the economy liable to devastating consequences from global capital forces. In a country such as Korea, with high savings and a balanced budget, the IMF's austerity programme transformed a currency crisis into a severe economic recession. Such painful contractions could have been avoided with less restrictive conditions placed on the macroeconomy (Feldstein 1998).

It further reinforces the post-crisis consensus that financial liberalisation without adequate regulatory institutions can be counterproductive, unless the country already has an autonomous and sound financial system. Although emerging markets may be intrinsically vulnerable to the volatile forces of external capital, the root cause of the Korean crisis must nevertheless be seen as originating from factors internal to the domestic economy. Many emerging economies will ultimately have to liberalise their capital markets. Until a fair, international regulatory system is established for disciplining global capital movements (Soros 1998), the developing economies owe it to themselves to take proper measures for self-defence.[24]

The process of liberalisation should thus be gradual and prudent, proceeding only when the domestic financial system is strengthened.

Secondly, the Korean case demonstrates the imperativeness of proper state governance in market reforms. Market forces by themselves cannot serve as a mechanism to correct various forms of market failure. They cannot be relied on to restructure the country's monopolistic corporate system. State intervention however could expedite effective restructuring by rooting out resistance from the anti-reform groups. Thus, Korea's embrace of market liberalisation is presumed to lessen statism, and yet it provides a new space to expand it. The Korean reform model has shown that it needs less state intervention in certain areas but more of it in others.

Such 'proper' areas for state governance, include the continued need to implement measures to enhance democratic corporate governance for the transparency and accountability of management; to monitor and regulate domestic financial institutions and corporations for potential insolvency; to provide social safety for those left behind in a liberalised market economy; to take preventive measures to minimise the potential damages of global capital forces on the economy; to develop national strategies to explore new opportunities in global and regional markets; and to strive for a long-term goal to build a knowledge-based economy, rich in human resources and intellectual capital.

The last, but by no means the least, significant element of the Korean reform is the DJ Kim regime's governing philosophy of a comprehensive structural reform (Kim 1999). It involves not only changes in policy matrix but fundamental structural changes in a wide range of social, economic, and political institutions. Success in policy reform should be seen as ephemeral, unless there is an assurance that a similar crisis will not be repeated. Financial reform in an emerging economy can serve only as the stepping stone leading to the next phase in comprehensive structural reform. Reforms of labour, business, rural economy, foreign trade, as well as government itself, must be implemented within the framework of a coherent whole. The need for such a comprehensive structural reform reflects the complexity of the problems a transitional polity like Korea may inherit, as well as the challenge of the new economic conditions. Its success however demands, among other things, the vision and determination of the political leadership.

Notes

1 That Korean banks had high proportions of short-term debt in relation to gross external liabilities was attributable to the banking reporting system. The

Korean government required borrowers to report any long-term loans being sought from overseas but exempted the reporting of short-term loans. Short-term loans were considered to be used mainly to fund trade activities and thus did not need to be monitored. Borrowers had an incentive to acquire short-term over long-term loans.

2 A country's macroeconomic stability is conventionally measured by such indicators as government budget deficits, inflation rates, debt-GNP ratio, and current account deficits.

3 It is worth noting one positive side effect of high interest rates on the restructuring of the chaebol. Given the already high debt-equity ratios, the higher rates forced the chaebols to stint on capital spending, which accelerated the process of restructuring of the chaebols as they began to shed non-profitable businesses and break the old ties between member firms.

4 The pace of the won depreciation actually tapered off soon after the president election, when Dae Jung Kim recommitted himself to complying with the IMF reform program and G7 countries announced their relief intention to Korea.

5 Income distribution improved in 1996 due to the downturn in the real estate market, which adversely affected the income growth rate of the affluent group. *Newsreview*, 6 June 1998, p. 27.

6 Critics were concerned that ongoing efforts for structural adjustment might fail if the government took pump-priming steps at a time when financial and corporate restructuring was incomplete. There was also the question of whether lowering interest rates would successfully expand the total money supply.

7 As of the end of September 1998, two of the 26 commercial banks that existed at the outbreak of the crisis, along with a number of other insolvent financial institutions, including 16 merchant banks, have been closed. Five banks have been acquired by stronger banks under government support (Claessens, Ghosh and Scott 1999: 90–92).

8 The series of mergers include, among others, one between two of the world's largest memory-chip makers (Hyundai Electronics Industries Co. and LG Semi-con Co.), which will be the world's second-largest DRAM-chip maker; one among the Samsung, Daewoo and Hyundai groups to combine their aerospace operations; and one among the Hyundai, Daewoo and Hanjin groups to consolidate their train-manufacturing businesses.

9 Completion of the chaebol's restructuring programmes by 2000 is seen to significantly boost their international competitiveness, and enhance Korea's external credit status. Hyundai alone is scheduled to reduce its debt-to-equity ratio from the current 333 per cent to 200 per cent by 2000, through offering of new shares or repayment of debts.

10 In reality, exports fell 2.6 per cent to $120.6 billion compared to the first 11 months of 1997. Imports plunged 37 per cent to $84.7 billion, which generated a trade surplus of $36 billion. Exports began to gain momentum after May 1998.

11 During the first nine months of 1998, the Financial Supervisory Committee ordered 5 commercial banks to close down and 11 to restructure. Out of 377 non-bank institutions, 34 were ordered to close, 21 were suspended from operating, and 20 were to restructure.

12 To begin with, Korea had a mild fiscal surplus at the time of the breakout of the financial turmoil in December 1997. The budget deficit gradually widened to 0.8 per cent in February 1998 and 5 per cent of GDP by November 1998.

13 Korea's imports for all of 1998 were estimated to fall short of $100 billion, for the first time in five years. For Korea's economy, which depends on imports of critical raw materials and energy, a serious fall in imports would adversely affect the nation's growth potential. In 1999, the import situation seems to have improved, as export expansion has been accompanied by balanced import growth.

14 The rest of Korea's labour market includes mainly small-scale establishments and the informal labour sector that consists of daily workers, part-timers, and employees in family business. Employment in this sector is unstable as workers can be laid off at the discretion of employers (Park 1999).

15 To date, the government's unemployment compensation scheme is most inadequate; unemployment benefits cover only a small fraction of the unemployed and the duration and amount of the benefits is very limited. Moreover, the current system tends to benefit relatively well-off workers, laid off from the modern sector firms. While temporary and day labourers represent the majority of layoffs, they are not covered by unemployment benefits (Park 1999).

16 Estimates by the National Statistical Office, Seoul, Korea.

17 National Statistical Office in Seoul. See *Newsreview*, 28 November 1998, p. 27.

18 The consumption slump was prevalent in all sectors except heating and lighting. Expenditure on clothes and shoes marked the highest contraction.

19 The survey data by the Federation of Korean Trade Unions.

20 For a comprehensive reform proposal on business, government, finance, and labour in Korea, see Root 1999.

21 Krugman's argument is based on Alwyn Young's estimates of total factor productivity. which is derived as the residuals from his production function regressions. No account is taken of the embodied nature of technology with new investments.

22 World Bank 1993: 58. Also 'The Asian Miracle: Is it over?' *Economist*, 1–7 March: 23–25.

23 According to the traditional Asian value system, family and personal relations are given primacy over and above any formal and legal rules. Clientelism and 'cronyism' has long persisted in such a corporate culture. Korea's economic institutions, which are deeply rooted in the culture of familism with a relatively low level of social capital outside kinship circles, will thus evolve into a system far short of Anglo-American style pluralism and liberalism.

24 China has avoided the fate of its neighbours as its capital market was closed to free international capital movements. The governing philosophy of the Chinese government is to slow down the liberalisation process until adequate control mechanisms are in place.

CHAPTER THREE

Shiping Zheng

Institutional Adaptation Under Pressure: China's Changing Economic Environment

Reform and restructuring in China took place in a different context from that of the other AMCs. But as with these other AMCs, the decade of 'post-Socialist reform' since 1979 has unleashed tremendously powerful, relentless and unruly market forces into the existing system. While these forces promoted competition and productivity and contributed significantly to the rapid economic recovery and growth, they also posted serious problems to the Chinese state in managing the economy, forced the governing institutions to reshape, and are ultimately redefining the state-market relations.

The power of the market forces seems to be no better illustrated than in the recent Asian financial crisis. It changed the 'simple' task of reform of the socialist system into something much more complicated. Initially, few in China seemed to have expected the regional financial crisis to prolong and worsen. For China, 1997–1998 would have been very good years. Entering 1997, China had already managed a 'soft-landing' of its economy under the shrewd leadership of Vice Premier Zhu Rongji. The galloping inflation that hit a record-high of 22 per cent in 1994 was brought down to one per cent without stalling the economic growth. Deng Xiaoping's death in February 1997 was much anticipated and therefore did not lead to any succession struggle as some analysts had predicted.

On 1 July 1997, China took over Hong Kong from the British government. Except for the downpours on June 30th, the end of the 156 year-old colonial rule of Hong Kong proceeded smoothly and orderly. In September 1997, the Chinese Communist Party convened its 15th Party Congress at which the post-Deng leadership had firmly consolidated its political power base. In October-November 1997, Chinese President Jiang Zemin paid an official visit to the United States, the first Sino-American summit in eight years. In March 1998, Zhu Rongji was confirmed as China's fifth premier at the Eighth National People's Congress (NPC). At his first news conference after becoming China's premier, Zhu Rongji announced an ambitious three-year plan to solve the problems of the state-owned enterprises (SOEs), while maintaining economic growth and low inflation. Against the backdrop of these more headline-grabbing events, the unfolding financial crisis in Asia seemed like anything but China's business.

However, as the financial crisis in the region not only prolonged, but also worsened, pressure on China began to build up. China's foreign currency market showed growing instability, attributable to rumours about a possible devaluation of the Chinese currency, Renminbi (RMB), and increasing activity of illegal foreign currency trading. Foreign direct investment into China, which had already been showing signs of slowing down prior to the Asian financial crisis, was now declining. China's export industry was hit by declining demands from the Southeast Asian nations. China's banks, financial institutions and SOEs, already burdened with bad debts, inefficiency, and corruption problems, now faced even more difficult times.

The Chinese economy, which had been growing at an average rate of 9 per cent over the previous seventeen years, was no longer sustainable at that rate. Even the 8 per cent growth rate set by the Chinese government for 1998 was not achieved. As the number of layoffs and unemployment rises, many disgruntled workers have taken to the streets to protest, causing grave concern about social instability.

The market pressure, intensified by the financial crisis, forced the Chinese government to make some aggressive and controversial policy changes and institutional adaptation. This chapter will look at this market pressure in the context of the new phase of China's reform and restructuring over the past 10 years, especially against the backdrop of the recent Asian financial crisis. Focusing on four separate but related functional areas, namely, currency management, reasonable economic growth rate through investment and export, state-owned enterprises reform, and banking system restructuring, the chapter will show how the new market forces affected the course of reform and the state's policy options, and how the government met the challenge through policy adjustment and institutional adaptation. The Chinese case clearly demonstrates that more than a social engineering project driven by a clear-cut ideological model, the transition in China is an example of a sophisticated interplay of the new economic dynamics, existing institutional arrangements, and planned actions and forced responses of the state.

The Challenge of A Stable Currency

The first and, indeed, the most frequently noted response to the Asian financial crisis from China is the Chinese government officials' pledge that China will not devalue its currency in the near future. Since the July 1997 devaluation in Thailand, on almost every major international occasion, Chinese leaders, from President Jiang Zemin and Premier Zhu Rongji to Foreign Minister Tang Jiaxuan, Foreign Trade Minister Shi Guangsheng, Finance Minister Xiang Huaicheng and China's Central Bank Governor Dai Xianglong, have assured the international community and foreign investors of China's commitment to keep the value of RMB stable. The repetition and frequency of China's pledge is both unprecedented and ironic.

On the one hand, China's decision not to devalue its currency is clearly not just an economic one, but also a political one. The Chinese state was endeavouring to calm the market, both domestic and international. On the other hand, despite repeated assurance by the Chinese government, the devaluation rumours continued, leading to more no-devaluation pledges from the Chinese leaders. The market thus relentlessly challenged the Chinese state's determination and ability to keep the RMB stable.

Analysts taking a cynical view of the Chinese government's pledge may believe that the Chinese leaders are simply playing the no-devaluation card in order to draw more international attention to China's newly acquired role in stabilising the financial situation in Asia, or to put more pressure on the Japanese government to stabilise the Japanese yen and revitalise the Japanese economy. Whatever the merit of the suspicion, it would be economically unwise and politically counterproductive for China to play the no-devaluation card as it would do more harm than good to the Chinese economy.

Since 1985, China has devalued its currency six times (1985, 1986, 1989, 1990, 1993, and 1994), from an exchange rate of 2.8 yuan per US dollar in 1985 to 8.27 yuan per US dollar in 1997. Each devaluation seems to have had a positive effect on China's export growth and consequently foreign currency reserves (see Table 3.1).

In 1997, the Chinese government decided not to devalue the RMB even though the currencies of other Asian nations depreciated dramatically. The initial decision to keep the value of the RMB stable was probably based more on political considerations, because currency devaluation would necessarily be a greater risk than no action at all. As the Asian financial crisis worsened and began to affect China's export industry, more economic calculations came into the equation. Economic admin-

Table 3.1 China's Exchange Rate, Export, and Foreign Currency Reserves 1986–97 (Billions of US$)

Year	*Exchange Rate RMB/US$*	*Export*	*Foreign Currency Reserve*
1986	3.45	30.9	2.1
1987	3.72	39.4	2.9
1988	3.72	47.5	3.4
1989	3.77	52.5	5.6
1990	4.78	62.1	11.1
1991	5.32	71.8	21.7
1992	5.52	84.9	19.4
1993	5.76	91.7	21.1
1994	8.62	121.0	51.6
1995	8.35	148.8	73.6
1996	8.30	151.1	105.0
1997	8.00	182.7	139.9

Source: PRC Statistical Bureau: *China Statistical Yearbook, 1998.*

istrators and managers in the Ministry of Foreign Trade, the export industry and southern Chinese regions like Guangdong, which accounted for 40 per cent of China's exports, called for a reconsideration of the devaluation of the RMB. They were worried that China's export competitors in the region, with their greatly devaluated currencies, would increase their market share in the world at China's expense.

Others, however, suggested that the Chinese currency was actually under pressure of appreciation, not depreciation, thanks to China's huge foreign currency reserves of more than US$140 billion and a trade surplus of US$30 billion in 1997. Although China's foreign debts reached US$138 billion in mid-1998, about 86 per cent of them were medium- or long-term debts. Moreover, while a strong RMB would make China's export less competitive, opponents of devaluation were not fully convinced that a depreciated RMB would necessarily boost China's export industry because devaluation of the RMB could trigger another round of currency devaluation across Asia. A devalued RMB would also make imports more expensive and so hurt exporters using imported components (USCBC 1998b). Ultimately, the Chinese leaders were concerned that devaluation of the RMB could undermine the Chinese citizens' confidence in the banking system, leading to economic turmoil and even social riots as seen in Indonesia, South Korea, and Malaysia. It would also destabilise the currency in Hong Kong and threaten the Hong Kong dollar's peg to the US dollar.

The Government's currency position has been relentlessly challenged by the domestic and international market forces. On China's black market, trading of foreign currency became increasingly active. At the same time, international currency speculators were attacking the Hong Kong dollar's peg to the US dollar and indirectly challenging the stability of the RMB. On several occasions, the People's Bank of China (PBOC) had to intervene in China's foreign currency market to keep the exchange rate stable, but these interventions were costly and often proved to be only partially successful.

Moreover, currency market intervention did not address the issue of outflows of foreign currency through unofficial channels. China's foreign currency exchange system has undergone several important changes in recent years. On 1 January 1994, China abolished the dual-track exchange rate system and created a unified rate based on a managed floating system by the PBOC. Since 1 July 1996, after the new *Regulations on Foreign Exchange Control* went into effect, all Chinese and foreign companies, Chinese institutions and government agencies, can buy and sell foreign currency through designated banks. On 30 November 1996, the RMB became fully convertible under the current accounts. However, without the approval of the State Administration of Foreign Exchanges (SAFE), trading of foreign currency by businesses and individuals is still illegal in China.

Nevertheless, because of loopholes in the control and monitoring system, and poor communication between banks, customs offices, and foreign exchange bureaus, billions of dollars were traded without the government's authorisation. Black markets, although illegal, existed in many cities. Street traders were often quoting higher buying rates for US dollars than the official exchange rate. Then, with fake contracts and forged customs declaration forms, businesses and individuals could siphon a considerable amount of the purchased foreign currency into overseas accounts.

To stem the outflows of China's hard currency amid rumours and fears that China would devalue its currency to match the depreciation in other Asian countries, the Chinese government began to take more drastic measures in the fall of 1998. First, in early September, the SAFE ordered Chinese bank branches to cease trading hard currency as from 30 September 1998. After that date, only the headquarters of Chinese banks would be allowed to engage in foreign currency trading (*DJN* 27 September 1998). In October 1998, the Government announced that as from 1 December 1998, all foreign exchange swap centres (which used to act as the official channel for foreign enterprises to adjust their foreign exchange requirements) would be closed.

These moves were designed to strengthen central control over the legal transactions of foreign currency. Furthermore, in an effort to prevent smuggling of large sums of foreign currencies out of the country, the Government, in August 1999, implemented a new rule requiring Chinese banks to obtain approval from the SAFE before they can issue exit permits for foreign currency leaving China in amounts exceeding US$4,000 for Chinese citizens and US$10,000 for non-Chinese citizens (*CD* 17 July 1999).

Second, the Government has adopted a new system for tracking foreign exchange outflows. The Import Customs Clearance Certification System, which was first tested in ten Beijing financial institutions and then in Shanghai and Guangzhou in early November 1998, was extended to the whole country on 1 January 1999. Under this system, all foreign trade companies are issued a digital identity card, which allows banks to verify customers' import declaration papers within seconds, protecting the banks against forged documents and preventing unauthorised parties from buying foreign currencies. Together with a national network linking banks, customs offices and foreign exchange bureaus, officials from the SAFE hope that the new tracking system will help control fraudulent foreign exchange transactions and improve foreign trade efficiency (*DT* 26 October 1998).

Third, in 1998 the Government launched a crackdown on illegal foreign currency traders, and firms that illegally obtained hard currency and deposited it overseas. The authorities believed that serious capital flight was the main reason for the stagnation of China's foreign exchange reserves, despite China's growing trade surplus (*SCMP* 20 October 1998). In August 1998 the official Xinhua News Agency announced that individuals who traded more than US$200,000 or made a profit of more than RMB 50,000 would be prosecuted, as well as companies found trading more than US$5 million or realising a profit of more than RMB 500,000. Middlemen who connected traders with clients would be charged if the trading exceeded US$1 million or if their profits surpassed RMB 100,000. This announced measure, which looks like a permit, rather than a crackdown on smaller illegal currency traders, highlighted the magnitude of illegal currency trading in China and the limit of the state's regulatory power.

Nevertheless, the state prosecutors have been able to crack a few big cases of illegal currency trading. One earlier case involved illicit foreign exchange transactions by 958 companies with a total profit of US$2 billion. A more recent case involved the Tourist Bureau of Xinhui City in Guangdong Province where bureau officials were charged with illegal gain in foreign exchange of US$36 million. In yet another case, managers from 334 firms were accused of holding US$773 million and HK$46.57 million offshore against government regulations.

The Standing Committee of the NPC has passed new laws, *Contract Law and the Securities Law*, against companies cheating the state by transferring or keeping their foreign exchange incomes abroad. Furthermore, since April 1999, the Government has waged an intensive nationwide crackdown on black market foreign currency trading which has resulted in destroying more than 50 illegal trading spots. In the meantime, hotlines have been set up in Chinese cities for people to report illegal foreign currency trading activities (*CD* 31 July 1999).

The long-term effect of the Government's actions to restrict bank transactions and control outflows of foreign currency remains to be seen. In the short-term, some of the measures are believed to have already stabilised the RMB and helped China's foreign exchange reserves reach US$145 billion at the end of 1998.

The Cycle of Market Economy

Along with its pledge not to devalue the RMB was the Chinese government's promise to keep Chinese economic growth at 8 per cent in 1998. Since the mid-1990s, China's gross domestic product (GDP) has shown a declining trend. The highest GDP growth rate of 14.1 per cent in 1992 was followed by 13.5 per cent in 1993; 11.8 per cent in 1994; 10.2 per cent in 1995; 9.7 per cent in 1996; and 8.8 per cent in 1997. Even though they are decreasing, these growth rates are nothing short of extraordinary. Indeed, a double-digit growth for an extended period is neither sustainable nor desirable.

Growth Target Under Market Conditions

However, the Chinese leaders believed that the Chinese economy needed to maintain a certain growth rate below which China would face severe consequences. In an interview with *Business Week* in 1994, then Vice Premier Zhu Rongji suggested that it would be dangerous to have an economic growth at 7 per cent 'because that would create major disruption to the economy. In addition, that kind of fluctuation would lead to social instability.' In late 1997, as the Asian financial crisis was unfolding, the Government set a target GDP growth rate at 8 per cent for 1998. Premier Zhu Rongji made it his personal commitment, as well as the top priority of his new cabinet, to reach that target.

While it was already a 0.8 percentage point lower than the actual growth rate in 1997, the 8 per cent target for 1998 became an increasingly questionable growth rate as the months went by. For the first six months of 1998, for instance, the GDP grew only 7 per cent. By the fall of 1998, official figures indicated that China's GDP grew only 7.2 per cent in the first three quarters due to declining export demand, the devastating floods in the summer, and sluggish domestic consumption. Some analysts suggested that the Government would have to boost the economy to 10.4 per cent growth over the fourth quarter of 1998 in order to achieve the 8 per cent growth rate set for the whole year (*AFP* 20 October 1998).

Theoretically, the Government could simply revise the target growth rate to reflect the changing realities, but a pledge to keep economic growth at 8 per cent seemed too much a commitment for the Chinese leadership, particularly Premier Zhu, to give up. Therefore, while the Chinese officials frequently reassured the public and the international community that despite serious difficulties, the 8 per cent growth was still attainable, the Government took a series of measures to sustain the economic growth, particularly by attracting more foreign investment, helping the export industry, and boosting the domestic demand.

Foreign Investment

From the early 1980s and until recently, China had been very successful in attracting foreign direct investment (FDI), thanks to bold policy initiatives, including the decision to open up China for foreign investment. In 1980–81, Special Economic Zones (SEZs) were set up in Guangdong, Fujian and later in Hainan. In 1984, Economic and Technological Development Zones (ETDZs) or Free Trade Zones (FTZs) were established in fourteen coastal cities, followed by several more FTZs in Dalian, Guangzhou, Zhangjigang, Tianjin and Shenzhen, and Pudong New Area in Shanghai. Moreover, in 1980, China joined the World Bank and International Monetary Fund and has since become the World Bank's largest borrower and one of the largest recipients of bilateral development assistance from advanced industrial nations. China has also become an important commercial borrower in the world.

Among China's sources of overseas direct investment, Hong Kong is by the far the largest, often accounting for more than half or two-thirds of the total foreign investments in China, followed by the United States, Taiwan, Japan, Singapore and South Korea (see Tables 3.2 and 3.3).

By the end of July 1998, among the 314,533 overseas-funded projects registered in Mainland China, 174,880 (55.6 per cent) were tied to Hong

Table 3.2 Foreign Direct Investment in China by Source Country or Region 1990–97 (amount contracted in US$ million)

	1990	*1991*	*1992*	*1993*	*1994*	*1995*	*1996*	*1997*
Hong Kong	3,833	7,215	40,044	73,939	46,971	40,996	28,002	18,220
Japan	457	812	2,173	2,960	4,440	7,592	5,131	3,400
USA	358	538	3,121	6,813	6,010	7,471	6,916	4,940
Taiwan	1,000	3,430	5,543	9,965	5,395	5,849	5,141	2,810
Others	1,948	3,405	7,241	17,759	19,864	29,374	28,086	22,410
Total	7,596	15,410	58,122	111,436	82,680	91,282	73,276	51,780

Source: USCBC, 'Foreign and US Direct Investment in China 1979–97.'

Table 3.3 Foreign Direct Investment in China by Source Country or Region 1990–97 (percentage of the total contracted amount)

	1990	*1991*	*1992*	*1993*	*1994*	*1995*	*1996*	*1997*
Hong Kong	50.5	46.8	68.9	66.4	56.8	44.9	38.2	35.2
Japan	6.0	5.3	3.7	2.7	5.4	8.3	7.0	6.6
USA	4.7	3.6	5.4	6.1	7.3	8.2	9.4	9.5
Taiwan	13.2	22.3	9.5	8.9	6.5	6.4	7.0	5.4
Others	25.6	22.1	12.5	15.9	24.0	32.2	38.3	43.3

Source: Calculated from the figures in 'Foreign and US Direct Investment in China 1979–97.'

Kong investors. Contracted and utilised capital inflow from Hong Kong reached US$288 billion and US$135 billion, accounting for 52 per cent and 54 per cent of the national total (*HKTDC* 1998). US investment in China has also been growing steadily. By the end of the first half of 1998, the United States had invested in 25,495 projects in China worth over US$43 billion (*AFP* 20 October 1998). Taiwanese investment had a contracted value of US$40 billion spread over 40,608 projects by September 1998.

As the figures in the two tables suggest, FDI in China has shown a downward trend in recent years. In 1997, while China's utilised foreign investment rose by 8.5 per cent to US$45.3 billion, contracted foreign direct investment plummeted to US$52 billion, down 29 per cent from the 1996 level. The number of foreign-invested projects and contracted foreign capital declined by 14.4 per cent to 21,028 and 29.4 per cent to US$51.8 billion respectively. Contracted investment from all China's major overseas investors decreased: Taiwan, by 45 per cent; Hong Kong, by 35 per cent; Japan, by 34 per cent; and the United States by 29 per cent.

There are multiple factors for the decline of FDI in China; some are temporary and others more structural. First, the economic recession in Japan and the financial crisis in other Asian countries greatly shrank the capital available for investing in China. For instance, during the first half of 1998, direct investment from Japan and South Korea plunged by 31 per cent and 32 per cent respectively. Second, the Taiwan Strait crisis in 1996–97 also dampened the enthusiasm of Taiwanese businesses for investing in Mainland China. Third, slower growth of foreign-invested projects and contracted foreign capital was at least partially caused by the Chinese government's decision to suspend tariff exemption for equipment and machinery imports enjoyed by foreign-invested enterprises (FIEs).

To the extent that China's economic growth has, over the years, become dependent on high flows of FDI, the decreasing rates of FDI were serious enough for the Government to act. One drastic measure taken by Beijing in early 1998 was to reverse its 1996 decision to terminate the investment incentive by reintroducing the duty-free and value added tax (VAT) free treatment for the importing of select capital equipment. Under the new policy, projects approved after 1 January 1998, if they are favoured by the Government and have completed feasibility studies, can apply to the local economic planning commission for a special certificate that proves to the Customs Office that the project is entitled to duty- and VAT-free import privileges (*USCBC* 1998c). Moreover, for the first time, the duty/VAT-free treatment also applies to domestic investments that fall under a separately issued list of *Industries, Products and Technologies for Which Development is Encouraged by National Policies.* China is also opening up its tertiary sectors, including wholesale/retail, information, legal advice, accountancy, and consulting services, to overseas investors.

As a guide for foreign investors, the Government has published a new *Guiding Directory on Industries Open to Foreign Investment*, which lists different types of projects that are either 'encouraged,' 'restricted' or 'prohibited'. Strongly favoured are investment projects that utilise high technology, especially in agriculture, raw materials, and environmental protection, and projects in pharmaceuticals, medical equipment, textiles, transportation, and electronics. Investment projects that utilise labour and resources from China's central and western regions are also 'encouraged.'

While China has been trying hard to improve its investment environment, high capital flows into China ultimately are contingent on regional recovery from the financial crisis and consequently the availability of large sums of capital. For the first half of 1999, new pledges of foreign investment dropped by 20 per cent and actual foreign investment fell by 9.2 per cent. Obviously, there are limits to what the Government can do to attract foreign investment and most experts agree that rapid growth of FDI in China for more than a decade cannot be sustained over the long-run. As of 1998, for the fifth consecutive year, China has been the world's second largest recipient of foreign capital after the United States.

Export

Twenty years ago, China's foreign trade was very limited and less than a dozen state trading corporations monopolised the industry. Since China began to open its door to the world, China's total foreign trade has been growing rapidly from US$21 billion in 1978 to US$325 billion in 1997 (*Xinhua* 1 November 1998). China's merchandise export volume reached US$ 182.7 billion in 1997 with a trade surplus of US$ 40 billion (*CMEI* 1998). Within merely two decades, China has become the world's tenth largest trading nation, with foreign exchange reserves of more than US$140 billion, second only to Japan. Foreign trade made up a mere 4.7 per cent of China's GNP in 1978, then rose to 10.8 per cent in 1988, and was as high as 38 per cent in 1997. Today, more than 300,000 firms in China are authorised to trade directly with foreign countries. Among China's top ten trading partners are Japan, Hong Kong, the United States, the European Union, South Korea, Taiwan, Singapore, Russia, Australia and Indonesia. These ten economies together accounted for 83.7 per cent of China's total foreign trade in 1997. Foreign trade, particularly export, has become another engine for China's fast economic growth in the recent decade.

In late 1997 and early 1998, however, China began to feel the impact of the regional economic crisis. Drastic currency devaluation by other Asian countries and outflows of capital and investment from Asia caused China's exports to these countries to fall sharply, particularly iron and steel, mineral fuels, and cotton. China was the biggest crude steel producer in the world in 1997 and the Asian market had accounted for 80 per cent of China's steel exports. In the first half of 1998, however, Chinese steel exports plummeted by 38.1 per cent (*CDBW* 18 November 1998). China's garment export, which was traditionally one of its strongest export industries and had grown at 10 per cent in previous years, grew only 6.25 per cent on average in the first nine months of 1998 (*CBN* 21 October 1998).

Even though China's exports to the United States and the European Union surged by 16.5 per cent and 21.7 per cent, and those to Africa, Russia, Latin America, and Australia surged by 18 per cent on average (*HKTDC* 1998), China's overall exports rose just 3.9 per cent in the first nine months of 1998, in contrast to a 20.9 per cent growth for the whole year of 1997 and well below the 10 per cent growth target set by the

Government for 1998. For the whole year of 1998, China's exports to Indonesia, South Korea, Thailand and Malaysia dropped by 44 per cent, 32 per cent, 24 per cent and 17 per cent respectively (*USCBC* 1998b).

As slumping exports weakened China's ability to maintain high economic growth and further worsened the job market situation for millions of workers already laid off by debt-ridden state-owned enterprises, the Government adopted one aggressive measure after another to promote exports. For instance, in 1998 the Ministry of Finance and the State Administration of Taxation raised the export tax rebate three times. Beginning on 1 January 1998, the export tax rebate for textile machinery was raised from 9 per cent to 17 per cent. Then on 1 June 1998, the tax rebate rate was raised from 9 per cent to 14 per cent for shipping exports; from 2 per cent to 11 per cent for steel and cement exports; from 3 per cent to 9 per cent for the coal industry; and from 9 per cent to 11 per cent for textiles.

Again on 1 July 1998, the Government raised the export tax rebate from 9 to 11 per cent for exports of seven special categories of machinery and electronic products and five categories of manufactured light industry products. When criticised for using export tax rebates as a form of export subsidy, or a disguised devaluation of the RMB, the Government officials pointed out that export tax rebates are a common international practice and China's rebate rates are in line with the rules of the World Trade Organization (*CD* 20 November 1998).

While export tax rebates may serve to promote China's export industry in the short-run, they are not sufficient to regain the export momentum that China had experienced during the previous decade. In the first half of 1999, China's exports still fell by 4.6 per cent to US$83 billion. Unless there are major improvements in the second half of 1999 China's trade surplus in 1999 will drop to US$ 20 billion from a record US$ 43.59 billion in 1998.

What is likely to have a more profound impact on China's competitiveness in the world market in the long-run are the ongoing major institutional changes of the Chinese export regime. For many years, enterprises under the Chinese export regime had to obtain approval from the State Economic and Trade Commission (SETC) and the Ministry of Foreign Trade and Economic Cooperation (MOFTEC) before they could engage in foreign trade business. In October 1998, the SETC officials announced that China would phase out the approval system and replace it with a registration system more in line with the international practice (*CD* 4 October 1998). Meanwhile, in certain areas, export quota or general licence control were being loosened.

Another major step toward deregulation in the foreign trade regime was the decision by the MOFTEC to grant direct import and export rights to China's private manufacturing enterprises and research institutes, effective from 1 January 1999, whereas before the policy-change, private enterprises had to go through state-owned foreign trade companies to carry out import and export business. Chinese private enterprises and research institutes will also be allowed to join export and import Chambers of Commerce (*CD* 16 October 1998). Chinese trade officials are hopeful that private enterprises will become a new dynamic player in promoting China's exports.

Domestic Demand

While trying to sustain the growth of FDI and exports in the face of the Asian financial crisis, the Chinese government also introduced several economic stimulus packages in 1998 to boost the domestic demand. One was the decision to accelerate the housing reform by abolishing the long-existing welfare housing policy and encouraging people to buy their houses. Commercial banks in China have relaxed mortgage policies to help the development of the housing market (*HKTDC* 1998). The Government also lifted a ban on car loans, offered by banks, which had been imposed in 1995 because of fear of inflation.

What is more controversial, however, is the Government's expansionary monetary and fiscal policy. On the one hand, the PBOC has eased the money supply by lowering the commercial banks' deposit reserve ratio and cutting commercial banks' deposit rates four times since October 1997. On the other hand, the Government has accelerated the state's investment in fixed assets and infrastructure. Following a 13.8 per cent increase in the first six months of 1998 over the same period in 1997, fixed-asset investment increased by 22.9 per cent, 26.9 per cent, 33.0 per cent and 28.4 per cent in July, August, September and October respectively. These increases exceeded the targeted rate set at about 20 per cent earlier in 1998 by the NPC (*SSB* 1999). In August 1998, the NPC approved the Government's plan to issue RMB100 billion (US$12 billion) bonds to state commercial banks to finance the increased in fixed-asset investment, especially in infrastructure development.

These economic stimulus measures, which may constitute China's 'new deal,' are highly controversial. China's MOF officials suggested that the newly adopted stimulus packages were only short-term policy responses to the Asian financial crisis and were unlikely be repeated in the future (*SSN* 3 November 1998). Some analysts, however, believe that China's market reforms are backtracking, with the Government using China's huge household savings to pump more money into the debt-ridden state-owned enterprises and shifting investment funds from fast-growing coastal regions to slow-growing interior regions (*WP* 3 December 1998). Others are worried that the new treasury bonds will put more pressure on fiscal revenues, and a swollen domestic money supply would place heavy inflationary pressure on the value of the RMB and exchange rates.

Will China's 'new deal' work or can China spend its way out of the Asian financial crisis? Early indications suggest that the success of China's expansionary policy is possible, but far from certain. In 1998, China's GDP grew at a rate of 7.8 per cent, not 8 per cent as insisted by the Chinese government, but that was no small victory in view of the worsening financial crisis in the region. In the first half of 1999, China's GDP grew by 7.6 per cent compared with the same period in 1998 and China should achieve the 7 per cent growth rate set by the Government for 1999. But this level of economic growth has been possible largely because of continuing government spending and rising government fiscal deficit.

Having incurred a fiscal deficit of RMB57.5 billion for 1994; RMB58.2 billion for 1995; RMB53 billion for 1996; and RMB57 billion for 1997, the Chinese government created a fiscal deficit of RMB96 billion for 1998. And the fiscal deficit for 1999 was budgeted to be as high as RMB150 billion, which nearly tripled the size of the annual fiscal deficit between 1994 and 1997. The Government has undoubtedly taken an enormous risk in trying to pull China through the most difficult times the region has experienced since the end of the World War II. Meanwhile, Chinese consumer demand has remained weak for almost two years and for the first half of 1999, retail prices fell 3.2 per cent and the Chinese economy faced a serious threat of deflation.

State Owned Enterprises

The state-owned enterprises have long been a financial burden on the Government and one of the key point of crash between the new market conditions and existing institutional arrangements. About two-thirds of the SOEs are losing money and 90 per cent of the bad loans by China's state banks are with SOEs. The Construction Bank of China, for instance, had over RMB200 billion (US$24.16 billion) bad assets. China's economic growth and banking reform is seriously hampered by the collapsing SOEs (*WP* 29 November 1998). In his political report delivered at the 15th National Party Congress in September 1997, Party General Secretary Jiang Zemin called for major changes in ownership and operation of China's SOEs (*CD* 12 September 1997). The Party congress endorsed a reform strategy aimed at 'grasping the large and letting go the small,' meaning that the state would help its large SOEs to become competitive enterprise groups while setting free all the small- and medium-sized SOEs by means of ownership reforms through public shareholding, workers' joint-stock companies, mergers, acquisitions, or bankruptcy.

The 8th National People's Congress held in March 1998 further called for deepening reforms of SOEs along with reforms of government administration and the banking system. At his first news conference in March 1998, Premier Zhu Rongji confidently told the audience that three years would be sufficient for China to bring most of its money-losing state-owned enterprises out of difficulty. 'We believe that we're absolutely able to attain the goal of bringing most state-owned enterprises now suffering losses, out of their difficult situation in a period of three years, or by the end of this century.' Zhu based his confidence on the calculation that while more than 40 per cent of the 79,000 industrial enterprises owned by the state are suffering losses, only 10 per cent among the 500 extremely large state enterprises, which account for 85 per cent of the revenues to the state, are suffering losses. In the meantime, Zhu ruled out the possibility that the Asian financial crisis would have an impact on the pace of China's reform of the SOEs.

By late 1998, however, as the Asian financial crisis continued, analysts began to question whether Premier Zhu's ambitious goal of 'lifting the great majority of state-owned enterprises out of difficulty in three years' remained realistic. In the first six months of 1998, for instance, the state sector continued to suffer heavy losses, reaching more than US$37 billion. Even Sheng Huaren, minister of the State Economic and Trade Commission, acknowledged that the SOE reform had proved more difficult than anticipated (*NYT* 1 December 1998).

The initial SOE reform strategy of 'grasping the large and letting go the small' essentially meant that the Government would select, for national development, large SOEs in strategic sectors and pump in vast amounts of state capital to restructure them and improve their performance, while 'dumping,' by way of sales, mergers, and bankruptcy, a large number of smaller enterprises which were either bankrupt or had limited potential (*KNI* 28 September 1998). Both the 'pumping' and 'dumping' elements of the SOE reform strategy encountered great difficulties, as the reform proceeded. The impact on the national economy caused by the collapse of a few giant corporations in South Korea and other Asian countries indicated to the Chinese leaders that bigger is not always better, particularly for those large corporations whose survival depends on financial support of the government.

On the other hand, in a rush to 'dump' the losers, local government officials often hastily put their SOEs up for sale, sometimes at bargain-basement rates. It was reported that 1,078 small and medium-sized SOEs located in 13 cities of Heilongjiang province, with a total of 320,000 employees, were offered for sale at a trade fair in 1998. Some provincial government officials even attempted to give away some of the troubled companies for free. Liaoning province, home to 10 per cent of China's SOEs, tried to sell off 1,500 of its unwanted companies through a promotional tour of major southern cities, including Shenzhen and Xiamen. Sichuan province sent a delegation to Hong Kong to look for potential buyers for a trial list of 52 SOEs. This rush of sales of the SOEs prompted Premier Zhu to order a halt in late 1998. Zhu accused local government officials of misunderstanding the SOE reform. Concerned that the half-sale, half-giving away of enterprises would result in great losses of state assets, Zhu suggested that sales should not be the sole way of reforming those enterprises (*CD* 30 December 1998).

China has been listing its SOEs on stock markets in Hong Kong, New York and London for more than ten years. While overseas listing has helped China's SOEs adapt to the requirements of the international capital market, its success as a way of raising capital is limited. Since 1993, China has given approval to 85 companies to issue shares overseas and only 45 have been listed, raising about US$10 billion by 1998. Of those listed, thirty-two are on the Hong Kong Stock Market (*CD* 7 December 1998).

Recently, China approved eight more companies for overseas stock listing, but much depends on how soon the Asian economy in general, and the Hong Kong Stock Market in particular, can recover. Overseas stock listing has to be a long-shot for rescuing China's ailing SOEs. Domestically, about 900 companies are listed on China's two stock exchanges, Shanghai and Shenzhen. There is an indication that the Government plans to allow more SOEs to trade a larger percentage of their shares on the domestic stock markets as a way of reforming the ownership of the SOEs (*WP* 8 August 1999).

A major obstacle to SOE reform is rising unemployment. China's SOEs account for two-thirds of urban employment, more than 100 million people. SOE reforms, plus such factors as an oversupplied domestic market and sluggish exports caused by the Asian financial crisis, have created an unprecedented number of layoffs and unemployment in China. According to official figures, the urban unemployment rate edged up to about 3.1 per cent by the end of 1997. In early 1998, an official government report suggested that an unemployment rate of five per cent would be acceptable as long as economic growth hit achieved at least nine per cent. However, some Chinese economists suggested that the urban jobless rate had already reached eight per cent in early 1998, twice as high as the official figure (*CET* 14 October1998).

Worse still, Chinese economic growth could only be expected to grow at below eight per cent over the next several years while more layoffs and unemployment are on the way. By the end of 1998, more than 10 million Chinese workers were laid off and another 8 to 10 million people could lose their jobs over the next two years. For instance, China's textile industry in 1998 began to implement a three-year plan to cut the production of spindles by 10 million and lay off as many as 1.2 million workers (*Xinhua* 7 November 1998). These figures do not include the unemployed in the rural areas who, in turn, have become what is known as the 'floating population', estimated at more than 100 million.

Growing unemployment has already caused serious concern about social instability. There have been many reports of people protesting in the streets in several provinces as well as in Beijing, demanding financial support from the Government. Local government officials who have to deal with the potentially explosive unemployment situation in their areas have intensified their lobby for the central government to slow down the SOE reform.

Premier Zhu Rongji, who in March 1998 declared that 'no matter what is waiting in front of me – whether it be landmines or an abyss – I will blaze my trail', strongly argued that trimming of state-owned enterprises had to continue even though many workers had lost their jobs as a result. In November 1998, while visiting China's northeastern 'rust belt', where most of China's money-losing SOEs are located, Zhu insisted that the main reason SOEs were losing money was because they had too many superfluous workers. 'They must lay off people if they are to stop losing money and improve efficiency. There is no other way out.'

To throw people out on the streets is, of course, politically dangerous. In the hopes of preventing massive protests and social turmoil from taking place as SOE reform continues, the Government has accelerated the reform of its social security system and taken several social protection measures to help laid-off workers, including income supplements and re-training programmes. In March 1998, the Government set up the Ministry of Labour and Social Security to develop and administer China's social security system. Meanwhile, more than 300 cities have established a minimum-income security system (*HKTDC* 1998). In 1998, the Government allocated RMB8 billion (US$970 million) for local governments and SOEs to open various re-training or re-employment centres for laid-off workers while temporarily covering their basic living expenses. Local governments were also urged to come up with more funds to help laid-off workers.

In the meantime, Premier Zhu placed pressure on SOE managers. In November 1998, Zhu warned that managers who proved to be unable to improve efficiency and re-employ the laid-off workers would be removed from their posts. Managers would be shown the 'yellow card' after one year's bad performance and 'sent off' the following year if they failed to turn business around. Zhu said auditors sent by Beijing would 'vigorously examine' the accounts of money-losing enterprises. Managers found to be responsible for bankrupting the companies would be 'fired without mercy.' Bosses who 'lived off the enterprises and profited themselves' and those who took bribes would be punished to the 'utmost of the law.' (*CD* 30 November 1998)

While SOEs, particularly large ones, still absorb the lion's share of the state resources, the Chinese non-state sector has become an increasingly important player in the national economy. The non-state enterprises, which include collective-owned and private-owned enterprises generated about 36.7 per cent of the overall retail sales of consumer goods and 63.1 per cent of the total industrial output in 1997 (*HKTDC* 1998). In response to the Government's call to stimulate economic growth and relieve unemployment pressure, China's state-owned commercial banks expanded their lending efforts in 1998 to small and medium-sized enterprises, many of which are in the non-state sector.

Finally, the Chinese government has also moved to restructure the government-business relationship through streamlining government agencies and 'de-linking' government institutions with economic units. In March 1998, the government reorganisation plan proposed by Zhu Rongji reduced the number of central government ministries and state commissions under the State Council from 40 to 29. According to the plan, the number of staff working in government institutions would be cut by half in three years' time, making redundant some four million government workers.

In the fall of 1998, the Chinese leaders ordered the military, police and judicial units to hand over control of their enterprises to civilian authorities by the end of the year, followed by another order in November 1998 for all Communist Party and government units to break their links with the enterprises that have been operating under them (*WP* 29 November 1998). These moves, if they prove to be successful, should not only help the Government regain the macro control over the national economy, reduce the state budget deficit, and fight corruption; but also pave the way for accelerating the SOE reform (*CD* 7 November 1998).

Banking System

China's banking system is just another major point of tension between the new market conditions and existing institutional arrangements. Unsound lending practices and lack of independence and transparency in the banking system are now considered to be the primary contributing factors for the Asian financial crisis. Yet banks are always the most cherished and protected property of the Government. Like the state-owned enterprises, many of China's banks are antiquated, poorly managed, deficient, and heavily influenced by political factors.

As China moves towards a market economy and becomes increasingly integrated with the world economy, it has become a top priority for the Government to develop a modern banking system that meets the international standard. In 1995, the NPC passed the *Central Bank Law*, *Commercial Bank Law*, and *Negotiable Instrument Law* that serve as legal frameworks for banking reform. In April 1996, a unified loan certificate system was introduced in most large- and medium-sized cities in order for the Government to regulate commercial lending. In April 1997, the PBOC began to institutionalise its monetary policy-making procedure by forming a 'Monetary Policy Committee' to adjust, monitor and manage China's monetary policies. However, it was the worsening Asian financial crisis that prompted the Government to take major steps towards restructuring the Chinese banking system.

The Chinese banking system originally consisted of several groups of banks. The first group was the People's Bank of China and its multiple layers of more than 2,400 branches at provincial, municipal and county levels. Until the most recent structural changes, branches of the PBOC were subject to dual control: the vertical administrative control from the head office of the PBOC in Beijing, and horizontal political control from provincial and local Party committee and government at the each same level.

The second group included three government policy-lending banks: the State Development Bank of China, the Import and Export Credit Bank of China and the Agricultural Development Bank of China. The third group included four major state-owned specialised commercial banks: the Bank of China, the Industrial and Commercial Bank of China, the Agricultural Bank of China, and the Construction Bank of China, more than a dozen specialised or local commercial banks, and over 60,000 rural and urban cooperative banks.

In addition, there were more than 240 international trust and investment corporations (ITICs) that were set up in the 1980s to attract foreign investment, raise funds for local development projects, and make investments on China's stock markets. Apart from the China International Trust and Investment Corporation, all the ITICs are controlled and backed by provincial and municipal governments. The total assets of China's ITICs were estimated at US$55 billion.

China's state-owned banks and other financial institutions are plagued by the problems of inadequate funds and a vast number of bad loans resulting from the past practice of policy-lending. By some accounting standards, about 25 per cent of the total outstanding loans of the Chinese banking system were non-performing loans, adding up to US$200 billion in 1996 or about 25 per cent of China's gross domestic product (*SCMP* 15 May 1998).

For many years, the PBOC hardly functioned as an independent central bank. Horizontal political control over the PBOC branches at provincial, municipal and county level gave local officials a good deal of influence over the bank's lending decisions. In the name of developing the local economy, it was common, and even seemed legitimate, for local officials to pressure the provincial branches of the PBOC to relax lending policies and approve loans for projects that turned out to be either duplicated or financially unsustainable.

To cover the operating losses, state-owned banks have essentially used individuals' savings. On the positive side, China's saving rate has remained high – between 30 and 40 per cent of Chinese household income. On the negative side, however, there are already scattered reports of depositors rushing to local banks to withdraw their savings.[1] Lessons learnt from the Asian financial crisis suggest that any attempt to fix the banking system after it is broken will be much more costly and dangerous.

Moreover, China's some 240 trust and investment firms bogged down with bad loan debts have already caused great instability in the financial sector. In September 1998, the Guangdong International Trust and Investment Corp. (GITIC) became the first to go by default. In the first half of 1998, GITIC had an 80 per cent drop in net profit. It was unable to pay loans up to US$6 billion and has an outstanding foreign currency debt amounting to US$1.38 billion. In October 1998, two more ITICs, the Dalian International Trust and Investment Corp. and the Guangzhou International Trust and Investment Corp. failed to make foreign debt repayments on the due date.

Despite the fact that the GITIC was set up and backed by the Guangdong Provincial Government, the PBOC, in early October 1998, ordered the GITIC to shut down by revoking its operating licence and right to trade foreign currency. All GITIC's accounts and assets were frozen by the court order. The Chinese Finance Minister Xiang Huaicheng predicted that more closures of local investment and trust companies would follow. Also, in October 1998, twelve local banks in the city of Beihai of Guangxi were ordered to close (*AFP* 29 October 1998). Earlier in June, the PBOC put the Hainan Development Bank out of business.

The Government also took aggressive measures to rectify its futures market. In November, the government announced that it would reduce the existing 14 futures markets to three (in Shanghai, Dalian, and Zhengzhou) by the end of 1998 in order to curtail excessive speculation in these tradings and to fend off the Asian financial crisis. This was a major reduction from the 60 futures markets in the early 1990s when the futures trading was at its peak (*AFP* 10 November 1998). These closures demonstrate the Government's determination to rectify the banking and financial institutions and avoid the financial crisis that has affected the economies of many of its Asian neighbours.

Restructuring the PBOC system is the core of China's banking reforms. At the national conference on financial affairs held in November 1997, the Government decided to reorganise the PBOC so that as China's central bank it will be authoritative and independent in performing its monetary policy-making, supervisory, and regulatory functions. According to the restructuring plan, all PBOC's branches at provincial and municipality level are to be abolished and inter-provincial, regional branches set up instead.

After a year of preparation, the PBOC announced in November 1998 its intention to implement the new banking system. The newly organised PBOC is represented by nine greater regional centres or 'megabranches,' each of which now has jurisdiction over several provinces and municipalities and their geographic responsibilities include:

1 Tianjin branch (Tianjin municipality, Hebei and Shanxi provinces, and Inner Mongolia);
2 Shenyang branch (Liaoning, Jilin, and Heilongjiang provinces);
3 Shanghai branch (Shanghai municipality, Zhejiang and Fujian provinces);
4 Nanjing branch (Jiangsu and Anhui provinces);
5 Jinan branch (Shandong and Henan provinces);
6 Wuhan branch (Jiangxi, Hubei and Hunan provinces);
7 Guangzhou branch (Guangdong and Hainan provinces, and the region of Guangxi);

8 Chengdu branch (Sichuan, Guizhou, and Yunnan provinces, and Tibet); and
9 Xi'an branch (Shaanxi, Gansu, and Qinghai provinces, and the regions of Ningxia and Xinjiang).

In addition to the nine regional centres, the Beijing and Chongqing branches are under the direct control of the Business Department of the PBOC headquarters. These organisational changes are intended to give the PBOC independence to implement its macroeconomic policies, to better monitor, supervise and regulate the nation's banking and financial institutions, and to reduce or eliminate the financial risks incurred by the intervention of local governments (*AFP* 17 November 1998).

While the PBOC is being made to function more as a central bank, the Government has also taken action to turn the four major state-owned banks, the Bank of China, the Industrial and Commercial Bank of China, the Agricultural Bank of China and the Construction Bank of China, into independent commercial entities closer to international standards. They will be given decision-making power over their financial activities and bear responsibilities for their own risks, profits and losses.

Following the cut in deposit reserve ratios by commercial banks, the PBOC abolished lending quotas for state-owned commercial banks on 1 January 1998, in favour of indirect loan-control measures. The PBOC also plans to move towards a market-driven interest-rate management system, which will relax interest-rate control and allow commercial banks to set their own floating saving and loan interests within a specific range.

In recent years, China has been cautiously but steadily opening up its banking sector to foreign banks and financial institutions. By the end of 1997, 64 banks from 16 countries and regions have been licensed to establish a total of 142 operational branches in China. Assets of these banks totalled US$38 billion by the end of 1997, up 27 per cent over 1996. More than twenty Chinese cities, plus Hainan Province, are open to foreign banks. Until the end of 1996, a major restriction was that foreign banks were, typically, not allowed to conduct RMB-related business. On 31 December 1996, the first batch of foreign banks, including the Hong Kong Bank, Citibank, Bank of Tokyo – Mitsubishi and the Industrial Bank of Japan, officially received licences from the PBOC to conduct RMB business in Pudong New District of Shanghai on a trial basis.

On 24 January 1997, the second wave of foreign banks, including Standard Chartered Bank of Britain, Sanwa Bank, Daiichi Kangyo Bank and the Shanghai-Paris International Bank, were also granted licences to offer RMB deposit and loan services to China-based foreign clients in

Pudong. By the end of March 1998, their RMB assets amounted to 916 million yuan (US$110 million). In April 1998, an official with the PBOC confirmed that another eleven foreign banks had met the government's criteria concerning assets scale, operational period in China, and performance record, and will therefore be licensed to do RMB business. In August 1998, the PBOC announced its decision to allow an expansion of foreign banks' RMB business outside Pudong New District, and in November 1998, two foreign banks in Shenzhen were licensed to conduct RMB business (*Xinhua* 25 November 1998)

Conclusions

Since the late 1970s when Deng Xiaoping's reform began, China's economic system has undergone major changes. While decollectivisation, decentralisation, privatisation or marketisation may describe some of these changes, none can fully characterise the complex process of the changing political economy in post-Mao China. It is obvious that China has been moving away from the Mao-style state economy, but it is less clear what kind of economic system China is moving to. What is clear are two things. First, the market has occupied an increasingly important position in the state's management of the economy. The government's predominant role in shaping the direction of the economy has undoubtedly become increasingly susceptible to market forces.

Second, despite, or perhaps because of, these changes, the state is still an effective manager of the economy. The Chinese government was not brought to its knees by protests and riots in the streets as happened in Indonesia, or by international financial institutions as was the case in South Korea. Nor was it incapacitated by slow changes in the economy as occurred in Japan for several years and still occurs today in Russia. Instead of seeking emergency aid from the IMF, China has pledged to the IMF US$4.5 billion for helping the Asian economies hit by the region's financial crisis and another US$540 million for assisting Russia to deal with its financial crisis (*AFP* 17 November 1998). Despite all the speculation, the fact that China has become an island of relative calm instead of the eye of the storm in the regional financial turmoil, raises interesting questions about the state's role in managing economic transition and sustainable development under the new market conditions and in meeting challenges from powerful and sometimes disruptive forces generated by global economic and technological changes.

It is tempting to suggest that China is simply lucky this time. By the mid-1990s, the Chinese economy had not been fully integrated into the global economy, though by some estimates it had already become the second largest in Asia and the third largest in the world (*IMF* 1993). Most importantly, the Chinese currency, the RMB, is not freely and fully convertible with foreign currency. The capital outflows from China are not easy, which presumably shielded China from the devastating assaults which other Asian countries faced from international financial institutions and currency speculators. Even if the 'RMB' or 'luck' factor initially stopped the domino effect and prevented China from becoming the next economy to fall in Asia, it cannot steer the Chinese economy out of the regional crisis nor solve China's own economic and financial problems.

Others suggest that China's huge foreign currency reserves are the ultimate weapon China has in dealing with any economic crisis. Foreign currency reserves, however, could only buy China some time, rather than provide a solution. Moreover, if China's state-owned enterprises continue to consume more than they produce; if China's export industry loses its competitiveness and market share; and if China's banking institutions are not made to become financially sound and efficient, China's foreign currency reserves could ultimately be depleted.

The Chinese state, whether it can be accurately labelled as hard-authoritarian, soft-authoritarian, or democratising, is certainly far from desirable. The way the Government directs, manages, or otherwise shapes the economy is not what some neoliberal economists would endorse. For others, market reform in China is still too slow and too little, and thus more severe consequences or crises are lying ahead. But ideological preferences and value judgement aside, one has to admit that for all the 'wrong' or 'right' reasons, China turned out to be more capable of handling the fallout of the Asian financial crisis than most of its neighbours.

As the World Bank is blaming the IMF for mishandling the Asian financial crisis and international financier George Soros and others are talking about the collapse of global capitalism, it seems all the more important for *national* governments to maintain some control over their economies. Governments should not substitute for or replace the market, for this has already proved to be a great failure in such command economies as seen in the Soviet Union and Mao's China. Nor should they become a hostage to, or a slave of, market forces. This approach to governance has also proved to be socially irresponsible and politically dangerous in the recent financial and economic crisis in Asia and other regions.

Between the two extremes lies a mixed economy in which both the state and the market can coexist and cooperate. While any kind of 'mixture' of the state and the market is open to criticism and modification, what matters most is to ensure that the market functions, rather than misbehaves and the government governs, rather than dictates.

As the Chinese government continues to battle with many serious economic and financial problems, it is a hazardous business to prescribe a 'right' recipe for China's problems, or to speculate what the Chinese economy might look like five or ten years down the track, or even to predict whether China will ultimately rise as a superpower with a stronger economy, better financial institutions, and a functional state-market relationship. What we can or probably should do is to understand the magnitude of the challenge of reforming a socialist system; complexity of the new market conditions; changing preferences of individuals, groups and society as a whole; and delicate, difficult and often risky policy options facing the Government. It is with this realistic understanding that the reform and the new relations and arrangements it has generated could be better understood.

Notes

1 One such run happened in November 1998 to several urban cooperative banks in the City of Huizhou City in Guangdong Province (*World Journal* 25 November 1998).

PART II

The New Political Conditions

CHAPTER FOUR

Peter Harris

China's Aimless State

Introduction

In elite circles in Beijing and Shanghai the belief is widespread that Chinese society, and by extension, the Chinese state, are entering into a qualitatively new phase of evolution, one that is uncharted and will entail untried opportunities as well as dangers. This proposition can be found expressed in a variety of discussion papers, books and articles published during the last two or three years. One example of a relatively cogent version of it is to be found in a report published in 1998 in *Zhanlue yu guanli* [*Strategy and Management*].[1] The report, entitled 'Short- and Mid-term Trends and Hidden Dangers in the Structural Transition of Chinese Society' (Sun, Li and Shen 1998), identifies three phases in the current Chinese reform process.

According to the three authors of the report, the first phase, already over, involved the erosion, that is the dismantling, of old socialist organisations and structures such as the people's communes. They do not mention a timeframe, but are evidently referring mainly to the period 1978 to 1984–85. The second phase, now coming to an end, consists of the transition to a market economy (the adjective 'socialist' in the authors' analysis is conspicuously absent), and has involved a shift in emphasis to the urban sector. The third phase is now starting and set to last ten years, and will, the authors predict, involve the 'comprehensive reconstruction' of Chinese society.

Implicit in this, and other recent Chinese commentaries, is an assumption not only of unprecedented social change, but also of a gradual transformation of the relationship between the Chinese state and Chinese society. This assumption is the outcome of discussions within China that have taken place alongside, and overlapped, a protracted debate among scholars and commentators outside China about the social implications of economic reform in China since the 1970s. This external debate is well-known among China specialists but worth rehearsing for those who are not.

The Debate

Much of the debate has concentrated on the extent – if any – to which the dismantling of the models and practices of the Mao era (1949–76), and the re-emergence of allegiances, sub-cultures, communities, groups, agencies and organisations around the edges of, or beyond, the state, may constitute the emergence of a civil society comparable to those elsewhere, notably in the states of central Europe in the 1980s.

The debates about civil society in central Europe in the 1980s were partly about the role newly developing civil societies might play in undermining Communist governments. Similarly, an undercurrent in the discussions about nascent civil society in China today has been the extent to which its growth could represent a challenge to the Chinese Communist state. Anxious, perhaps, to avoid such implications, some scholars have conducted the discussions about China not so much in terms of civil society, but rather in terms of a public sphere – the social domain in which public opinion can be formed – taking as their point of departure Habermas' analysis of the role of the public sphere in the development of European capitalism (Habermas 1991).[2]

Like the concept of civil society (Gellner 1994, for example), the Habermasian concept of an emergent public sphere is firmly grounded in European experience, and in the divergence of public and private, state and society, which, in his view, is an essential historical characteristic of bourgeois capitalism. In the Chinese case, scholars have been divided as to how applicable, if at all, either the Habermasian concept of a public sphere, or the concept of civil society in any of its European senses, is to contemporary China, or indeed to China at any time during the last one hundred years or so.[3]

As far as contemporary China is concerned, opinions vary as to whether or not a form of civil society has emerged in the post-Mao era. Some, such as White, have indicated that the growing non-governmental sector in China may have some of the attributes that characterised civil society in central Europe in the 1980s, in the sense that while they have an ambiguous and complex relationship with the state they presage important changes in the balance of power between state and society, and contain 'the seeds of both political construction and collapse' (White, Howell and Shang 1996: 215).

Others have been more cautious and sceptical about the applicability of the concept of civil society to what they argue is still an authoritarian or corporatist state, one that now offers a limited degree of autonomy to individuals and social groups, but remains deeply intolerant of such groups or individuals playing anything approaching an antagonistic role outside the ambit of the state (Chamberlain 1998: 69–81 and Harris 1998).

Either way, many commentators agree with the Strategy and Management researchers that China today is experiencing a significant, perhaps extraordinary, transformation within the broad nexus of state and society, however that is defined. The transformation consists, among other things, of new forms of social diversification and stratification, changing distributions of wealth and major alterations in gender roles; the growth of a new, more confident and worldly class of managers, entrepreneurs and urban intellectuals able to function partly or wholly outside the framework of state-owned institutions and *danwei* [work units]; and a wholesale shift in mood, especially in coastal cities and among young people, away from politics and the nostrums of the Communist Party and towards the many facets of contemporary mass culture, including more open and frank forms of public discussion of many aspects of life other than formal politics.

There is thus a somewhat ill-defined sense of new social and political forces at work, reinforced by memories of the unprecedented expressions of public discontent embodied in the 1989 Tiananmen crisis, and by the reports, often stifled inside China, of vain but persistent efforts by dissidents to expand the scope of legitimate political activity. It may be too soon to say whether these newly emergent forces presage a major redefinition of the balance in China today between public and private, and state and society; but what is clear is that they embody and complement a gradual evolution in the purpose of the Chinese state, and the role it plays *vis à vis* society, which it is not too soon to assess.

The Teleocratic Tradition of The Chinese State

The most effective way to make such an assessment may be to consider these emergent forces and changing social circumstances from a point of view somewhat different to the one discussed until now. Rather than considering the state of Chinese society, it may be better to analyse the state of the state – that is, to diagnose the condition and intentions of the state with which the society is so intimately interleaved.

If that is so, it may also be possible to benefit from definitions and descriptions of the state that derive from the European experience but are less tendentious than concepts such as the public sphere and civil society. It is arguable that there is common ground between European and Chinese intellectual and political traditions regarding the nature and aims of the state which can provide us with a fruitful means of assessing the significance of changes affecting the Chinese state today.

Given the tendency nowadays among social scientists to respect the particularity of cultural traditions, establishing such common ground is a hazardous undertaking. But reasonable misgivings about glib comparisons and orientalist prejudice should not prevent us from applying models or hypotheses that offer broader, more fruitful perspectives than those of specific cultures, however strongly defined and irreducible some aspects of these cultures may be.

Despite their many underlying differences, it is reasonable to suggest that the two political traditions – Chinese and European – share a number of understandings about the basic condition of the state. For the present purpose one among these is particularly important. This is that by its nature the state – and before the modern state, the pre-modern state in China (Chan 1984) – tends to fall into one of two fundamentally different categories.

The first, which is close to, though still well removed from, a state of nature, provides only a bare framework for the untrammelled association of men and women in society, and has no other motive or design than to provide a morally neutral setting in which its peoples can pursue their interests and lead their lives. The second, qualitatively different from the first, is purposive, teleological and hence often directive in nature, its rulers and officers perceiving themselves to have an end or ends to which the state and its panoply of powers should be orientated.

In a European setting these two poles, or ideal types of the state, have been best described and analysed by Michael Oakeshott who, in tracing the emergence of the state, has drawn a fundamental distinction between the state as *societas* – an association of people acknowledging the authority of certain rules of conduct, but indifferent to the pursuit or achievement of a purpose – and the state as *universitas* – an association of people engaged jointly and exclusively in satisfying a common substantive want (Oakeshott 1975: 201–5).

The state as *societas* is unobtrusive, inclusive, tolerant of autonomous groups within society, and primarily concerned with providing security, order and a rule of law. The state as *universitas* takes a directive role with a strong state apparatus and is intolerant of those standing in the way of the fulfilment of its overriding goal or purpose. This is so whether that purpose is clearly and acutely defined in terms of specific goals, as in the case of states governed by a Communist party whose aim is to bring about a condition of communism, or whether it is cast in less stringent, more general terms, as in the case of a state whose avowed aim is the modernisation and economic development of its people.

Again in a European (and more specifically Spanish) context, Victor Pérez-Díaz has usefully described these two types of state slightly differently, as respectively the nomocratic type – a state governed by law and custom – and the teleocratic type – a state governed with an end or purpose in view (Pérez-Díaz 1998: 251–52). One can go further, and postulate not just two types of states, but rather a spectrum ranging from the purely purposeless state through forms of the state that are purposeful but only in a very broadly defined way – the common want being a want of the most general kind such as national wealth – to states whose grandest purposes are perceived in terms of realisable, all-embracing ideals such as those of Leninist Communism or Fascism.

Within the Chinese philosophical tradition (as in other parts of the Sinic world), there has been little or no explicit analysis of the two types of state along the lines undertaken by Oakeshott. The contours of these two types of state are, however, historically well defined within different elements of Chinese political theory and practice. A radical form of the first of the two types of state is the view of the state envisaged by early Daoist philosophers, and in particular Zhuang-zi and those associated with his name.

Zhuang-zi's admonitions against the moral high-mindedness of kings and their ministers reflect a broad distaste for intrusive politics and a deep sympathy for a minimalist state that have remained an abiding influence on Chinese political thought for two millennia.[4] The sections of the book *Zhuang-zi* that deals with the role of government prescribe a policy of almost complete non-interference that is entirely in keeping with this view. At the most, the writer accepts the need for order only to curb excess, otherwise the 'best policy is Doing Nothing' (Graham 1989, p. 310). More generally, while accepting the existence of a political order as inevitable, Zhuang-zi moves further than any ancient Chinese thinker (as Schwartz puts it) 'in the direction of denying [it] any function ... in "correcting" things.'(Schwartz 1985: 231–32).

In a completely different and much harsher form this view of the state, or at any rate of the rule of a king and his servants within a state, was also the view of some of the early Chinese philosophers later called legalist. (Legalism has always been associated in Chinese history with a ruthless authoritarianism, but at issue here are not the methods used by legalists to govern, but their overriding purposes).

It is not always clear from the writings of early legalists – *fa jia*, Chinese proponents of *realpolitik* for whom the English name of legalist is somewhat misleading – whether their authoritarianism is predicated on any larger aim or intention than the effective wielding of power. Shang Yang, the legalist minister of the early state of Qin, declared that the state did indeed have aims, those of 'the enrichment of the state and the strengthening of the army'. But the outstanding early legalist, Han Fei-zi, appears not to have subscribed to even this mildly teleological policy.

As Graham has convincingly argued, Han Fei came close to taking a non-interventionist view of the state, so much so that his views paralleled the views of the Daoist classic the *Lao-zi*. Whereas the *Lao-zi* advocated adapting to uncontrollable order, however, Han Fei sought to uphold 'an automatic social order' through the strict and pervasive application of rewards and punishments, an order in which the ruler himself would be 'reduced to one component in the machinery of state'.

From this perspective there is much less qualitative difference between the way early Daoist philosophers and Han Fei conceived the role of the state than is usually thought. Neither saw the state as having a purpose or aim, a teleological role; what they disagreed profoundly about was the extent and severity of the application of order needed to curb social excess and provide a framework in which society could function undirected (Schwartz 1985: 256; Graham 1989: 267–92).

In a less unqualified form this understanding of the state is arguably the view, or comes close to the view, of those Chinese ministers and officials, typified by the conservative Song dynasty scholar and statesman, Sima Guang, who regarded good government as nothing more nor less than the just and benign management of social order and the proper application of the law. In Sima Guang's conservative view, which echoes views and practices prevalent during the Tang dynasty, the state had a purpose, but only a limited one – to ensure political unity and stability.

A line had to be drawn between public responsibilities and private interests. Sima believed that it was, in Peter Bol's words, 'profoundly irresponsible to advocate policies to refashion the world according to an ideal model' (Bol 1993:148, 151–192, and 187). At its starkest, Sima's view of the ruler and the state had something in common with that of early legalists like Han Fei. Once the structures of a state (*guo*) had been put together by the founder of a dynasty, the task of the ruler was to maintain that structure with practical good sense, good will and determination. Sima told successive emperors that 'achieving order depends on but three things: first, the assignment of offices; second, reliable rewards; and third, necessary punishments' (Bol 1993:153).

Proponents and practitioners of the second, teleocratic version of the state represent a much more pronounced strand in Chinese political thought, and in recent centuries, particularly this century, have come to be seen as constituting an overridingly influential mainstream. In a moderate form, teleocratic conceptions of the state underlay the views of early Confucians such as Mencius, whose advice to kings about the state and government was informed by a nostalgic idealism, a desire to work towards the restoration of the rituals and observances of the early sages, and to achieve benevolent government and government policy in which morality is nurtured and the people's livelihood ensured.

Like many of his successors Mencius presupposed that the state and its ruler had a clear, even utopian purpose to fulfil, and that state policy should be formulated and carried out accordingly. In a different, more pragmatic way, this view of the state was also the view of the philosopher Mo Zi, whose utilitarianism was also underwritten by a moral purpose, the 'unifying of morality' (Graham 1989: 45).

But in the course of time, the somewhat restrained idealism of the early Confucians came to inform a more vigorous determination to shape the imperial state or realm through firm, pervasive moral guidance, combined with comprehensive policy-making and interventionist government. This determination was typified by ambitious reformists such as Wang Mang, founder of the Xin dynasty, and Sima Guang's Song dynasty contemporary Wang Anshi.

Wang Anshi's plans for reform, comprehensive as they were, were based on a conception of the state whose government and society were indistinguishable, whose ruler looked to the ancient sages for perfect models of the ideals he and his subjects pursued, and whose institutions met every need and desire, public and private. It is little wonder that Wang has often been regarded as the first precursor of Chinese state socialism.

Despite the critical view of Wang Anshi's reform programme taken by orthodox Confucian scholar-officials both at the time and afterwards, his strong state-centred moralism, if we may call it that, later became a hallmark of the Confucian bureaucracy, and was reinforced by the political and educational philosophy of Zhu Xi, the twelfth century Confucian synthesiser and founder of the School of Principle [*li xue*] and 'neo-Confucianism'. The trend was sustained or even increased throughout much of the Ming and Qing dynasties.

Exceptional scholars such as Huang Zongxi and Gu Yanwu may have sought, by one means or another, to temper the despotic, centralising tendencies of the imperial state (Huang by emphasising the moral conduct of princes and the importance of the law; Gu by advocating decentralised administrative authority). But even such rare critics of the established order remained firmly within the mould of the neo-Confucian *telos,* which was otherwise unchallenged, and indeed strengthened in practice by the absolutism of powerful emperors such as Hongwu, Kangxi, Yongzheng and Qianlong (Brook 1998: 30–32).

In a more radical form, this second tradition of the state was espoused in imperial China by leaders of political movements outside the established order, eschatological and utopian rebellions, some devoted to Buddhist or other millenarian beliefs, others subscribing to venerable concepts of great peace [*tai ping*] or great community [*da tong*] (Wakeman 1973: 101). The views of such rebels – men such as Hong Xiuquan, Heavenly King of the Taipings – were often based on utopian visions of a communistic society with new, more benign forms of governance, rather than a society governed by a strong state.

With the exception of the occasional Chinese ruler such as the Tang empress Wu, who portrayed herself as the bodhisattva Maitreya, the more explicit of these salvationist visions and aspirations were beyond the pale of Confucian orthodoxy, though their intellectual origins were not, and in their explicit utopianism they shared some ground (though not the communistic ideal of shared property) with the anarchistic idylls of poets such as Tao Qian. Paradoxically, when put into practice, the ideals of such utopian rebels tended to fall far short of, and even contradict, their intent, as they did during Taiping rule in Nanjing, and ultimately during the rule of the Chinese Communist Party (CCP). In much the same way chiliastic and other utopian movements in Europe – including, most recently, the Communist movement of the Third International – have tended to result not in anarchic utopias but in strongly controlling and directive states.

In combination with an increasingly influential range of European ideas, this intellectual legacy was reflected in perceptions of the state that were articulated in China during the late Qing and the early years of the Republic. In this formative period, when China found itself having to come rapidly to terms with the Western world, and with it the post-Westphalian system of states, the outstanding trend – anarchists and conservative Confucian influences apart – was towards a new but equally concerted and directive view of the state.

In response to the impact of Western imperialism, the corrosion of dynastic authority and the growth of regional and local interests, leading Chinese reformers advocated the creation of a strong, wealthy and centralised state, just as their Meiji counterparts in Japan were doing. The efforts of federalists to promote their cause, highlighted by Prasenjit Duara (Duara 1996, pp. 47–8), were eclipsed by advocates of a new Chinese nationalism, variously statist and ethnic, who emphasised the need for a new form of political unity and legitimacy capable of creating a robust state that could hold its own in the recently-discovered international state system.

The most outstanding advocate of this view was Liang Qichao, whose conservative republicanism and sympathy for Germanic statism corresponded well with his advocacy of state-centred citizenship – it was with good reason that he described the citizens in his famous work *Xin min shuo* [*On Renovating the People*] as *guomin,* people of the state – and of a new national *zheng tong* (Chang 1971: 149–219 and 238–71; Fogel and Zarrow 1997: 3–38; Liang 1989: 1–162).

In his early years Liang's thinking was influenced by the leading reform-minded scholar Kang Youwei, a monarchist with a strongly utopian turn of mind expressed in his *Da tong shu (Book of Great Community).* The *Da tong shu* appears to have been inspired by a mixture of Hua Yan Buddhism, a popular American novel about a utopian future, and the evolutionary view of the world (from chaos to *taiping)* of the *Gongyang Commentary* on the *Shu jing (Book of History),* which had gained popularity as a result of a revival of New Text Confucianism in the eighteenth and nineteenth centuries (Bernal 1976: 11–32; Hsiao 1975: 109–10; Cheng 1997: 61–81).

The ideas of these and other late Qing reformers were, in some form or other, teleocratic, in the sense that their prescriptions for society were all based on a shared perception that the common aim was the political, economic and social transformation of China, an aim that (Kang's ultimate goal of *da tong* utopia notwithstanding) could only be realised by means of a strong, directive state. The same was true of revolutionaries such as Sun Yat-sen, Wang Jingwei, Dai Jitao, Li Dazhao and Chen Duxiu, though it was not until the death of the anarchist Liu Shifu in 1915 and the diffusion within China of Leninist ideas about the state and revolution after the Bolshevik revolution, that those advocating a strong ruling party within a strong state predominated over anarchists and others of a less teleological frame of mind (Hoston 1994: 189–90 and 195–204). What monarchists like Kang, republicans like Liang, revolutionary republicans like Sun, and socialists like Chen and Li, disagreed about was not the nature of the state as such, but rather the political agency of transformation within it.

Thereafter the teleocratic trend in Chinese political thinking about the state was reinforced by the eclipse of the federalist idea, by the preoccupation of the May Fourth generation with the need for a unified, centralised state in the face of external aggression and internal fragmentation, and by the influence of Soviet Communism and Stalinist conceptions of state and society on both the Nationalist Party of China (KMT) and the Communist Party of China.

The intellectual break with the past brought about by the spread of socialist ideas in China was striking but not complete by any means. Even though the abolition of the state examination system, along with other changes in educational practice, and the social background of many of the new political leaders and intellectuals meant that they were not steeped in Chinese intellectual traditions in the same way as Liang Qichao, Kang Youwei and their generation had been, the new political elites were still influenced by many of the attitudes towards the state – its legitimacy, its territorial dimensions, its status as the embodiment of the nation, and its role in ensuring the nation would grow wealthy and strong – of their immediate predecessors.[5]

As a consequence, the People's Republic of China (PRC) was established in 1949 as an intensely purposeful state, with two overriding aims. The first of these was to build a wealthy, powerful, self-confident, ethically secure China, a China shaped by a strong, unified state defined territorially along much the same lines as the late Qing (the principal exception being Outer Mongolia, which retained its independence despite Mao asking Khrushchev in 1954 if China could have it back). The second was the desire to construct a socialist state, an aim which commanded a consensus within the new elite, and continued to do so until Mao and a minority of radical ideologists around him championed a new, more radical Leninist despotism against the growing scepticism, foreboding and, finally, disillusioned fear of their peers.

There is no need to revisit here, in any detail, the history of Mao's increasingly destructive, and in many ways expedient, pursuit of these two aims – the founding aims of the People's Republic of China. One aspect of the two founding aims is, however, important to note. This is that although they appear to have been in contradiction with each other (a point frequently made in recent years by Chinese officials decrying the impact of so-called leftist policymaking on economic modernisation), they were, in fact, largely self-reinforcing. The aims were self-reinforcing in the sense that many ambitious, hopeful Chinese intellectuals and politicians in the 1940s and 1950s perceived in Communism the best vehicle for the restoration of China's national strength and dignity, and only abandoned their support for it with the utmost reluctance.

They were also self-reinforcing in the sense that the construction of a socialist state was dependent upon a strong teleocratic state, one that served the cause of national construction just as much as the cause of socialism. This had been the case in the Soviet Union, where the planned creation of 'socialism in one country', with all that that entailed for the role of the state, had gradually emerged as the central tenet of official policy once it had become apparent, as it did to Lenin in 1921–22, that the Bolsheviks' earlier goal of state-free Communism – proletarian internationalism – was unachievable. Despite its early aspirations, Soviet Communism had thus turned out to be an effective way of strengthening the state, rather than diminishing or dismantling it. The same applied to Chinese Communism under Mao.

Not that for Mao, as for Stalin, the pursuit of Marxian internationalism within the framework of socialism in one country was altogether straightforward. There were bound to be contradictions and dilemmas. Like Stalin before him, Mao dealt with these dilemmas by muddling through, sometimes dwelling on internationalist aspirations – as he and his colleagues did to some degree in their support for anti-imperialist movements and Marxist-Leninist Communist Parties in the 1960s and early 1970s – but more often inclined to approach domestic and foreign policy in realist and statist terms.

If internationalist communism was a distant aspiration, socialism in one country was not, and the framework for its realisation had to be a well-armed, wealthy state. Indeed, the poorer the prospects of international communism, the sturdier the protosocialist state had to be if it was to deal with its enemies and antagonists at home and abroad. So although the arrangement sometimes seemed incongruous, the CCP's successive formulations of socialism, and Mao's own idealistic intentions, were firmly conceived within the framework of a teleological state.[6]

The problem, and there turned out to be one, was not the incongruities implicit in the concept of Marxist-Leninist socialism in one country, or in the twin founding aims of national reconstruction and socialist construction. Those could have been relatively manageable ambitions, similar in kind to post-war ambitions to construct a socialist welfare state in, say, the United Kingdom or India. It was, rather, the fact that the CCP leadership, and more particularly Mao himself, were devoted to more far-reaching, even utopian socialist ideals. These ideals characterised the policies of the CCP in the 1950s, 1960s and 1970s, policies Mao and, to a decreasing extent, other CCP leaders were committed to. Being state-based rather than internationalist, they further reinforced the teleocratic tendencies of the state.

This utopian idealism took two forms, or rather, had two intertwined strands. The first strand was the old goal of *da tong* which Mao, on the eve of the founding of the People's Republic, explicitly recognised for both domestic and foreign audiences as an element in the CCP's *weltanshauung*. Chinese scholars began to explore this *da tong* ideal again during the Great Leap Forward, even if, as it seems, they never took their explorations very far (Mao 1975: 414 and 418; *CASS* 1959; Schram 1974:115–16), and though it faded away thereafter, Mao himself never seems to have entirely forgotten it.

The second strand was the Stalinist socialism that CCP leaders had learned from their Soviet comrades, and perceived themselves as taking more seriously – arguably, *did* take more seriously – than the 'goulash communists' in Moscow, the second generation Soviet leaders under Nikita Khrushchev.

It seems odd to describe post-war Stalinist socialism, associated so clearly now with corrupt and discredited modes of governance, and with the enormities of the Stalin era, as being a source of utopian idealism. But in the 1940s and 1950s the CCP was still very far from disenchanted with the Bolsheviks, their lineage and their legacy. In its early years, at any rate, the CCP leadership embraced the aims and intentions of Stalin's policies and Soviet development strategy with concerted dedication.

Mao was occasionally critical, but at least until the debacle of the Great Leap Forward, and in certain respects for much longer, CCP leaders managed to sustain something close to a consensus, in public anyway, on the need to follow the basic parameters of the Soviet Model. This meant, above all, achieving and maintaining a high level of public ownership of the means of production as a prelude to full Communism, with the emphasis on state ownership in heavy industry and concessionary, mainly collective policies in rural areas in temporary acknowledgment of existing conditions and of peasants' class nature.

Many of the policies central to CCP state-making were based on the policy framework Stalin had used between 1928 and his death in 1953. They included the nationalisation of much of China's industry in the 1950s and 1960s, which eventually resulted in de facto state ownership or control of industry in the collective, as well as the avowedly state-owned sector. They also included the marginalisation of private enterprise; the creation of an agricultural production system based on state farms and collectives (even if the collectives were downgraded after the disaster of the Great Leap communes); and the ascendancy of the five-year plan and the state planning system, with allocated distribution of products and services.

In politics they included the persistent emphasis on class struggle; the existence of a large security apparatus based on the use of terror justified by the need to extirpate class enemies; and a huge system of labour camps beyond the reach of the law. All these policies were founded on the assumption, however little articulated, that a form of sharing, communitarian Communism in China would soon prevail, and was the utopian end justifying the means.

Only in a few important respects did CCP policymakers differ from the model developed by Lenin and more especially Stalin. Their vision of a decentralised communised system with intensified and unified central political control,[7] which they espoused under Mao's influence during the Great Leap Forward, and which Maoist radicals returned to in 1967–68, echoed a brief policy initiative undertaken during the Stalin era (the large-scale collectives of 1928), but one that Stalin never carried through. The determination of the elderly Mao, and a group of radical Marxists loyal to him, to instil proletarian values into the superstructure at all costs, (which was the rationale, to the extent that there was any, for the 1966–69 phase of the Cultural Revolution), was a more explicit assault on the ruling party and a more urgent measure to promote a higher stage of socialism than Lenin or Stalin (let alone Khrushchev) had ever undertaken.

From quite another policy perspective, the initial tolerance of a new people's democracy towards some other class interests, the basis for the Chinese People's Political Consultative Conference, promised a broader base of support for the CCP to build on than the Communist Party of the Soviet Union (CPSU) had ever sought, though the whole idea was discarded during the Great Leap Forward and again between 1966 and 1978. In addition, the early emphasis on the remoulding, rather than the destruction, of recalcitrant intellectuals seemed designed to secure the support, rather than the alienation, of a critical sector of Chinese society.

Most of these deviations from the Soviet model were designed in one way or another to create a faster, more effective road to Communism. They thus underlined, rather than undermined, the view within that CCP that the prospect of realising Marxian Communism was greater in China than in the Soviet Union. For most CCP leaders, they reinforced the view that Soviet-style Communism in China was a realisable national goal, that is, a goal to be achieved within the bounds of and under the direction of the Chinese state, and within a generation or so.

Not everyone within the CCP leadership saw this as plainly as Mao. Mao laid his plans for the Cultural Revolution by taking the lead in denouncing Soviet revisionism, notably in the polemical disputes between the CCP and the CPSU during the period 1960 to 1965, in particular the 'Nine Criticisms' published in 1963–64, as well as in notes he wrote in 1961–62 on Soviet economic policy. In these notes, not openly published at the time, he mapped the road to national, rather than international, Communism with single-minded clarity of purpose.

'After a good many years,' he wrote, 'after ownership by the people's communes has changed into ownership by the whole people, the whole nation [sic] will become an indivisible system of ownership by the whole people. This will greatly spur the development of the productive forces. For a period of time this will remain a *socialist* system of ownership by the whole people, and only after another period will it be a *communist* system of ownership by the whole people' (Mao 1977: 68–69).

Others within the CCP leadership seem to have avoided such sweeping predictions. However, most CCP leaders participated actively in the polemical debate with the Soviet Union and, despite differences of view, seemed ready enough to uphold the general Chinese – and more specifically Mao's – line right up to the mid-1960s. Only the assault on the established CCP leadership, and the crippling of essential elements of the Party and state apparatuses (Xiao 1998: 19–20) during the Cultural Revolution, alerted the CCP majority to the practical outcomes of Mao's train of thought.

Consequently, the sense that Stalinist policies represented a means of achieving a socialist utopia soon, even very soon – certainly sooner than the Russians, and certainly with more dramatic material achievements than those of the capitalist world – added determination to the sense of purpose with which the twin goals of ordinary socialist construction and national restoration already infused the CCP and its sympathisers.

From the 1970s on, *da tong* rarely figured in official discourse. Informally though it has continued to be cited by senior officials as one of the ultimate goals of Chinese socialism. So, too, though less and less noticeably, did the sense that somewhere in the future a *da tong* could be achieved. Given that both these strands of socialist utopianism depended upon a strong, directive national authority, shaping, guiding and justifying the steps being taken towards achieving them, they both served to strengthen the *telos* of the post-1949 state to the point where it became all-embracing.

The State without Purpose

If we now traverse the two decades or so from the time of the Third Plenum of the Eleventh Central Committee of the CCP in December 1978, when Deng Xiaoping returned to power, it is apparent that the state in China, while still pervasive and authoritarian, has lost much of the confident sense of purpose that justified it, and that it embodied, in the first decades of the People's Republic.

In the first place, the utopian idealism that Mao and his supporters sought to put into practice is now an anachronism. Consideration of collective utopias, whether of the *da tong* or Marxist-Leninist varieties, play almost no part in public discourse, and to the extent that they are still discussed, the utopian ideals of scholars such as Kang Youwei are now considered more in the context of the history of Chinese democracy (Xiong 1987: 232–41). It is left, once again, to popular religious fads and cults to carry the tattered banner of utopian fantasies.

At the state level, Deng Xiaoping did much of the demolition work on radical socialist utopianism within a short time of regaining power. The wholesale debunking of so-called leftist or collectivistic, class-based, propagandistic approaches to education, health, welfare and culture that took place during the period 1979–81, when the Cultural Revolution was being officially reassessed; the detention or marginalisation of leading leftwing political figures such as Hua Guofeng, Chen Boda, Jiang Qing, Zhang Chunqiao, Yao Wenyuan and Wang Hongwen; and the partial suppression of leftwing thinking in academic circles – all these measures served to prevent any resurgence of Maoist sympathies, other than in the form of an exotic popular cult of Mao and Mao memorabilia (as was allowed to happen in the early 1990s).

Other steps were taken to remove teleological elements of the state, most notably by dismantling the people's commune system from 1980–81 on, and by progressively downgrading centralised state planning and the role of the State Planning Commission. The people's communes had not, by and large, served as more than a loose frame for rural collectives since 1960–61, when administrative and, more specifically, budgetary authority had been devolved to so-called production brigades and production teams (whose telling titles were abolished in 1981–82 along with the communes).

But their very existence, and their name, reflected a purpose-driven view of the goals of socialism which Deng and his supporters steadily distanced themselves from. This gradually became the case, too, with the central planning apparatus. True, Mao had allowed this apparatus to be curbed during the Cultural Revolution, his delusory intention being to rule through a select group leading a new, Maoist party, invigorating the people down to the grass roots so as to press on more quickly to a higher level of socialism. But the decision to move away from central planning in the mid- to late 1980s and thereafter was motivated by a completely different consideration – the need to let the market take the lead, a first step towards relinquishing in theory as well as in practice the state's capacity both to direct the economy and to enlarge public ownership so as to promote more advanced forms of socialism.

The turning point in this process came at the Thirteenth Congress of the CCP in 1987, when the then acting general secretary of the CCP, Zhao

Ziyang, declared that 'the general pattern of economic operations' in China 'should be one in which the state regulates the market', and that current conditions in China were characteristic of the 'initial stage of socialism', which had begun in the 1950s and would last for at least a hundred years (*CD* 1988: 144–6). With these policy statements Zhao, to all intents and purposes, announced that socialist utopianism was dead.

When he returned to power Deng Xiaoping had only the sketchiest plan of action. To the extent that he had a plan at all, his intention seems to have been to restore a form of political orthodoxy based on the norms and values of the 1950s, reinstate the goal of realising the Four Modernisations first announced by the then prime minister, Zhou Enlai, at the Third National People's Congress in 1964, and open the way to modest economic reform so as to promote rapid modernisation.

In economic affairs Deng did indeed start to 'cross the river by feeling for the stones underfoot [*mo shitou guo he*]', to use what became a cliché to describe the CCP's reform efforts. He worked in an ad hoc way, building on experiments tried in the early 1960s, and on Zhao Ziyang's experiences in Sichuan province in the late 1970s when Zhao was governor there. Deng summed up his approach to the then West German chancellor Helmut Schmidt, when the two men met in Beijing in 1984: 'I have only a very limited understanding of economics' Deng told his visitor. 'I simply made the very general suggestion that we enter on a more flexible policy. Others must take on the job of turning this into reality . . . I am convinced that reform is necessary' (Schmidt 1989: 346).

Deng's aim was to 'seek truth from facts', as he often emphasised, and avoid the grandiose aims of his predecessor. In political and social affairs, Deng's intentions were somewhat clearer. He reinstated or strengthened the institutional structures and corporatist style of government that the CCP had first introduced in the 1950s (Schmitter 1993: 195–8; Unger and Chan 1996: 95–129; Lee 1991: 153–79). These consisted of a hierarchical structure, often overlapping, of the Communist Party, armed forces, civilian government and People's Congresses (parliament), complemented by legal, procuratorial and public security systems, and mass line organisations to serve as Stalinist 'transmission belts' for CCP policy.

Through the reinstatement of this structure, Deng had the explicit intention of realising socialist prosperity in China under the leadership of a Marxist-Leninist CCP. To this extent his aims were teleocratic. But at most, they reflected the more moderate goals of national construction in a socialist framework embodied in the two founding aims of the People's Republic discussed above. What remnants of socialist utopianism there may have been in his outlook, and in the outlook of other senior colleagues, were evident only in a reluctance to abandon such Stalinist shibboleths as the public or collective ownership of property, especially agricultural land.

Since then the teleocratic nature of the Chinese state has been gradually undermined, both economically and in other spheres. In tandem with this the corporatist structure that Deng reinstated on the 1950s model has been corroded and weakened by the multiple effects of rapid economic growth and social diversification.

In economic policy, successive trends and political decisions have contributed to this process. They include steps taken after the abolition of the systems of people's commune and the production brigade and production team to endorse family-based farming on the basis of long leases on (though not yet outright ownership of) agricultural land. They also include the steps taken from the mid-1980s on, often in response to popular pressure, to relax restrictions on labour migration and modify the *hukou* or household registration system in cities (the latter admittedly still at an early stage of development, even in progressive cities such as Shanghai).

They also include the important redefinitions of the Chinese economy that have been agreed on since Zhao Ziyang's statements at the Thirteenth CCP Congress in 1987. These have included the gradual endorsement during the early 1990s of the concept of a 'socialist market economy', now sometimes referred to just as a 'market economy'; the decision, taken in stages in the 1990s and currently being put into effect, to undertake fiscal and financial reform, primarily by giving the central banking system a more independent role; the steps taken in 1998 – the outcome of which it is still too early to judge – to separate the People's Liberation Army from its extensive web of interests in business; and the measures taken by Zhu Rongji since he became premier in March 1998 to reduce drastically the size of the central government (*CD* 1998: 453–6).

One motive for these latter measures has been efficiency, the need to cut costs and prevent a large central budget deficit; but another has been to rationalise and reduce further the role of the central authorities in the planning and management of the economy, following the curtailment of the role of state planning from the mid-1980s on. Some Chinese scholars regard these measures as no more than the latest and most concerted of various attempts taken since 1949 to check the otherwise inexorable growth of the Chinese bureaucracy. Others, more optimistically, see in them the beginnings of a qualitatively new approach to government (Xiao 1998).

Perhaps the most important developments in the present context have been the moves in the 1990s to restructure and redefine state-owned enterprises (SOEs). Initially the emphasis was on encouraging SOEs to shed their community responsibilities in such fields as health and welfare. But the policy announced by Jiang Zemin at the Fifteenth CCP Congress in 1997 of pushing for diversification of ownership in all but a thousand or so enterprises in the public sector has the greatest significance. As has become clear, it is a decision that opens the door wide not just to diversification of ownership but to outright privatisation. It thus presages a further shift away from orthodox forms of state ownership and control in favour of a variety of other forms of ownership and asset management, including limited shareholding companies and shareholding co-operatives (Baum 1988; Walker 1997; Foo and Cheung 1997; *World Bank* 1995).

This particular measure apart, the outcome of these developments has been the marginalisation of the theory and practice of collective agriculture; a growing acknowledgment of the need to clarify property, including land rights; a weakening of the theory and practice of the *danwei*, or work unit; and an increasing intolerance, at least among those working with or in sympathy with Zhu Rongji, of the political controls and influence exercised through the state sector in industry and through the banking system, and indeed of the excessively interventionist role the state still plays in the economy more generally (Fan, 1998; Lawrence 1998).

There has been a growing enthusiasm for share ownership, especially in more developed cities and provinces – though, at least until recently, publicly trading corporations have all been publicly owned; and an extraordinary intermingling of the public and private in ownership and management, typified at the local level by the strong entrepreneurial elites of officials straddling government and business (Oi 1995).

The extent to which the strength and authority of the state has increased or diminished as a result of all these changes is debatable. At the village level there are good grounds for arguing that 'though still strong, [the state] has pulled back dramatically from its earlier efforts to directly control what occurs' at that level (Unger 1989: 134). Certainly the apparatus of the CCP in rural areas appears to be unprecedentedly weak, and decaying.[8]

On the other hand, local government officials-turned-entrepreneurs now enjoy a stifling array of economic powers, replacing the political powers they may have foregone. Bowen and Rose, for example, have argued that a new form of 'state corporatism' – by which they mean the state as a corporate or business actor, not the state as *estado corporativo* – is maintaining a fiscal chokehold on local enterprise (Bowen and Rose 1998; also Lardy 1998). And partly as a result of the fiscal reforms of 1993–94, the central state has not been weakened financially as a result of the decentralising aspects of the reform process as some had earlier feared – or hoped – it would.

For the present purpose, however, the relative strength or weakness of the state is not the issue. The point here, rather, is that as far as economic policy and practice are concerned, several fundamental elements of the *telos* of the CCP state have faded away. These include component parts of teleocratic state socialism such as central state planning, rather than the use of the market, and the maintenance of large-scale collective units in the countryside as a first step towards full public ownership of the means of production in the agricultural sector. Less radically, they include the determination and the capacity to create an avowedly socialist state, and to manage national economy policy towards this specific end.

This latter aim is still paid lip service to, but in an attenuated form, expressed as it is by means of vague formulations such as, to paraphrase Jiang Zemin, the transition from the primary stage of socialism after a hundred years, and the construction of a material and also spiritual civilisation in accordance with the theory of Deng Xiaoping. More explicit goals relating to the construction of socialism are no longer taken seriously by any except a small handful of theoreticians (Link 1992; Barmé 1999; Liu 1997; Meisner 1996).

As a consequence, the overall aims and purposes of the state in the economic field have become progressively less clearly defined, and may indeed be in the process of being fatally undermined. There remains the less orchestrated goal of economic modernisation – Jiang Zemin's material civilisation. But that has become weak in purpose and meaning, and blends readily into the accepted aspirations of a large part of world – aspirations pursued in a globalising era by many means and through many media, not just the state.

In a similar way it can be argued that a number of developments in other fields, notably those relating to law and legality, politics and government, and social structures and organisations, are in the process of weakening the teleocratic condition of the state. These developments have occurred in a wide range of settings, only a few of which will be considered here.

As far as law and legality are concerned, the revival and development of a legal system under the rubric of the Party's longstanding policy of promoting 'a socialist democracy and legal system', a slogan dating back to the 1950s and reasserted from the mid-1970s onwards, has reintroduced an element into Chinese state and society that for all its deep and persistent flaws has become more than just an instrument of official policy.

To some extent the renewed emphasis on the law has reflected an appreciation that as market-based transactions and foreign trade and investment supersede state planning and economic autarky, laws become an economic and administrative necessity.

Indeed, the official view of China's achievements to date in enacting a range of civil laws is that the state, or more specifically the National People's Congress, has 'basically attained the objective of constructing a primary legal framework that suits the development of [a] socialist market economy' (*NPC* 1998). But there is more to the achievements than that. The CCP's commitment to a form of Soviet-style law in the early 1950s, and its later experiences with the lawlessness of Maoist ideology, seem to have reinforced the determination of Deng Xiaoping (and other first generation CCP colleagues, notably Peng Zhen) to reinstate the law as a *political*, as well as economic, necessity essential for ensuring order and equity in a nation that would no longer consist of classes but of citizens.

As in other aspects of China's reform process, however, the progressive evolution of the legal system since 1978–79 has impacted on the state in ways that the CCP leadership could not have anticipated. As Potter puts it, 'once a principle of law is enunciated it becomes part of the public domain and open to uses that the regime [i.e. the state] may not be able to control' (Potter 1994). The impact of the law on the state has manifested itself at two levels – at the theoretical or conceptual level, and through the enactment and application of legislation impinging on the actual, day-to-day authority of the state and altering its relationship with society.

At the theoretical level there has been a slowly growing official recognition of the need for law, and for officials to 'act in accordance with the law' [*yi fa ban shi*] and allow rule by law rather than rule by man. There has been an increasing acknowledgment of the need for the rule of law rather than rule by law – the two phrases being expressed in Chinese by two homonyms, both pronounced *fazhi*, the first implying a much broader scope for law as a concept than the second – and of the need to uphold civil or citizens' rights (*gongmin quanli*). In his speech to the Fifteenth CCP Congress in September 1997 Jiang Zemin referred to the need to protect citizens' rights, and to ensure that no one was above the law, though when he spoke of *fazhi* he continued to use the first of the two terms, 'rule by law'.

This, in turn, has encouraged discussion by relatively liberal thinkers within the Chinese Communist establishment about reinstating a conception of citizenship consonant with the rule of law (Xia 1995; Liu, J. 1998). With the demise of the Marxist-Leninist formulations about class and the mass line which effectively eclipsed the idea of citizenship from the 1950s onwards, there is some prospect of the notion of a state of citizens being restored to the place in elite thinking which it enjoyed in the early years of this century, at the time of Liang Qichao's *Xin Min Shuo*.

The actual impact on the state of the enactment and application of the law has been notable in a variety of ways, but particularly in the case of two types of law – criminal law and administrative law. In both cases there has been a slow, but perceptible, shift in the relationship between the ordinary person, or citizen, and the state. In the case of criminal law, there has been an increasing, though often grudging, acceptance of the need for the rights of defendants to be observed, particularly as far as their rights to counsel are concerned, and for trials to become more transparent processes in which the defendant's guilt is not wholly presupposed. Such considerations are reflected in the revised Criminal Procedure Law adopted in 1996, which for all its many shortcomings is a highly significant development.

As one well-informed review of the Criminal Procedure Law has pointed out, it demonstrates 'that China has begun to reorient its basic approach to criminal justice away from a dominant preoccupation with social control toward a somewhat greater concern for the protection of defendants' rights ... [while setting] a stricter standard against which the government's actions ... can be judged' (Hecht 1996: 79, also, 1–18). It marks, in other words, an early phase of what may be described as a trend towards Chinese citizens having both the right and the capacity, however circumscribed, to defend themselves against the directive encroachments and controls of the state, and to define the function of the state in a different way.

The same can be argued of the administrative laws that have been passed in recent years, most notable among them being the 1989 Administrative Litigation Law.[9] This law seeks to make the state more accountable by allowing citizens and other parties, private and public, to seek redress from the courts for administrative decisions perceived to threaten their freedoms or economic interests. Opinions as to the impact of the law vary. It is certainly far weaker than comparable laws elsewhere, partly because it does not extend to decisions taken by the CCP.

However the law has been widely used, with several tens of thousands of cases recorded each year. The implication of these figures is that inside China the law is seen to be of some value. This is borne out by a sample analysis undertaken in 1996–97, which showed that more than half the plaintiffs studied, the majority of them workers, peasants, private entrepreneurs and state-owned enterprises, obtained favourable or partly favourable court rulings. An incidental finding of the analysis was that citizens in China are becoming more assertive of their rights and more knowledgeable about laws relating to those rights (Pei, 1997; Potter 1995: 168–70).

There are various implications for the relationship between state and society of China's administrative laws, as well as other laws dealing with aspects of civil rights In an immediate, practical sense, if tolerably well applied – and to date their application is severely constrained by such factors as the relative shortage of lawyers, particularly private lawyers, and the limited autonomy of the courts, especially at the local level – such laws will provide a means for citizens to express grievances and the state to respond to them.

More broadly, the laws lay the groundwork for a more critical, even adversarial relationship between citizen and state, and afford the citizen means for redress against the state, in a manner that runs counter to long-held assumptions within China about the omniscient, controlling nature of the state and its role. Having earlier been a confident, directive instrument of national policy the state is gradually being placed in a more qualified position, off its pedestal, as one party among a number engaged in routinised processes of mediation and dispute management.

As for the broader implications of the gradual reinstatement of the law, it would be incongruous at this early stage to claim that it is even beginning to constitute part of a social fabric of law and custom knit loosely together by the state, as law and custom in nomocratic states are construed to do. The most that can be said, perhaps, is that Chinese society has taken a first tentative step in that direction.

Several significant changes in political practices during the last twenty years have also affected the nature of the Chinese state. Among them has been a gradual evolution towards a less stage-managed, more active parliamentary system. People's Congresses have had their roles reinstated and enhanced as a result of Deng Xiaoping's reforms, and as individual deputies attest (at least in Beijing and Shanghai), are now real forums for certain civic activities and certain types of debate. In this respect they have regained, and are building on, the leeway given to them in 1979–80, then lost again in the aftermath of the 1989 Tiananmen crisis.

The National People's Congress in Beijing is also becoming increasingly well equipped to take on the task of drafting laws, though such skills have not yet been acquired at the provincial level. At the same time at least some lower-level People's Congresses are better able than before to monitor the work of government, in particular its adherence to the law, and respond to the needs of ordinary citizens. This is particularly true at the provincial level and in municipalities of provincial status such as Shanghai, where the People's Congresses' standing committees now meet as they should by law for three to five days every two months.

The system of People's Congresses still bears very little resemblance to parliaments in functioning political democracies. Indirect elections, at best, are the norm above the country or district level, and real political interest groups and parties (as opposed to the notional new democratic parties) are quickly suppressed (Liu 1999). Senior CCP leaders and scholars still talk in terms of a very slow transition to universal suffrage, and a prospect of multiparty democracy in the distant future, if at all (Li, 1998 and Liu, Z. 1998). Nothing has come of discussions in the 1980s about strengthening the ineffectual Chinese People's Political Consultative Conference so as to create a functioning bicameral system. And on most important decisions, the Congresses bow to Party pressure and Party priorities.

The People's Congresses are also beset by a number of practical and logistical problems that are still at an early stage of being dealt with. Among these are the fact that they still meet in plenary session too infrequently; are still often dominated or directed by the CCP, whose members are estimated to constitute seventy per cent of all deputies; still fail to provide deputies with agendas well before their meetings; have too few specialist staff members; and offer deputies far too little logistical and administrative support. As one leading Chinese specialist in the Congress system noted recently, the main problems the Congresses currently face can be summed up as: too little time for meetings, too few financial resources for back-up, and too weak a history of democracy nationwide to ensure their potential is realised.[10]

As a result, the People's Congresses are still just starting to find ways of serving as effective mediums for continuous debate, undertaking detailed scrutiny of government budgets, drafting and enacting province-level laws, servicing their constituents' increasingly diverse needs and interests, and serving the various other functions given to them by law.

Nonetheless the political culture of People's Congresses has developed to the point where some province-level Congresses, at least, have achieved an institutional life of their own (MacFarquhar 1998). Even if this development is not going to open the way to pluralist democracy, it has certainly encouraged a more openly critical attitude towards the state, one that calls into question and even undermines the state's directive authority.

This shift in parliamentary culture has been matched by the emphasis that the central authorities have been placing during the past decade or so on democratic elections at the village level (Kelliher 1997; Choate 1997; *MCA* 1993, 1994 and 1996). Again it would be easy to overstate the significance of these elections, which are not multiparty competitive and are managed for its own purposes by the CCP. Overseen by the conservative Ministry of Civil Affairs at various administrative levels, the elections are carefully distinguished from People's Congress elections, which, it is said, belong to a different institutional system (*tizhi*). And despite – or perhaps partly because of – its obvious showcase appeal to foreign governments and donors keen to promote democratic reform in China, the election programme has evinced little enthusiasm from many local officials and power-brokers within the Ministry.

Even so, the authorities have pressed ahead, evidently seeing the programme as an important way of reconstituting village governance, and during the last five years village-level elections are reported to have been carried out in some form or other throughout most of China. These elections have sometimes involved some effort to introduce secret ballots and other appurtenances of non-Communist election practices, and can be seen as a step towards changing ordinary people's attitudes to cadres and other local powerbrokers. As Li Jingpeng, a senior political scientist at Peking University, puts it:

> the basic-level democratic elections being promoted in villages in some places at the moment should be carried out in cities as well.
>
> Some people think the village elections have meant doing a lot of mobilising of people, because the turnout has been very high. Without being mobilised at all, ordinary people wouldn't be much interested, and no way would the turnout have been so high. So some people doubt whether these kinds of democratic elections have any substance. I see them differently. If ordinary people just take part in elections, and cadres are chosen by election, they're bound to have a sort of sense of responsibility towards the people. . . . This'll be far better than the old way of just being answerable to those above them.' (Liu, Z. 1998: 165).

Indeed, it can be argued that in terms of the state in China, the village-level election programme has been significant for two reasons. On the one hand, it seems to have been born out of an official realisation that the reform process under Deng Xiaoping and Jiang Zemin has been eroding the status and influence of the Party and the state at the village level, to the point where they are both in danger of becoming ineffectual. In many parts of China village cadres have been shedding their loyalty to any higher purpose (and exacerbating farmers' sense of grievance in the process) in a caricature of the get-rich mentality promoted by the reforms (Shevchenko 1996).

The village-level election programme has thus been motivated by a grudging acceptance of the need for the state to find new ways of legitimising its grassroots authority. On the other hand, the programme has the potential to alter the relationship between the state (in the form of local cadres) and villagers, by adding to villagers' capacity to question and doubt state authority. In both respects, the programme reflects and reinforces the declining importance of the purposeful state.

To these limited but significant changes in the political culture of China must be added the more striking developments that have occurred in society at large. As we have discussed earlier, the last two decades have witnessed the emergence of increasingly varied, often inchoate, social conditions. This is not the place to describe the elements of this rapidly changing society in detail. But it is worth pointing out that among its essential components are many institutions and individuals on the fringes of the state, among them non-governmental organisations of various kinds, profit and non-profit, including businesses, business councils and trade associations, professional associations, charities and issue-orientated groups, as well as old, revived United Front agencies that have changed with the times.

In the early years of the reform process, the state encouraged the development of these so-called 'social organisations' [*shehui tuanti*] or 'people's organisations' [*minjian zuzhi*] as a means of improving institutional and professional networking, especially horizontal networking, which had earlier been very weak. To begin with, the resulting networks were managed along orthodox corporatist lines, with clearly defined hierarchies of exclusive institutions or associations, often supported by, and dependent on, a state institution (the so-called *gua kao danwei*, or parent unit). The eight mass organisations, United Front 'transmission belts' for Party's mass organisation and mobilisation, were revived, and the more energetic of them formed the core of notionally non-Party agencies dealing with activities in such fields as women and youth affairs, trade unionism, industry and commerce and culture.

In recent years, however, rapid economic growth and social diversification have engendered a growing number of institutions, groups and individuals often only loosely connected to the state apparatus, and frequently occupying an ill-defined middle ground between the state, private enterprise and non profit-making or profit-making non-governmental organisations. The current pace of social change in China is so great, especially in coastal areas, that it is not yet possible to characterise this trend in detail. Nor is it possible to map the changing attitudes among these institutions, groups and individuals with any degree of accuracy, especially given the self-restraint many still exercise in responding to surveys and questionnaires on sensitive social issues. Nonetheless it seems reasonable to suppose that the growth of the non-state sector and, in particular, of a range of non-governmental organisations, has influenced the way intellectuals and decision-makers perceive the role of the state.

This influence is perceptible in a variety of settings. To take just one example among many, twenty years ago it was widely accepted that responsibility for social welfare rested with the CCP, the unit or the collective. Concepts such as philanthropy [*cishan*] and non-profit organisations [*fei yingli jigou*] were barely understood, even in specialist circles.[11] Today one well-placed source estimates that perhaps ten per cent of China's emerging middle class are ready to undertake unofficial philanthropic work, now seen to be an essential element in the proper functioning of society.

At the same time, more than a thousand charities and foundations have been established at 'the local level' (which in this context usually means the province) in the 1990s, not counting a growing number of private schools, clinics, volunteer groups and organisations with some kind of charitable intent, all of which must have altered – that is, diminished – the role of the state in the eyes of those concerned (Yang 1998).

What is important to emphasise here is that while the authorities have done their best to manage this newly emergent social sector, it remains connected to, but no longer entirely subordinate to, the state. Not even new, restrictive regulations for non-profit non-governmental (and quasi-governmental) organisations (*Xinhua* 3 November 1998) are likely to restrain or systematise it. It now takes so many forms, and has so many alternative ways of organising itself, that the corporatist framework in which it was originally allowed to develop can no longer contain it. It is almost certainly too weak to separate itself from the state apparatus on which it still depends for registration, protection and (in many cases) financial support, and thus too weak to create a truly autonomous social zone in which the seeds of political change might germinate. But it is open and responsive to changing circumstances, and offers organisational and intellectual alternatives to the state in ways that deprive the state of the directive authority it has long enjoyed.

Moreover, the alternatives offered are reinforced by the increasing exposure Chinese citizens have to the resurgent influences and traditions of

China's local and regional cultures, languages and outlooks (Friedman 1994b and Xin and Ni 1995) and by their easy access to relatively unfettered sources of information and analysis, from the internet (which some five million Chinese are now estimated to have the use of) as well as from television and radio talk shows and hot lines, local newspapers and magazines, video stores and bookstores, some with a wide range of contents. The significance of these trends, in a society long accustomed to a wholly intrusive and directive state, outweighs the immediate constraints that new, non-state actors in society have to function under.

Conclusion

It would be premature – indeed, highly incongruous, given the persistent intrusion of the authoritarian state into everyday affairs – to draw on all these developments so as to portray the state in China as becoming a state as *societas* in Oakeshott's sense of the term. Besides, there are few signs as yet of interest within China in the alternative views of political structure and purpose expressed by less idealistic and teleocratic political philosophers and philosophical traditions, among them the Chinese traditions discussed at the outset. These are, however, there to be tapped when the time is ripe.

In the meantime, and in summing up, developments in China in the last twenty years have opened the way to new, more critical assessments of the state. Among these developments have been the measures taken to dispense with utopian idealism once and for all, and to replace a planned economy based on Stalinist ideals with a market economy only loosely guided by the state. Among them too has been the slow – often painfully slow – establishment of a society based on the rule of law and accepted practice, rather than the dictate of cadres, and on citizens rather than classes.

It is a society struggling to restore half-forgotten loyalties and try new forms of association as it emerges from the rubble of the Mao era, and from the corporatist straightjacket of the Deng transition – a cluster of communities with common interests coming to terms with the loss of moral authority of the state, corrupt in both theory and practice. All these trends are depriving the state of its *telos*, its purposes, and moving it inch by inch in the direction of a state as *societas*. Like the other shore of a wide river, the aimless state in China is still out of reach; but its contours can be made out in the distance.

Notes

1 The journal of the Society for Strategy Management and Research (Zhongguo zhanlue yu guanli yanjiu hui), a profit-making non-governmental organisation based in Beijing and linked to influential elements within the military which has, in the past, provided a forum for controversial assessments of the Chinese reform process.

2 The literature on civil society and the public sphere in China is too extensive to list here. For Chinese perspectives on the issue in the 1980s, see Ma 1994, and Huang 1993.

3 The debate about civil society in China today has been paralleled by a debate about civil society in China during the late Qing and the Republic (1911–1949). See Wakeman 1997 and 1998.

4 To cite just one notable example of his influence, Zhuang-zi was much respected by the late Ming scholar Wang Fuzhi, whose ideas about Han Chinese culture foreshadowed aspects of modern Chinese nationalism, and whose opposition to Manchu rule was admired in this century by Mao Zedong and others. Wang argued that Zhuang-zi's 'doing nothing' [*wu wei*] view of the role of government represented a far better political philosophy than the moral reformism and legalist strictness of most *ru* scholar-officials (Yan 1997).

5 To take just three examples of this: 1) Mao Zedong was strongly influenced as a very young man by Liang Qichao and Kang Youwei, and by Liang's ideas about *xin min* – including, presumably, its statist assumptions; 2) Sun-Yat-sen and Chiang Kai-shek defended the concept of *zheng tong*, and both the KMT and the CCP advocated the creation of a united, multiethnic state coterminous with the territorial realm of the late Qing. In the CCP's case this was consistent with Stalinist doctrine about the national question, and also with the nationalist views of late Qing reformers like Liang and Kang; and 3) Mao grafted on to the teleological Stalinist model a lifelong admiration for many aspects of traditional Chinese statecraft, including – famously – the despotic (though as we have seen, not necessarily purposeful) style of government of the legalist emperor Qin Shi Huangdi (Schram 1966: 25, 27, 38; Wakeman 1973: 151–2. Chan 1984: 133–4; Harris 1998: 111–124; Leys 1979: 54–60).

6 The arrangement was evidently incongruous to Maoist radicals such as Zhang Chunqiao and Yao Wenyuan (both members of the so-called Gang of Four), who at the height of the Cultural Revolution seem to have seen less need than Mao did for the socialist state. In a conversation with the two men in early 1967, Mao resisted the idea of turning China into a collection of people's communes – organisations which Zhang and Yao, like Karl Marx, appeared to regard as a critical precursor to the final dismantling of the state, and which for that very reason Mao was unwilling to sanction (Schram 1974: 278).

7 Jonathan Unger argues that while in the application of his radical policies Mao may have wanted decentralised administrative control, at the same time he sought unchallenged, unmediated CCP control right down to the village level, so that 'villages across China had to march quick-step to a single drum beat' (Unger 1989: 126).

8 According to Minxin Pei, official data show that eight per cent of village-level Party cells cannot function or have collapsed, while sixty per cent are 'mediocre.' (Pei 1998).

9 The *xingzheng susong fa*, also known in English as the Administrative Procedure Law. Other relevant laws include the Administrative Sanction Law, the Administrative Supervision Law and the Law on State Compensation. In drafting this administrative legislation, Chinese legal specialists drew on the experiences of several other states, including France, Germany and Japan.

10 These and other comments in this section are drawn from interviews the author conducted on 23 and 27 November 1998 with legal scholars at Fudan University, Shanghai, and in the Research Service of the Office of the Standing Committee of the National People's Congress in Beijing. See also Pu, Ding, Sun and Hu 1995.

11 To be more precise, these concepts had been thoroughly forgotten, since charitable activities have a well-documented history in China going back at least as far as the Ming dynasty. I am grateful to Duncan Campbell for pointing this out.

CHAPTER FIVE

Seiji Endo

The Japanese State: Surviving Neoliberal Political Economy

The Problem of the Japanese State

There was a time when scholars from the United States and Japan talked much about the hegemonic cycle and the possibility that Japan might overtake the U.S. as a hegemony, and that Asian economies as a whole were becoming the prime engine of growth in the global economy. American manufacturing was losing competitiveness and the U.S. markets were filled with cheaper, and sometimes better, products from Japan and other AMEs. Not only was the US declining as an industrial power but also its management of the economy was deemed to be undisciplined and the biggest source of instability in the world economy. The U.S. was importing much more than it earned and consequently accumulating huge fiscal deficits.

After the Plaza Agreement in September 1985, the U.S. lost any intention and perhaps ability to support the value of the dollar. Japanese capital flooded into American financial and real estate markets only to increase the current account deficits of the United States. Washington ceased being a benign and benevolent hegemony and began instead to be a more self-centred and self-interested one. Its allies, irritated by this manner of exploitative hegemony, advocated that the U.S. should put its own house in order before demanding that other nations contribute to the stability of the world economy.

Some American scholars were seriously worried about the decline of the country's economic power and tried to identify its causes in various ways. Confidence among the American public was low with regard to the competitiveness of the American economic model in facing the challenge from Japan and other AMEs. Many Japanese scholars, however, believed that Japan should not rush to replace the United States as the number one hegemonic power, as the sooner you get to the hegemonic position, the sooner you would be replaced, as the logic of the hegemonic cycle dictates.

In contrast to the American public, the Japanese people seemed to be generally satisfied with the efficiency and competitiveness of their economic system and development model, as well as the discipline of the work forces and the civic qualities of the society as a whole.

This may sound like a story from the distant past but it was, in fact, just less than ten years ago. Now the tables have turned (around, upside-down, or whatever). The American economy is very vigorous, showing little sign of inflation or slowing down for a substantial period of time. The Administration has achieved a fiscal surplus rather than stuck with a budget deficit. Many economic indicators are setting historical record. Key industries such as computers and computer assisted high-tech manufacturing have been pushing the economic growth even further. The financial market is the strongest and leading the global trends. The American economy has survived the painful industrial adaptation and restructuring and regained the competitiveness it lost to Japan.

In addition to the new level of economic power and dynamism, American companies are buying into Japanese markets, where real estate is surprisingly cheaper than it used to be during the era of bubble economy. Now it is the American economy, with its greater flexibility and little regulation by the state, that seems to be the model for the future, rather than the developmental state of Japan. In a reversal of the hegemonic competition 10 years ago, we are seeing the start of another round of the competition between the United States and Japan, and it is now Japan's turn to put its house in order.[1]

Nevertheless, it is simply unrealistic to consider Japan as a hegemony in the current situation. Japan's economy has been in a seemingly unending depression over the past several years, and in 1998 its real GDP shrank by 2.8 per cent. It was at its lowest level in fifty years, worse than in 1973 when the oil crisis hit the world economy. Its unemployment rate is 4.3 per cent with about 3 million people unemployed, which is, again, the worst since the end of the World War II. The Government is running a huge fiscal deficit now amounting to a year's GDP of the country and the number of bankruptcy cases is incredibly high. It is said that the large banks have almost cleared their non-performing loans and the worst is now over, but in doing so they have depleted their available assets in order to pass the regulations of the Bank of International Settlements (BIS). In addition, there are the loans to Asian countries whose situation became worse during the financial crisis.

Japan has come to be seen as the problem rather than solution to the regional economic difficulties, despite the fact that, as the biggest economy in East Asia, it is contributing a fairly substantial amount to help other

Asian economies. Because of the weak economy, the yen depreciated rapidly, almost like a free-fall, during the first half of 1998, and it nearly triggered another drop in value of other Asian currencies. With the stagnant Japanese economy, it has been difficult for Southeast Asian countries to export to Japan and earn the much needed foreign currency to assist them to recover from the financial and economic crises. The prospect of reduced export earnings in East and Southeast Asian countries in the first half of 1998 prompted many to talk about fears of a Great Depression emanating from Japan.

As far as the United States was concerned, the Japanese government did not understand the gravity of the situation. Recognising the critical state of the Asian economies, the Clinton administration gave up the subtle and benign manners of persuasion and openly demanded that the Japanese government take stronger fiscal measures, such as greater deficit spending and a permanent income tax reduction. The Japanese government, on the other hand, insisted that they had been doing their best and that the market was not properly taking into account the fact that the Japanese economy was a fundamentally healthy one.

In the early part of 1999, the Japanese economy, having hit rock-bottom, began to show some signs of recovery. At the same time, Asian economies are slowly getting back on the track of recovery. China, despite mounting difficulties in various aspects of its society and economy, continued growing more than seven per cent. The new developments seem to indicate that the worst of the crisis may have been over. It may well be possible that, in due time, the Asian economies will have recovered sufficiently enough for us to remember this crisis as simply another episode of mismanagement of the macroeconomic policy by some Asian countries and the overshooting of the market forces. If we believe that the global market is fundamentally healthy and the current policies of austerity and continual financial liberalisation are correct cures for the dislocated economies, then we may simply have to wait and see whether these policy measures would produce desirable results.

The issue, however, may have less to do with whether the governments of Asian countries could take correct and timely policy measures, or whether they were experienced in managing the crisis, however important they may be in their own right, but more to do with whether appropriate and necessary institutional arrangements are in place, so that these policies could effectively work. Contrary to the belief of some scholars that the market is self-regulating and will bring about equilibrium in the longer run, market mechanisms do not work in an institutional vacuum. Strong institutions are required to provide order, security and discipline if the market is to function properly and effectively. At the core of these institutional arrangements are the determination and capacity of the political leadership and consequently the effectiveness of the state power.

Traditionally the United States was instrumental in providing the political and military support for East Asian economies during the Cold War era. With the end of the Cold War, the Washington has become more self-centred and reluctant to carry the burdens of a hegemony. The vacuum created by the decline of US hegemonic presence has not been filled in by an effective and authoritative regional structure as we have seen in Europe. With the decline of the traditional U.S. provision of political support, and without a regional structure for consultation and cooperation, effective national political leadership became crucial in the increasingly freer global capitalist system. Unfortunately this has also been lacking – at least in Japan. The developmental state of Japan has reached a point where it could no longer provide the type of state power at home which was essential for the prioritising of national interests, allocation of resources and organising of a competitive national economy; nor it could supply the type of political leadership in the region which has been naturally expected in view of the decline of US hegemonic presence. This lack of political leadership has been a major source of uncertainty and ineffectiveness in Japan's reform, restructuring, and search of a new model of economic growth and social development.

With this underlying concern in mind, this chapter will focus on the provision of necessary institutional support for a sustainable growth and development in Japan, and the consequences of the lack of it. It will first investigate the cause of the decline of the Japanese developmental state. It will then look at how the Japanese government tried to deal with the structural problem by seeking institutional support from some possible form of regional arrangement. In both instances, the chapter will examine how the United State, and indeed the neoliberal global regime it represents and promotes, fitted in. The chapter will argue that it is the neoliberal global order that has been primarily responsible for the decline of Japan's developmental state and that the weakening of the Japanese state will further the tensions between Japan's national interests and arrangements on the one hand, and the dominant neoliberal global order on the other.

The Decline of the Japanese Developmental State

It is the view of this author that the current economic problems experienced in Japan for the past decade can be better explained by looking at the problems on the political and institutional side than on the side of economic policy and operations. In a general sense, it is the mismatch between the globalising neoliberal political economy and Japan's developmental state that caused many of her problems.

For the last two decades, the Government has been trying to liberalise and deregulate the economy in a belief that more dynamics can be generated with the fading out of the state from managing the economy. It began when the Nakasone Administration proposed in the 1980s that the private sector should be the leading force in the restructuring of the Japanese economy and embarked aggressively on the privatisation of the national railway system in the mid-1980s, followed by that of the telecommunication industry. One can see that the seeds of neoliberal political economy have been long planted in Japan.

The neoliberal experiments however left a mixed record because the tradition of developmental state was powerfully at its heyday then under which the economy was indeed governed by the Government. Even into the 1990s, against the backdrop of the prolonged economic recession, the Government still used methods associated with the development state model in battling the recession: deficit spending, special income tax cuts and the reduction of interest rates to an historic low to create effective demands.

On the other hand, the Government continued to push their neoliberal programme and targeted the financial deregulation as the key for revitalising the economy, as up until the first half of 1997, the economy was not as bad as it would be late – at least it continued to grow. The Hashimoto Administration promised that it would implement a Japanese Big Bang to promote financial deregulation and restructuring. These policies were aimed at making the Tokyo financial market as useful and attractive as other financial centres and restructuring the industry-based Japanese economy into a finance- and service-oriented one.

To this end, the Hashimoto Administration took several steps. In terms of the financial sector reform, the Government successively passed a series of reform bills in June 1997 in the hope to build the trust with the international capital that the Japanese government would be able provide a healthy environment for international capital to operate without unnecessary government intervention or interruption.

One of these laws, passed in the Diet on 11 June 1997 and going effective in April 1998, separated the Bank of Japan from the mighty Ministry of Finance and gave the bank political and institutional independence and central monetary policy making authority. Parallel with this was the division of the Ministry of Finance. The Ministry had a strong grip on the national budget and supervisory power over private financial institutions. A new law, passed on 16 June 1997 and implemented in June the following year with overwhelming support from the public, broke the Ministry up into sections, and created a new independent Financial Supervisory Agency to take the responsibility of supervising private financial institutions. These new laws, along with others, signalled a new safe guard that that the Government would not be in a position to use monetary policy at its whim.

Further drastic reforms were recommended in a report by three consultative bodies of the Ministry of Finance on 13 June 1997. Their recommendations included the abolition of the rigid division among banking, securities, and insurance sectors by 2001 and full deregulation of control over the commission of stock sales by the end of 1999. Legislation of these issues was finalised on 5 June 1998, thus inducing the globally mobile capitals to enter the Japanese market.

In the area of fiscal policy, the growing government deficit, which could result in inflation in the future, was of great concern for the international capital. The Government was determined to follow the prescription favoured by the United States, the European Union, and institutions like IMF. A law went into force on 28 November 1997, which required the Government to reduce the budget deficit to 3 per cent of GDP by the year 2003. Also, to enlarge the revenue base for national budget, the Government had already increased the consumption tax from three per cent to five per cent as of April 1997.

It is clear that by taking these deflationary policy measures, the Hashimoto Administration was following the neoliberal prescription almost in a textbook fashion. The Government might have judged that the Japanese economy was then just in the process of recovery and strong enough to survive these severe measures. The now weakened Japanese financial sector needed these measures to keep Tokyo as a major global financial centre, and the Government hoped that these measures would help the financial sector regain its strength. Things seemed to be working as expected initially. Just prior to the introduction of the higher consumption tax in April 1997, the Japanese people rushed to buy goods. This created some rebound from stagnation and it looked as though Japan was finally recovering and the Government's judgement and policies were right.

But they were not. While consumption picked up, it was only temporary, with people being keen to buy most of what they needed before the introduction of the higher consumption tax. The financial sector continued to keep their lending tight to secure their financial position and satisfy the BIS regulation. The stock market stagnated and short-term capital kept dripping away from Japan. The strict deflationary policy was very unwise for a weakening economy and the timing of these measures was ill chosen as they were taken just before the Asian financial crises and remained unchanged until July 1998.

By the time the budget structural reform bill passed the Diet, many large financial companies had run into serious difficulties and it had became clear that a public fund would be needed to save the financial system from breaking down. On the other hand, the crisis of the Thai economy spread to other countries in the Asia-Pacific. Korea in particular was beginning to show signs of serious difficulties. Japan at this critical juncture was caught in a political inertia of the neoliberal policies and could not promptly change its course.

The difficulties since late 1997 can be attributed to the misjudgements and failed policies on the part of the Government in response to the dynamic national and regional economic conditions. But it seems that the problem is not just a matter of policies, but also, and perhaps more importantly, a matter of the deep-rooted problems of the Japanese state.

Nature of the Failure

The Japanese state as an effective model of national economic management has been responsible for the post-World War II Japanese economic growth and expansion. Under this model, the state is structured into a complex of networks which allowed the state apparatuses to take on the important function of coordination among industries. As with other countries, it is the purpose of the developmental state to promote and protect the interests of national capital in the global competition for profits and a greater share of them.

There are continuing debates on how to characterise the role of the Japanese state in this catch-up process (Johnson 1984, Murakami 1984 and 1992) and I do not have the space here to explore them in details. It is worth stressing though that the state, (in)famously represented by the Ministry of International Trade and Industry (MITI), has not been all that powerful and almighty in organising and creating the economy of Japan. There have been many mistakes and failures by the various governmental ministries, and their interventions have quite often blocked the creative initiatives of private firms. Industries have often disobeyed the government instructions and succeeded. The MITI may have been a powerful machine up until the early 1960s, but after that there have not been many recorded successful projects.

The Japanese state used a complex of available measures which are more the coordination of industries and companies than the order and authority which companies had to obey. It provided information about the activities of foreign companies and available technologies and financial incentives and inducements for companies to follow the instructions of the bureaucracy. The state sometimes created ad hoc bodies among competing companies which focused on research and development for newer products. Once the work is done, the coordination and cooperation among these companies would disappear and they will harshly compete with each other on the open market.

In this way, the Japanese state actively intervened in the functioning of the economy in order to help its industries, especially the manufacturing one. It does not, however, mean that the state centrally controlled the whole economic system as many of us would believe, but rather that it tried to set the conditions under which the competition among corporations would be fair and less destructive. There are always winners and losers in the market. What the Japanese state attempted to do was to control the damage competition could do to the losers through financial aids for companies in difficulties or arranging mergers among competing companies. The state also tried, up until very recently, to keep different markets separated and rarely did they allow companies to operate across different markets. Thus, the state was successful in directing companies to compete in a well organised market environment.

Built into this system were the social relations between the private sector and the state. Private companies often sent their employees as trainees to governmental ministries as a way of expanding human networks and getting to know the people and functions of the government. Also included was the treatment of bureaucrats by private companies to expansive restaurants, golf courses and provide them with gifts, etc.

The late economist, Yasusuke Murakami, pointed out that the methods used by the Japanese state could work if the industries were all Japanese and players the competition all followed the unwritten codes set by the Government. As has been pointed out earlier, the Government may not have been an active market player but it set forth the conditions of competition. The basic rules or social norms are often unwritten, in the way that the different sectors are organised in which companies are allowed to compete with each other. They could remain unwritten as far as the market players were all Japanese and in close contact with the state apparatuses (Murakami 1984). Globalisation, however, means that foreign companies are coming into the Japanese markets with totally different understandings of the rules of the markets. Thus, although Japan has been an active player in globalising political economy, it has institutional weaknesses in meeting the challenge of globalisation.

It is also important to note that the Japanese state has essentially been interested in nurturing the manufacturing sector whilst the banking and other financial sectors have simply been tools used for mobilising resources for manufacturing, even although the keiretsu, or groups of companies, are organised around major banks. Rarely has the competitiveness of the service and financial sectors been national policy issues. Even at its zenith, the Japanese economy was never viewed as a strong and competitive service and financial giant.

The opening up of the financial sector means that the regulation of the market will have to be in written rules and their open and equal application to all players. There is little room for discretion which has been an area of bureaucratic control in Japan. In addition, because the state-of-the-art financial market has become more sophisticated with advanced techniques, the regulators need to be really knowledgeable experts in the field. The current system of recruitment of the bureaucrats, however, does not provide such experts. Generally, the bureaucrats are not trained to be experts in any field; rather they are required mainly to have general ideas about the functioning of the government. They change their positions in the government about every three years, which makes it difficult for them to have knowledge of global financing comparable with that of those working in the markets. Thus, even it is its intention, the Government, even its most powerful organ the Ministry of Finance, may not be able to perform the regulating job effectively.

Aiming at these weaknesses, the Government has been trying to restructure the state institutions, and in doing so has highlighted the complex interactions between politics and economy. Companies with global profile are the fore runners in the globalisation process and they wanted a more liberal and internationally oriented government so that their global operations can be built upon on a safer and more predictable national political basis. Such an preference for a liberal and internationalist government is further reinforced by that fact that they have become strong enough to get rid of the governmental guidance and support.

These companies also prefer a politically and diplomatically more sensible government. Because of the history of Japanese aggression in Asian countries, Japan and its capital have not been received with a hearty welcome. Adding to these difficulties have been some conservative politicians who have often made the relationship between Japan and other Asian countries strained by making historically unwarranted statements, only to remind other Asian countries that Japan has not changed since its defeat and that it may not relinquish its political appetite for Asia. This is the most unwelcome aspect of Japanese politics for the globalising international capital both home and abroad.

Those globally profiled companies found such a politically and diplomatically sensitive government in the Hosokawa Administration, with many runaway politicians from the Liberal Democratic Party (LDP). The Hosokawa Administration opened up a way to improve Japan's relationship with other Asian countries. The Hosokawa Cabinet unfortunately dissolved in inter-party rifts in the coalition. After a brief period of minority government, the Socialist Party (JSP), which was part of the governing coalition in the Hosokawa Administration, decided to form another coalition government with the LDP only to leave disarray among the public. With a socialist prime minister in the Government, reform of the Japanese political economy seemed to come to a halt. The public interest, once mobilised to reform and modernise Japanese politics subsided rapidly; they were merely consumed and people are now deeply dismayed by politics and politicians.

The bureaucrats have also added to the public's dismay of the government. The series of scandals among government officials have only increased the level of concern among the Japanese people. When the wave of scandals in the Ministry of Finance were exposed, the people were persuaded that the Japanese bureaucracy had been deeply contaminated by the money culture. The resistance by the bureaucracy against the reforms of the Hashimoto Administration made the bureaucrats look like a bunch of people who were more interested in their own interests than those of the public. The trust of the people in the 'talented and clean' bureaucracy had long disappeared.

Encouraged by such a political mood, the Hashimoto Administration embarked on a series of institutional reforms. It decided, as discussed previously, to break up the regulatory and policy-making authority of the state over the financial sector and give the regulatory power of the all-powerful Ministry of Finance to the new Financial Supervisory Agency. The comprehensive restructuring of the bureaucratic system was urged despite continued bureaucratic resistance. Given the magnitude of the reforms, it was surprising that the Hashimoto Administration was successful in having these measures passed through the Diet relatively easily, but what was more surprising was the low public interest in the matters.

With the depression and the run on the yen, the Hashimoto Administration changed its direction by 180 degrees and decided to suspend the fiscal reform; to reintroduce a temporary income tax cut; and to revitalise the economy through increase in public spending with a supplementary budget of 16.6 trillion yen ($120 billion). It is interesting to note that while other advanced industrial countries are heading toward the IMF prescribed model of economic recovery and revitalisation with the reduction of spending by the public sector, Japan seems to be heading in the opposite direction: more deficit spending.

This policy change was welcome by the public. Given the state of Japanese economy, the fiscal policy with deficit spending was perhaps the best way to combat the economic problems. The change, however, was so drastic that it could not be sustained with the same Prime Minister in power who ardently argued for cutting the budget deficit. It was not until Obuchi came to power that the policy change was on its full wing. The Obuchi Cabinet decided, as soon as it came to power, to implement a unique 15-month budget which combined the Supplementary Budget to the fiscal year 1998 Budget and the budget of fiscal year 1999. In November 1998, it introduced an emergency economic policy which consisted of public spending of 20 trillion yen and a tax cut of 6 trillion yen. It is clear that the Japanese developmental state, while weakening, is not completely dead just yet.

One can thus argue that the Japanese state is a halfway house between the traditional developmental state and the neoliberal one modelled on the United States. This being half way creates an ambiguity in the ongoing changes in the political economy of Japan. The old structure of the developmental state is hard to die. One can see elements of the Keynesian policy of deficit spending in the economic policy of the current administration. Many Japanese are not necessarily in favour of the American style of economy and society where competition is so stark and the rich take most of the fortune and the poor take just a small portion of the fruits of economic growth.

On the other hand, it is also difficult to ignore the growing presence of the neoliberal economic policies and the effects of deregulation and liberalisation of the Japanese economy. Deregulation and liberalisation through the Japanese Big Bang will continue to be pushed, as many Japanese financial institutions are lagging behind their American counterparts in terms of internationalisation, and are desperately trying to find partners from the United States as their helping hands. Only further regulation and liberalisation would help the deepening of the internationalisation process, even it will take a long time to create a new state structure based on the American model.

Moreover, even the public distastes the American style of economy and society, they are not very much interested in politics at all and will probably not do much to challenge the restructuring of the state. Oppositions, be they political parties or social movements, are not well organised as effective political forces. Political parties from the left are atrociously disorganised; trade unions are very weak; and consumer movements are basically irrelevant. People are more concerned with the tangible effects of economic policies rather than the structural agendas involved. In this sense, the public's attitude to politics opens a window for reform actions of the Government.

It leaves, however, very serious problems that any democratic polity may have to face. The lack of public interest in the restructuring of the state will create a situation where people are unmobilised in response to the changing conditions, in which case the whole project of restructuring may fall apart because of the lack of public participation and even support. Political reforms are very much needed and people are not satisfied with the way things are happening. But without enthusiastic participation of the public, none major political changes could really take place. And without tangible signs that things are changing, the public will continue stay away from the political and policy process viewed as being run mainly by distrustful and ineffective politicians.

The foregoing analysis shows that there is an increasing tension between the traditional Japanese development state and the neoliberal political economic order advanced through global dynamics. While we still have to wait and see if and in which way the restructuring of the Japanese state is really moving, it is clear that the declining development state in Japan can no longer effectively fulfil the responsibility of managing the economy of modern complexity, dynamism and global scale. On the other hand, the neoliberal regime has not firmly established in the Japanese state either. Consequently we are seeing a very ineffective and undetermined government, uncertainty and contradictions in the direction of future economic movements, and weak governability of the overall Japanese state. Some form of effective governing structure is indeed called for.

Building Political and Institutional Support: A Regional Alternative

With such a political vacuum at the national level, a regional alternative seems to be attractive. Indeed much of what the Japanese government has done to promote a regional structure of cooperation and consultation can be interpreted as such an institutional alternative.

East Asia does not have any region-wide institutions, such as in the European Union, which could provide a framework for coping with common problems that cannot be effectively dealt with at the national level. It is often argued that this is because of the Asian way of making international cooperation, which is supposedly far less formal or clear in legal or institutional terms. Even the process of building such informal cooperation tends to be incremental rather than radical or dramatic as we have seen in the European Union. Included in this informal regional framework are perhaps consultative bodies such as ASEAN, APEC and ARF.

It is this important background against we could better understand Japan's efforts in search of alternative institutional arrangements for a sustainable growth of its economy at the time when the old developmental state was experiencing increasing difficulties to continue to function while the neoliberal regime is not able to operate effectively either. Here we will first look into the historical roots of the weakness of institutional building in East Asia before we examine Japan's subsequent efforts.

The US and Regional Structure in East Asia

During the height of the Cold War, it was the United States, especially when John F. Dulles managed its foreign policy, who tried to build an anti-Communist alliance in Asia through a complex network of bilateral and multilateral treaties. For various reasons, however, the multilateral framework backed up by the United States failed, but a series of bilateral arrangements centred on the United States survived(Fujiwara 1992). At the same time, some form of informal regional economic cooperation emerged in line with the U.S. Cold War political and military strategy in Asia. This informal regional economic structure had a unique structure, with the United States as a hub and other Asian countries as spokes. It survived the political and economic changes over the decades (Endo 1995).

With the regional structure as such, the far greater power the United States had, and an overwhelming priority of regional cooperation against Communism, Japan was designated as the centre of industrial activities and perhaps the engine of economic growth and development in the region, early on in the Cold War, at latest since the Korean War. Initially, Japan, in search of a large export market, thought China was potentially indispensable as a market for Japan's economic recovery. However, with the emergent confrontation between the Western bloc and the Communist world, the United States leaned to seem the importance of keeping Japan within the Western bloc, politically, strategically, as well as economically, away from mainland China. Instead of allowing Japan to move into the Chinese "market," Washington encouraged Japan to move into Southeast Asian. But the region was not able to absorb a sufficient amount of exports from Japan, hence the United States "incidentally" became the main absorber of the Japanese exports (Lee 1993).

With the economic recovery of Japan, it soon began to move into Asian markets, first with its reparation and compensation for the war damage from the late 1950s, then trade and official aid through Official Development Assistance (ODA) in the 1960s. With the regained industrial power and the stable current account surplus, Japan started in the early 1970s to invest into Asian countries, and the amount of investment by the Japanese grew rapidly. It was, however, the Plaza agreement in 1985 that drastically increased the value of the yen against US dollar that pushed the Japanese to redirect their investment to the US markets, Europe and East Asia. The change in the value of the Japanese yen and consequently growing enthusiasm in foreign direct investment were the driving force between the restructuring of the global presence of Japanese economy.

By the mid-1980s, Japan had developed enough manufacturing and financial power to shape the economic order in the region. Major multinational companies of Japanese origins extended networks for the supply of parts and assembly lines across East Asia, mostly through their capital investment. Let by Japan's industrial leadership, Korea, Taiwan, Hong Kong and Singapore started their own process of industrialisation and the pattern of multi-layered catch-up process, or flying geese, in East Asia emerged (Cummings 1984; Bernard and Ravenhill 1995).

Japanese multinational companies retained their research and development in Japan along with high-tech products, while standardised products using plain technology are produced in Southeast Asian countries and China. And gradually, the regional economic structure changed from a simple hub-and-spoke centred on the U.S. to a more complex one with Japan as another economic centre.

There was one old element left intact in the emergent structure: Japan was still not an absorber of exports from East Asian countries. It remained primarily a supplier of capital and products to other Asian countries, and continued to accumulate trade surpluses with these Asian countries. Consequently, not only did Japan rely on the US markets, but also did Southeast Asian countries and China become dependent on the United States for exports. Even with rapidly growing intra-regional trade and investment Pacific Asia, no other major country can import as much as the U.S. does; hence the U.S. remains to be the largest final market. This is perhaps one of the reasons why, even with the declining US military and political presence, no effective closed regional arrangements could have genuinely developed.

On the politico-military side of the regional structure, the American power is more significant. Since the end of the Cold War, Washington has taken steps to maintain its pivotal position in East Asia and project itself as an indispensable among in mistrusted Asian countries. Japan, on the other hand, with its right wing political forces, still has not won the trust of other East Asian nations, even after so many years of its persistent efforts and with its much respected economic influence. It is still considered untrustworthy.

There are some activities related to Japan's renewed or enlarged commitment to the U.S.-Japan Security Treaty. Some in Asia rather think that this may be a good thing for them as it would keep Japan on a lace or as a cap on a bin. For others, this may appear otherwise. China, for example, is fiercely opposing the new security Guidelines Japan signed with the United States. There are still others such as Taiwan, who expect Japan to take the leadership position and see this as a positive development for the security and political order of the region. Japan, caught up in these competing interests of its Asian neighbours, has just been too weak to take any side. It has been painted, rather reluctantly, into a potential power broker in the region and but has just not been able to master a clear strategy and necessary resources, and the art of diplomatic manoeuvre to become one.

Adding to the difficulties for Japan to build a Japan-led regional order is the China factor. China is a growing economic and military power and the sheer size of its population is a real source of threat. No other East Asian country can be a counter-weight against this rising power. But because of its imperialist history, current human rights record, and authoritarian nature of the regime, China cannot be a trustworthy leader of East Asia, at least not yet. Though Japan is the second strongest world military power in terms of military spending, it cannot really be a reliable military ally for smaller East Asian countries in the event of their conflicts with China. The military power of the United States and its political commitment to the stability and security in East Asia, therefore, is still much needed by small countries as a reliable counter-balance against China.

The question is whether Washington can still deliver the much needed presence. Militarily, perhaps still yes. Politically, yes or no, as there is a widespread sense of uncertainty involved in US relations with many Asian countries. Economically, perhaps no, especially as China is increasingly expanding the powerhouse of East Asia. With the uncertainty in US relations with Asian countries and its conflicting interests in the region, a regional framework for political and economic cooperation seems to be necessary and urgent. But neither China nor Japan was ready to take it seriously. Without their endorsement and provision, such a regional framework can never be substantially effective.

The Financial Crisis as An Opportunity for Japan

The Asian financial crisis came right against this very backdrop. With the blessing from Washington that Japan should take the leading responsibility in helping countries in Asia to cope with the crisis, Japan, in contrast to its low key diplomacy in the past, took some unusual steps initially, in the hope to protect Japan's economic interests in the region, and at the same time, to recast its regional and international leadership profile. In retrospect, one can indeed see this as a golden opportunity for the restructuring of the regional structure where Japanese leadership could be founded on a more secure basis.

Many at the central banks in East Asia had realised the danger of the rapid withdraw of short-term capital before Thailand was hit by the currency crisis in the summer of 1997. After the peso crisis of Mexico, they began to consult and share information about the financial situation of each country. But this process did not result in any formal policy programme to prevent a currency crisis of similar nature in the future in Asia, nor any arrangements for crisis management.

When the Thai crisis did occur, the Japanese government took unusual active steps offering bilateral and multilateral financial assistance to Thailand. In the month of August 1997 alone, Japan provided US$4 billion to Thailand on the bilateral basis. When the crisis spread to other Asian countries, Japan again actively organised a series of bilateral and multilateral assistance to crisis management in Indonesia, South Korea, the Philippines, and others, in cooperation with the IMF and the United States as well as international entities such as APEC, IMF, ADB, G7, etc.

The seriousness of the Japanese government in taking leadership in the crisis management is reflected in the forms and substances of its assistance programmes. Almost one and half years after the eruption of the crisis, the Japanese government suggests that its financial assistance to East Asian countries has four principal goals and five major policy programmes. The four goals are: economic recovery and revitalisation, restructuring of the economy and rebuilding of human capital; special assistance to socially vulnerable people who suffer most during the crises; and the stability of foreign exchange. The five assistance programmes include: a special package called the New Miyazawa Initiative; the special yen loans; the ASEAN-Japan programme to build human capital; assistance in kind such as the supply of rice and medical goods; and a programme to strengthen the stability of foreign exchange.

The Government's figures show that Japan committed itself to a total US$80 billion package to help East Asian countries heavily damaged by the economic crisis.[2] By the end of November 1998, the Government had provided or committed to provide a total of US$44 billion: $19 billion to the IMF; $22.5 billion to assist trade finance and other economic activities; $2 billion for economic restructuring and human capital building; and $150 million for the socially disadvantaged. In addition, Japan expressed its intention to introduce a new policy package called the New Miyazawa Initiative, with $15 billion for mid- to long-term financial assistance, $15 billion for short-term financial assistance, $30 billion to Asian Currency Crisis Support Facility which will be installed in the Asian Development Bank (ADB), $5 billion for the special yen loan for economic recovery and restructuring. According to the Japanese government, some $57 billion has already been set for implementation out of the total of $80 billion by February 5, 1999.

It seems that the Japanese government has been rather active in organising an international effort to help other East Asian countries, despite the mounting economic problems within Japan. It certainly appears that the Japanese government is changing its normally slow reactive, rather than proactive, style. But such policy initiatives left the impression that they were too piecemeal and did not have a sufficient impact upon the global financial market to fence off the forces of global capital.

What is more critical here is that over the course of the crisis management, the Japanese government was confronted with several serious conflicts with the U.S. and international financial institutions such as the IMF which no doubt will have great implications for the future of East Asia. One of the conflicts occurred in the autumn of 1997 during the volatile first phase of the crisis when the Japanese government appeared to be interested in the idea of setting up an Asian Monetary Fund. The idea was to create a special fund for supplying emergency financing and credit to Asian countries in difficulties without the severe conditions normally associated with similar assistance packages from international financial institutions such as the IMF. It was perhaps the belief of the Japanese government that most of the Asian countries would not have to undergo tight monetary control and severe deflationary measures, as the problems in these countries were different from those in the Latin American and African countries during their crisis in the 1980s which involved public deficits, steep inflation, and current account deficits.

The United State and the IMF however strongly objected to the idea of the AMF. They feared that the unity of the international monetary system and the standard practice of international financial institutions in attaching conditions to their rescue package might be impaired by the new entity and the idea behind that. They believed that the economic problems in these recipient countries cannot be fundamentally dealt with without these severe conditions and austerity programmes. But beyond the economic concerns, one can also see the political nature of the controversy. It is not just a matter of economic logic or ideology, but more a political problem of who has the power to control the distribution of global capital and credit. For the U.S., a new, independent fund, with a different economic ideology and in the hands of Asian countries could only mean the rise of Japanese (or perhaps Chinese as well) power at the expense of the American influence. It was this concern about a regional structure centred on Japan that made the United States, the IMF, and ironically China suspicious of Japan's move.

Faced with these strong objections, Japan backed down and gave up the idea, at least for now, even though it has become clear that Japan was never completely wrong on that issue. There was growing frustration among Asian countries, particularly those hit hard by the crisis and forced to take IMF package, for their unnecessary suffering under the austerity package. The Japanese government has good reason to believe that its diagnoses were more accurate about the economic situation in Asian countries. While the Japanese government still stresses that the IMF should be the central institution coping with global financial and currency matters, it became more critical of IMF prescribed economic programmes.

Since then Japan has quietly trying to reframe the idea into one of the schemes of the ADB. On the other hand, the IMF itself seemed to have a critical second thought about its handling of the Asian crisis. Does this then mean that the conflicts are settled between the Japan, and the neoclassical IMF and the United States? Probably not. At least for the Japanese, they have learnt a bigger lesson. The question is not really whether Washington wants Tokyo to play a leading role in East Asia; nor whether Japan is determined or capable of taking the responsibility. Rather it is the confrontation between the powerful global neoliberal political economy and the particular nationalistic way the Japanese economy has been organised and promoted that set the stage for the Japanese government, US government and international financial institutions such as the IMF to play. And it is in this confrontation that we see the fundamental weakness of the Japanese state.

The Hegemonic Japanese State: A Forever Remote Dream

There are, at least, two critical lessons Japan learned from its own recent economic problems and the Asian financial crisis. First, the Japanese have realised that the recent financial and economic crisis is not Asian or East

Asian in nature but of the global capitalist system. Second, Japan has the highly expected responsibility but only a limited power to deal with the regional economic crisis. Learning from the experience, Japan now has more concrete ideas about the future of East Asia and Japan's role in it.

Japan's experience of the recent economic crisis taught itself a lesson about the power of global capitalist system and the destructive potential of global capital. For Japan, the relation between global, regional, and national political economy has never been more clear and critical. Japan for example was expected to be the chief financier of the last resort during this crisis and it indeed tried hard to live up to the expectations and plaid the role quite earnestly, But one way or another, for countries in and outside the region, it was the stagnant economy of Japan itself that was the main source of the economic problems in the region. The problems the Japanese encountered in the region, with its neighbouring countries or with the United States or the IMF, may ultimately come back to the problems in Japan itself. At the same, like in the domestic context, the weakening Japanese state is left with very limited space for political and policy manoeuvres with those powerful external forces, and fewer resources and policy tools available.

There are quite many in the Government of Japan viewed the crises more in terms of the instability of the global capitalist system than the failure in macroeconomic management by governments of individual Asian countries. In fact, much of the problems in macroeconomic management at the national level can be attributed to the instability of the global system. This reading of the capitalist system's instability as the primary source of the economic problems has important implications. It recognises for example that the release of the market forces from the grip of the state power proved to be very problematic. Japan's "soft" resistance to Washington's pressures in its battle against its own economic problems and the Asian economic crisis suggests that liberalisation of the financial market without the support of proper institutions and management skills could be very damaging.

Moreover, as the Government went great length to argue, it is useful, and often necessary to have effective regulation and control by less developed countries over the movements of short-term capital, especially outgoing capital. Although the government would not go too far as to advocate capital control by Japan or other industrialised countries, it indeed emphasises the need for strengthened monitoring and surveillance over capital flows, especially over short-term capital investment. This view reflects the idea that the economic difficulties in Japan and East Asia cannot be remedied just by learning skills of market management; and that not only East Asia and Japan, but the world system as a whole will need an institutional overhaul, with which necessary political and institutional support could develop at the national, regional and global level for the desired function of the market.

It appears that Japan is aimed at a broader realignment of the institutional power balance between political authority and the market forces. For quite a period of time, the Japanese state lacked an effective political leadership and necessary institutional tools to manage newly released market forces both at home and in the region. For Japan to have a sustainable economic growth at home and build a political economic order in the region, such a political leadership and institutional arrangements became extremely important.

The necessity of such political leadership and innovative institutional building reflected in Japan's handling of the problem of exchange rate in the recent economic crisis. In view of the dramatic fluctuation of exchange rates during the crisis, the government came to believe that there is a need to develop new institutional arrangements for the stable working of the exchange rate regimes. One of the causes of the economic crises in East Asia was believed to be the difficulties for fixed exchange rates to respond to the changing economic conditions in an orderly fashion. Most countries in the region pegged their currencies to U.S. dollar, even although in theory they were allowed to move within the defined "basket." At the same time, Japan also had its yen tied to U.S. dollar. Even when it intended to help Asian countries out of the financial crisis, it could not really do much with this dependent Japanese yen.

On the other hand, the successful launching of the euro seemed to have moved the Japanese further to think actively of the possibility of building the yen as a third global currency, similar to the dollar and the euro and with the backing of regional economies, and using it as the basis for a possible Asian currency zone. The Europeans realised that stability in currencies and exchange rate has great significance for a stable regional trade and financial system. Moreover, European currencies had been vulnerable to the fluctuations in the global financial market over the years since the early 1980s. It became clear to them that each individual country would not be a able to counter the massive power of global capital, which are basically operating in the US dollar. A new European currency was an important institutional innovation to cope with the powerful dollar based global capital and market forces. They made an important strategic choice in creating a new unitary currency. With the support of a single currency, the Europeans are in a better position to compete with the Americans and perhaps Asians as well and re-energise European economies.

The idea of the yen as a third global currency and a yen-based Asian currency zone is significant also from the perspective of the century-long efforts by the Japanese to build an effective regional order. The pre-war efforts aside, the post World War II order in East Asia was built primarily upon Japanese economic power and American military power, a fact which simply denied the necessity or effectiveness of any other formal regional arrangements. With the defusing of the military tensions in the region since the end of the Cold War and increasing competition among global capitals in the region, manifestant particularly in the recent economic crisis, Tokyo has found that a manageable regional order it has sought to build lacks the necessary institutional support. A regional, if not global, yen and further a yen-based Asian currency zone may well indeed fill in this vacuum.

Technically, the yen's share as a currency in world trade and financial activities has been extremely low, out of proportion to the world share of its products and capital. According to government figures, the yen's share in the world trade was just five per cent in 1992 and its share in the foreign reserve was only 4.9 per cent in 1997. As a comparison, in 1996, Japan's share in the world GDP was 15.8 per cent and in the world trade was 7.1 per cent. The share of the U.S. dollar in the world trade was 48.0 percent in 1992, and in 1997 the 57.1 per cent of the foreign currency reserve was in U.S. dollar. 31.0 percent of the world trade was in European currencies at the end of 1997 and 22.4 percent of foreign currency reserve was held in European currencies. In the same year, the yen was used for 35.8 percent of import and 22.6 percent of export. The yen's shares are very low compared with the dollar and the euro (Ministry of Finance). This fact added some urgency to the idea of an internationalised yen.

Having a good idea is one thing, and how to turn it into a reality is another. And often the Japanese are not necessarily as good in this regard as in industrial manufacturing. The idea of an internationalised yen has been known for more than a decade. A consultative body was created and it issued a report in March 1985 and 1985 which called for the expansion of use of the yen in international transactions. But things didn't work well(Kamikawa and Uematsu 1997). The Plaza Agreement resulted in a steep appreciation of the yen against the dollar. Asian countries who borrowed from the Japanese government in the form of the yen suffered an huge increase in payable debt.

Since the financial crisis, the Government started to pick up the idea again. On July 8, 1998, a Special Consultative Committee was set up and has since been very active in a detailed cost-benefit assessment of an internationalised as well as regionalised yen. A new interim report detailed issues involved the process of its implementation. At least in some corners of Japan, people are starting to have a more serious thought about the idea and the regional institutional arrangements it requires.

Problems, however, cannot be discounted. The public are not enthusiastic about any government policy initiatives. There is no consensus among the elites, particularly the bureaucrats, media producers, and academics on the Government's policy proposals, perhaps because the strategic geo-economical thinking is just not their style. Bureaucratic infighting is always a problem. But the real problem is the Japanese state itself. The Government is really inexperienced in making policy cases to the public in a more open and competitive political environment. Added to that is the instability of the Government which has led to frequent changes in policy directions. Politicians do not necessarily well understand the entangling issues of the relationship between Japanese economic policy and domestic politics. The overall Government structure is caught up between the old habits and arrangements of the developmental state and the new neoliberal political economic dynamics. This has left the state with no determined political leadership and no effective institutional support.

Concluding Remarks

The problems with Japan's developmental state have existed for years. Neoliberal political economy, whether we like or not, will perhaps continue to dominate. We have already seen signs of the shift in many AMCs including Japan. The problem is that this neoliberal model of development, if we are to call it development, is not sustainable as it is built upon, rather than helps to close up, the gap between the rich and the impoverished. While the old model is dying, the new one may not be a very happy choice for the majority of people after all.

It is obvious that Japan, with the weakening Government at home and the challenge of global neoliberal dynamics, has rather difficult times ahead. There are social forces in Japan that have been trying to 'restructure' the Japanese state into some kind of the neoliberal model. But it is just not easy for the interventionistic developmental state to restructure itself, primarily because various interests it represents are still there, alive and powerful. Moreover, one cannot expect the weakened and tension-ridden state to take on itself the kind of responsibilities, such as heavy handed involvement in the economic recovery in the name of effective political leadership, proposed ironically by those who otherwise would think these responsibilities are just the unnecessary legacies of the

Asian model. It is all too easy to criticise the incompetence of the Japanese government in the management of its economy and in response to the economic problems in the region. But the problems are deep-rooted and structural, and being structural, it is all the more difficult to resolve them.

While Japan's weakening state is not something easy to change, the Government is trying to build some form of institutional framework beyond Japan as an alternative to the much needed but indeed lacked political leadership and effective state back home. These ideas, from the Asian Monetary Fund to the yen based Asian Currency Zone, may not be in the spirit of the neoliberal momentum, are at least good attempts to address the problem of ineffective Japanese state resulted from the tension between the old development state of Japan and the neoliberal global dynamics.

Moreover, the regional alternative will provide a framework in which the problems in Asian economies could be dealt with on a basis of more regional sensitivity. It will direct more attention to ensure the fairness of new arrangements for the management of the new economic dynamics. It is very clear that there are many stumbling blocks in the way and it is not easy to build a new form of regional political economic order that would be completely immune from the neoliberal dynamics. These regional efforts by Japan indicate therefore that Japan is under pressure to find a credible and effective solution to the problems arising between its traditional developmental state model and the increasing liberalisation of its economy. For those who think that through these regional efforts, Japan is building its path to a hegemonic power in the region, this view may help to open more thinking space.

On the other hand, the prospects for the efforts to deal with the problem of the weakening developmental state are uncertain and perhaps even risky. Policy makers in Tokyo may expect their regional efforts will bring new dynamics into the troubled economy, which continues to be balked by the arrangements and attitude associated with the declining developmental state, the unstable and ineffective political leadership, and the ambiguous relations between the state and various corporate and social forces. But the apparent uncertainty of the prospect of a regional framework, and because of that, the possible emergence of a more competitive and confrontational regional environment will push the Japanese economy further into the neoliberal dilemma and further weaken the Japanese state. A vicious cycle in the transitional polity of the Japanese type may materialise for very different reasons.

Notes

1 The discussion of the hegemonic cycle was mainly an American phenomenon. Despite all the signs of resurgence of the U.S. hegemony though, there is little interest in the issue of U.S. hegemony now. It seems that as long as the U.S. remains the dominant power, there seems to be no real 'scholarly' need to talk about hegemony of any kind.

2 As a point of reference, Japan has implemented an Emergency Economic Policy for itself with a total of more than 20 trillion yen or US$167 billion, as the Government believes its own economic recovery is the best assurance for the recovery of other East Asian economies.

PART III

The New State-Market Nexus

CHAPTER 6

Xiaoming Huang

Contested State and Competitive State: Managing the Economy in a Democratic Taiwan*

Chalmers Johnson used the term, 'developmental state,' to characterise the unique methods of growth in Japan (1982). The model has since been applied to growth in other Asian countries (for examples, Deyo 1987; Berger and Hsiao 1988; White 1988; and Chu 1989). The studies examining and debating the model have consequently formed a dynamic research paradigm.

The Johnson paradigm depicts a national campaign of development and modernisation orchestrated by a determined, capable, and effective government with the political will, administrative skills and ability of social and corporate mobilisation (Johnson 1982, especially, Chapters 1 and 9). But the popular interpretation that an East Asian-type growth tends to be associated with an authoritarian state has gone beyond what was intended by the concept of the developmental state, and has consequently led to confusions and intense debates.

At one level, the development state is often related to the corrupt and oppressive party-family-state found in many AMCs (Lingle 1996 and 1998). Indeed, the type of authority structure did leave its mark on the economic record of these AMCs. But the development state, or state activism in general, was not necessarily the function of an authoritarian structure. The same active and effective state can be found in different authority structures (Chu 1989: 671) and as the case this study is to make, the state is still assertive and effective in post-Cold War Taiwan where a democratic political structure has replaced the authoritarian party-state. If there is less evidence for the direct causal relations between the corrupt and authoritarian authority structure and state activism, one has to rethink the nature of the relationship, specially in the context of Asian development.

* An earlier version of this chapter was also presented at the Annual Conference of the International Studies Association held in Washington DC, February 16–19, 1999. The author thanks Professor Edward Friedman and Professor Ralph Pettman for their comments.

One needs to understand the real nature of the 'mark' left by the authoritarian structure and, indeed, the institutional foundations of East Asian development.

What the authoritarian structure provided, which leads to a second popular interpretation of the developmental state model, was a political environment in which investors would have confidence in their investment, and the state would have a relatively free hand in pursuing unpopular economic policies and programmes. The first aspect is mainly an empirical one. As the Harvard IIE/ADB 1997 Report, echoing a 1994 study by Lindauer and Roemer, pointed out: '[s]ustained political stability in most of these countries enabled governments to be consistent in their approach and to implement longer-term economic strategies. Almost all of the successful Asian economies had stable political leadership, with few changes in heads of state and little shift in underlying economic direction' (Radelet, Sachs and Lee 1997: 51; also Lindauer and Roamer 1994).

There is nevertheless a need of caution here. While political stability can indeed be measured by the fact that 'few changes in heads of state' (presumably a key indicator of the authoritarian regime as well) as in the 'miracle' period in Asia, it is not a *necessary* condition for political stability. Political stability could well be achieved, for example, through regular, predictable and democratic transfer of political power. Perhaps 'little shift in underlying economic direction' is closer to what political stability means.

In respect of the second aspect, it was in this political environment that the government was shielded from unwanted interference from a society that collided with the government's overall economic agenda. Certainly, state autonomy (Evans and Rueschemeyer 1985, and Evans 1995), as an institutional condition helping strengthen the state's capacity to turn a developmental ideal into economic reality, is much easier to exist in an authoritarian structure than in a democratic one.

It is thus natural to assume that a new democratic structure would re-establish the missing link between the state and society and the corporate community in particular, and therefore would seriously weaken, if not eliminate, state autonomy. Under the new environment of freer flows of political capital, there is, according to Susan Strange, a 'sideways' shift of authority from the state. The state, rather than being autonomous, becomes 'defective' (Strange 1995 and 1996). The questions that interest us here are: could the state still retain its 'capacity' with its presumably weakened autonomy? Does state autonomy matter in the new environment? If yes, how does the state continue to preserve its autonomy?

Finally, there is a third group, particularly those economists and public policy specialists, who find state capacity at the core of the Asian Model.

Instead of viewing Asian development as an effect of a particular political structure, they focus on the institutional capacity of the state. The World Bank's 1993 'miracle' report, for example, believes that the essence of the miracle is 'rapid growth with equity,' which is the function of sound public policy, long-term macroeconomic stability, institutional collaboration, appropriate strategy of capital accumulation, and efficient use of resources. All these require an active and capable state (World Bank 1993). A strong state, as Linda Weiss carefully points out, is 'not a coercive state but one with the organisational capacity for governing industrial transformation' (Weiss 1997: 15, note 31 and 1998). For this group, state capacity is essential for the strong economic performance of East Asia (Weiss and Hobson 1998 and 1995).

State capacity is a set of institutional arrangements underlying the effectiveness of the government's policy formulation and implementation, while authority structure is a set of relationships among primary forces in a given social environment that reflect, as well as enforce, a distribution of political power. In an authoritarian polity, the state would be the central carrier of both political authority and policy functions. In a democratic order, the state ought not to be the centre of political authority, but may still well be the primary policy maker and enforcer. The notion of state capacity as a core institutional foundation of Asian development serves as a useful basis for the hypothesis that the replacement of the authoritarian structure by democratic institutions would not affect the state's capacity to manage the national economy. The Asian Model is still very much alive and effective, with or without the authoritarian structure.

It is this line of thinking that has inspired this study. In the following sections, I will first examine the democratic redistribution of political power in Taiwan over the past decade and its institutional restructuring centred on liberalisation, decentralisation and the opening up of society, and thereby demonstrate the changed nature of its authority structure. The second part then will investigate the dilemma the state faces under the new democratic and market conditions; whether the government is still active and effective; and how it actually performs its interventionist functions in the new environment. With the democratic nature of the new authority structure confirmed, and the state's continuing activism demonstrated, the third part of this chapter will explore a theoretical explanation that hopefully will help us better understand the state's governing functions in an emergent democracy.

Building on the literature of institutional selection, I will argue that an interventionist state could emerge from a market situation as a preferred institution for better market coordination and adjustment. This is particularly so in an economy, such as Taiwan's, which consists mainly of small and medium-sized enterprises (SMEs) that tend to be shaped or moved rather than a shaper or mover in the global market. It is particularly so also in a society, such as Taiwan's, where mutual dependency is 'embedded' between the state and various social forces. The new democratic order works actually better to ensure that individual and group preferences will be effectively transformed into national actions for which institutional disadvantages can be compensated.

A Democratically Contested State

The period from the end of the 1940s (when the Kuomintang, or KMT, government moved to Taiwan) to 1986 (when the principal opposition party, the Democratic Progressive Party, or DPP, was founded and subsequently President Chiang Ching-kuo, towards the end of his life, ordered the lift of Martial Law banning free press and political parties) is regarded as the authoritarian era in the recent history of Taiwan. The following decade from 1986 to 1996, when 'founding elections' had been successfully held and for the first time the President was directly elected through popular vote, is generally considered as the period of democratic transition.

Thus, while some may see an earlier 'juncture,' for example, in 1977 when the ruling KTM suffered the first major setback in local elections and its local factions allied themselves with opposition forces in a rebellion against the KTM (Chen 1995: 268), many, including this author, see 1986 as the 'starting point' of the process of democratisation (Tien and Cheng 1997:1). For Tien and Chen, 1986 as the cutting-off point involves a sophisticated theory of democratisation. For this author, the year separated two very different historical periods in terms of the distribution of political authority. The authoritarian era featured the predominance of the party-state with political power concentrating in the hands of the state, the KMT, and its two successive chairmen, Chiang Kai-shek and Chiang Ching-kuo. The democratisation, in essence, was a redistribution of the political power. Instead of the state being the sole power holder, political authority was relocated to the citizenry, exercised on their behalf by representative institutions: branches of national government, competitive political parties and local government.

The decade-long democratic power redistribution can be seen in three areas. The first was the establishment of a competitive party system. The rapid growth of the DPP and reorientation or revitalisation of the KMT led to the emergence of a competitive party system with the dominance of the two major political parties. Second, a series of steps in constitutional reform streamlined relations among branches of the national government distorted under the authoritarian party-state of the Cold War. The democratic power redistribution also took place intensively between the local and central government. As will be demonstrated in this study, the democratic process not only restructured the authority distribution, and provided legitimacy for the new political order, but also turned the state into an institution whose actions are accountable to the public, constrained by legal procedures, and subject to credible challenges from contending political forces and interest groups.

The Formation of A Competitive Party System

The new party system grew with the rapid rise of the DPP and a simultaneous decline of the KMT. With the KMT being the symbol of the party-state regime and the greater China identity, the DPP was launched on a platform aimed at the collapse of the KMT state and the promotion of a 'Taiwanese identity.'[1] This was the political foundation upon which the DPP built itself. The past ten years of the DPP's growth and expansion can be roughly divided into two phases. The first one, from the mid 1980s to early 1990s and with a wide range of radical methods of mass mobilisation and issue campaign, was to break the KMT's monopoly on the state machinery and national resources.

Through decades of building up favourable institutional arrangements and a personnel network, the KMT developed a high level of control of the state apparatus and the society, from the military to the economy and from police to mass media. The consequent 'quasi Lennist party state' (Cheng 1989 and Dickson 1997) was an effective, coercive and often brutal system of marginalising, neutralising and eliminating political oppositions, a system that effectively produced what might be called 'institutional violence' that the DPP and other opposition forces had to overcome. In its 'formative' years, 'physical' violence became an important aspect of the DPP's political participation and mobilisation. 'Violence against violence' was a main form of political contestation between the emerging opposition and the KMT-dominated state.

The DPP's campaign was advanced on several fronts. In the Legislative Yuan, the DPP used procedural measures such as filibusters, as well as physical interventions, to challenge the KMT's 'majority dictatorship.' 'Parliamentary violence' however had a limited effect on the political reality in the Legislative Yuan where the KMT held an overwhelming majority. The DPP had to take violence into the streets. 'Street violence' had a strong anti-system appeal and its operations were less constrained by the existing institutions. Parliamentary and street violence frequently occurred in the early ice-breaking years of the democratic transition. 'Violence' was also reflected in the DPP's radical approach to many key national issues.

The most significant among them was the DPP's position on the problem of national identity concerning the constitutional status of Taiwan in relation to mainland China. The 1991 amendment to the party constitution claimed an independent Taiwan as its ultimate goal. Technically, the DPP's position was aimed at the weakening of the constitutional foundation of the KMT regime and therefore de-legitimising the KMT's rule.

Into the 1990s, political conditions in Taiwan had changed significantly. The ambiguous 'ideological' reorientation of the KMT, with the triumphant rise of the 'mainstream faction' in KMT leadership,[2] effectively reduced the national identity's appeal of the DPP. Factional fightings within the KMT and consequently the weakening of the ruling party itself, accompanied by the gradual installation of new democratic institutions and procedures,[3] also made less relevant the DPP's attack on the KMT's authoritarianism.

The DPP also came under great pressures to project itself as a responsible and national interest-minded political party that could be trusted with national responsibilities, in order to further the prospect that it would become the ruling party, or lead a coalition government with the KMT.[4] These new conditions narrowed the range of issues that the DPP could play and how it plays, and, at the same time, demanded the DPP to expand its political basis and move toward the 'vital centre.'

Particularly, the DPP had to deal with the two mutually excluding elements on its political agenda: the party platform for an independent Taiwan; and the campaign to win 50 per cent voters, 50 per cent of seats in the Legislative Yuan, and ultimately the presidential election. The party platform confined the DPP's political basis to a fixed set of constituencies (stable at about 30 per cent of the voters in the past 5 years) while the national power drive demanded the DPP to reach beyond these traditional constituencies.

As far as the Taiwan Independence clause is concerned, while the majority of the people may not necessarily want to return to mainland China, they did not consider an independent Taiwan a feasible and reasonable option.[5] It was apparent that the DPP needed a new party platform of broader appeal to maintain a credible challenge to the KMT, and to further the redistribution of political power from the KMT. The

DPP needed a transition of itself from a 'revolutionary' party to a professional one.

The transition was put on the Party's agenda and into concrete political and policy moves under the leadership of the moderate faction within the DPP led by Hsu Hsin-liang and Shih Min-te. Professor Xu Bodong, a leading observer in Beijing of the DPP politics, identified four elements of the DPP transition (Xu 1998). On the Party's independence platform, the DPP reinterpreted its position and claimed that Taiwan is already independent and has no need for a public declaration. This position was further confirmed by its 'China policy' which emerged from a major internal party debate in April 1998.

The second element is the method of mass mobilisation and participation. The Party called for abandonment of various forms of 'violence.' In fact, parliamentary and street violence has rarely been seen in recent years. On industrial policy, the Party reached out to the business community in an attempt to change its image as the champion of social groups such as environmentalist groups and labour unions. In April 1998, the DPP called a national conference to develop an 'industrial policy' [*chanye zhengce*] aimed at making the DPP a constructive force in the sustainable growth of national economy and building positive relations with the business community.

Finally, the DPP also took steps to 'democratise' the Party itself. Organisational changes were made and are further proposed to turn the Party from a political force challenging the establishment to one that is a critical part of the new democratic order it helped build, and ready for effective national leadership. The DPP was the first among the major political parties to replace the method of the Party Centre's nomination with direct elections of party candidates for public offices. The DPP also planned to reorganise its central leadership to give it more decision-making efficiency and less constraints by factional politics (*CT* 2 April and 31 December 1998). Professor Xu, echoing what Hsu, then chairman of the DPP, argued, that the DPP's victory of 43.3 per cent voters over the KMT's 42.1 per cent in the 1997 county and city magistrates elections vindicated the success of the Party's transition.

The democratic redistribution of political power was materialised in the first instance through the painful rise of the opposition party breaking the monolithic authority structure and its transition to a credible and effective agent of political power. This same process was also the one in which the KMT lost its monopoly. What happened in Taiwan though was not just a one-way transfer of such power from the old guard ruling party and eventually its collapse, as we have seen in many other transitional polities in recent years. In many ways, the political power redistribution was ironically a process controlled and managed by the defending KMT. Through internal party leadership reshuffling, reorientation in party ideology and political platform, and a series of initiatives in the reform of the political system itself, the KMT managed to slow down the process of its 'chronic shrinking' and retain its dominant presence in the emergent new democratic environment.[6]

The transformation of the KMT was much more difficult than the rise of the DPP. It was a transition from a revolutionary quasi-Leninist party (with an ideology to pursue) to a bureaucratic professional political party (with elections to win), coupled with tensions around the leadership succession, the ideological division in the KMT, and, consequently, the reorientation of the KMT from a party of Sun Yat-sen's Three People's Principles to a party of 'Neo-Taiwanesism.'[7] It was a process in which the Party searched for its identity, rebuilt its legitimacy, and ultimately demonstrated the relevance of its continual existence.

The challenge that the KMT faced in the democratic redistribution was to exit gracefully from the old party-state-society complex and emerge as a 'kindlier and gentler', as well as effective and capable new KMT. As in any other transitional polities, the process of self-transformation was difficult and dangerous because of the impact it would have on the existing interests and established arrangements. Unlike many others though, the KMT leadership succeeded in controlling the process from being turned into a violent one between the KMT and the rest of the political society.

A key to such a unique experience was President Lee Teng-hui's political entrepreneurship in seeking broad political support beyond his KMT party apparatus and positioning himself as a force 'outside' the KMT establishment. The 'Lee Teng-hui syndrome,' an ambivalent feeling the opposition DPP developed towards Lee based on the belief that Lee may be closer to the DPP than to the KMT conservatives on many issues the DPP held dear, led to a sophisticated political game played out among Lee(and his mainstream faction), the DPP and the KMT conservatives. This eventually resulted in the consolidation of Lee's leadership within the KMT as well as his rise as a broadly accepted national leader.

The success of the transition also related to Lee's tactics of facing his enemies one at a time in phasing out resistance within the Party to his leadership and programmes. There were several major campaigns from 1988 to 1996, in which Lee managed to isolate and marginalise his major opponents. Each served as a major stepping-stone in the consolidation of his leadership. Each round of the political wrestling ended with the replacement of the leading figure in the opposition by another who would in turn become a new target in the next round. The past decade saw the rise of the mainstream faction of President Lee to the dominance and the marginalisation of the opposition forces within the Party into the nominal 'non-mainstream faction.'

The leadership change in the KMT laid down the political foundation for the successful execution of the Party's reform programmes. A key aspect of the reform was the reorientation of the KMT in terms of its political constituencies, ideological foundation and fundamental interests, a process referred to as '*bentuhua*,' or indigenisation, in which the KMT transformed itself from a greater-China-based political party to a Taiwan-based one. In addition to an increasing number of offices in the Party and the government being held by native Taiwanese, the reorientation was most aggressively pursued in the KMT's redefinition of Taiwan's relations with mainland China.

In 1990, the KMT called a National Affairs Conference, where a new Party-line emerged on the issue. It proclaimed that Taiwan and mainland China both were 'political entities with their own authority of jurisdiction' (MAC 1994). In 1993, the Foreign Ministry issued a *Foreign Policy White Paper* setting forth the idea of 'one China, two entities and phased equality' [*yige zhongguo, liangge Shiti, jieduanxing fenzhi*] (MOF 1993). The idea was advanced further as the result of the first visit to mainland China in 1998 of the chief of Taiwan's quasi-government body dealing with mainland China, *the Foundation for Cross-Strait Exchanges.* As one commentator pointed out, behind the notion of 'equal status' was a subtle shift from 'one divided China and two political entities' to 'one divided China and two equal states'(*CT* 19 October 1998). In July, 1999, Lee made an even bolder move to proclaim that from then on, Taipei's relations with Beijing should be dealt with on a 'state-to-state' basis.

The new mainland policy was the most important element of the KMT's reorientation, as 'social cleavages' in Taiwan are formed primarily around the issue of national identity and consequently the voter basis of political parties is divided mainly by that issue (*CT* 31 December 1998). The new mainland policy changed the image of the KMT from a party for the greater China to a party for Taiwan. Consequently it helped the KMT build a major issue basis for the legitimacy of its rule; revitalise the public's trust in the Party; and alleviate its relations with the DPP who was fiercely against the traditional KMT policy line on the cross-strait relations.

Lee's ambiguous position on national identity, while reflecting his world view and personal philosophy, effectively limited the room for the DPP's manipulation of the issue and forced it into either moving to the vital centre or taking a more radical and less popular position.

Consequently the DPP, moving to the vital centre, had to shift its focus to those more costly and less effective issues such as social welfare or environment protection. Those who felt strongly about the issue broke from the DPP and formed their own parties. The DPP was further weakened.

On the other hand, Lee's position also helped Lee's mainstream faction firmly control the policy agenda within the KMT. With the support of the public for Lee's new thinking on China relations, Lee managed to isolate and discredit those in the KMT establishment who were reluctant to support, or even challenged Lee during the Party's leadership succession. Lee's campaigns against the KMT conservatives were assisted by the tensions generated by the issue. The KMT conservatives were exposed to an effective Party chairman and his growing number of loyalists; an aggressive DPP whose main interest was to destroy the KMT, particularly its conservative faction; and a concerned public, the majority of whom have little confidence in the traditional KMT line on the issue. The fate of the conservatives was not hard to imagine.

There were also signs of reform in the KMT's internal 'party affairs.' The KMT, like many other 'permanent' ruling parties around the world who used to operate in a feigned democracy, relied heavily on transfer of cash benefits to voters through grass-roots party workers; in return for their political support for the Party. Within the KMT itself, hierarchy and centralism, legacies of the Party's Leninist past, are still very much alive, after years of its surviving the national process of democratisation.

The KMT tried to do something about the traditional link between the Party and its constituencies and the methods of mass mobilisation. In the 1997 elections, for example, the Party made a minor change in its campaign tactics. While still relying on local Party 'footers' to keep the old machine up and running, the KMT 'parachuted' several senior government officials to run for local offices, hoping this could be a new way of party mobilisation without the burdens of having to appease local factions. All these three instantly converted candidates failed in their bid. In the 1998 elections, the Party went back to the old way.

The rise of the DPP and the fall of the KMT over the past decade reflected the breaking down of the monolithic party-state authority structure. The subsequent reform, adjustment, and reorientation in both parties led to the emergence of two strong, competitive and credible political organisations. This in turn made them a logical holder of the redistributed political power and primary destination of political capital flows. By the end of the1990s, a stable national power distribution has been established. Elections in the past three years have consistently returned a roughly 30–40 per cent of votes to the DPP and 45–55 per cent to the KMT. The new competitive party system provided the new political power distribution with legitimate and effective carriers, and established necessary mechanisms for the democratic politics to function.

Restructuring of Government Organisation

The democratic redistribution of political power also took place in a series of institutional changes and modifications in government bodies at the highest level. The constitutional reform was necessary for several reasons. First, the 1947 Constitution was never actually 'abolished,' but only 'suspended.' In place of the suspended Constitution during the authoritarian era was the Temporary Articles. After the abrogation of the Temporary Articles in 1991, the legal basis of any new political order had to be found back in the 1947 Constitution. There was, in a sense, a restoration of political order based on the 1947 Constitution.

Second, the 1947 Constitution was designed for the whole China, including Taiwan and Mongolia, which the KMT government then constitutionally ruled. The structure of government and procedures of its formation, laid out in the Constitution, could hardly be relevant over the territories the KMT government controlled in the late 1980s. Adjustment was seriously needed to match the Constitution with the land, the people, and the state that it actually governed. Third, the 1947 Constitution was uniquely modelled after the five-power structure framed by the founding father, Dr. Sun Yat-sen: the President, the National Assembly, the Executive Yuan, the Legislative Yuan and the Control Yuan.

The Constitution had never really been put into practice after its proclamation. The decade of its actual function after the restoration indicated that there were serious problems in such constitutional design. There was, for example, no clear justification for the line of authority and responsibility among the branches of government. Functions among the branches of government were overlapping. Consequently, the government was ineffective, inefficient, and, most importantly, unsatisfactory for the democratic and presidential politics in post-Cold War Taiwan.

The constitutional reform has been carried out in a series of constitutional amendments passed by the National Assembly from 1990 through 1999 (Tien and Cheng 1997: 3–9; Tien and Chu 1996: 1151–54). The pattern usually was that the President convened a National Affairs Conference where a consensus was formed among contending political parties and interested groups and the National Assembly would turn the consensus into concrete constitutional amendments.

In 1990, the first National Affairs Conference was held and a general consensus was reached regarding the substance of the initial constitutional changes. The overall mandate to the National Assembly was: to amend the Constitution where necessary so that the state would have an appropriate and indisputable constitutional foundation and the government would, with an improved internal arrangement of authorities and responsibilities, function effectively and efficiently in the new political environment. The mandate led to subsequent constitutional amendments that fell into three categories.

The first round of change was aimed at the reconstruction of the constitutional foundation of the state, reflecting the view that the government no longer ruled the territories the Constitution had defined, and public offices should be elected by the people over which the government had actual jurisdiction. The revoking of the Temporary Articles was not simply a return to the original Constitution. In fact, the sitting assemblymen were forced to vote the 4-decade-old National Assembly into history as the new National Assembly would have only members elected from within Taiwan. Following that, new amendments were adopted for the President as well as the provincial governors to be selected through direct popular vote rather than indirect vote by the National Assembly as in the past.

The second category was designed to shape the type of the government in terms of the primary location of the government's executive power, an institutional choice between presidential system and parliamentary system. There was an intense debate as whether Taiwan needed an American (presidential), Japanese (parliamentary), or French (semi-presidential) system. In the second phase of the reform between 1992 to 1994, several amendments were passed which were intended to strengthen the office of the Presidency in relation to the Prime Minister, the National Assembly, and the Legislative Yuan. The President can now make cabinet and other government appointments without the Prime Minister's endorsement. Direct election of the President through popular vote also makes the President accountable to the voters rather than to the National Assembly. The Prime Minister is appointed by the President, subject to the Legislative Yuan's confirmation. In a new set of amendments in 1997, the power of the Legislative Yuan was further weakened with a higher threshold on its non-confidence vote and impeachment of the President.

Those changes intended to streamline the jurisdictions among branches of the government fell into the third category. In addition to the clarification of division of labour among the five branches, efforts have been intensified in recent years to restructure the government organisation through two major undertakings: 'Province Diminution Plan' [*jingsheng an*] and 'Government Restructuring Plan'[*zhengfu zaizhao zn*]. The first one, accomplished in 1998, reduced Taiwan Province from a major layer in the constitutional structure of the government to a nominal intermediary organisation without popular mandate. The other one, still in the process of forming a multi-party consensus, is the restructuring of the National Assembly and the Legislative Yuan, or 'parliamentary reform' [*guohui gaizhao*].

Key political forces agreed that the reform shall move in the direction of turning the National Assembly and the Legislative Yuan into one parliament, but disagreed as to whether the new parliament should have one or two houses. If a bicameral legislature, then the National Assembly would be the Upper House and the Legislative Yuan the Lower House. The DPP favoured the abolishment of the National Assembly altogether and therefore a unicameral legislature. The KMT took a position of 'improving the existing system,' that is, combing the existing Legislative Yuan and the National Assembly into a bicameral parliament. The parliamentary reform was seen as the last leg of President Lee's decade-long crusade for constitutional reform.

All the undertakings in the constitutional reform can be seen as part of the effort to restore constitutionalism. But it was not just a simple restoration of the suspended constitution. Rather it was an innovative and entrepreneurial experience of institutional building. More importantly, the reform rebuilt the constitutional basis for the emergent new political order and provided legitimate and modern institutional justification for the representative and executive powers.

The Challenge of Local Politics and Local Government

The democratic redistribution not only institutionalised social cleavages in national politics in the form of party politics, and rationalised the organisation of government by way of constitutional reform, but also forced political attention, along with resources, to shift to local politics and government.[8] Local politics tended to be underdeveloped under an authoritarian regime. This applied also to Taiwan. Such underdevelopment in Taiwan, however, was additionally a consequence of Taiwan's Chinese-style political tradition and the suppressive regime of the Cold War.

Under the Presidency of the two Chiangs from 1949 to 1986, local elections still took place even during the era's darkest times. But these were isolated events, and not part of the normal function of a political system of open competition. There was little political contestation involved. With

Marshal Law in place and the Constitution suspended, there were no opportunities or incentives for the citizens to exercise their civil rights or pursue their individual interests through open political competition. The KMT, through various state institutions, deeply penetrated and controlled the society. The society was 'incorporated' into the party-state system.

The revitalisation of local politics was no less significant than the development of party politics and the reorganisation of the national government. The new constitutional order vests the ultimate authority in the hands of the voters. Political parties become a primary carrier of the public's interests and their chief representative at national level. The government is given the mandate to organise the satisfaction of citizens' interests. The open and competitive electoral system ensures that not only the people's access to public authority is fair and open, but also the relationship between public office holders and the authorising public remains 'democratic.'

This new fundamental structure, or, an anticipation of it, directed the flows of political capital 'downwards.' It created new dynamics in the political system. First, there was a change in the public's attitude to politics. The public became more assertive than in the past and saw politics as a way of personal gain and civic life rather than just remote 'state affairs.' Such an attitude, plus the bottom-up election process, has been effective in forcing public office seekers to shift their attention and resources to the level of individual voters.

Second, it was not just individual voters but also the local government which became more assertive. Under the old regime, the local government was only a functional extension of the central government and designed to implement or enforce policies of the central government. Local government did not have the political mandate or executive rights independent of those of the central government. It collected taxes for the central government and relied for various functions on the budget allocation from the central government. Chief local government officials were appointed by the central government. Police, fire fighters, and others serving in public services, were salaried by the central government.

With the active involvement of the citizenry in the political process and local elections becoming substantive in recent years, local government began to redirect its services towards local constituencies and tried to build a sense of accountability to local voters. At the same time, local government significantly reclaimed executive authorities from central government, including jurisdiction over personnel appointments, entitlements to local taxes and self-sourced revenue. These developments intensified the political confrontation between central and local government.

A new central-local relationship could no longer be delayed for a fair and sensible division in administrative responsibilities as well as financial and personnel authorities between local and central government. Since late 1997, bills have been proposed in the Legislative Yuan addressing the problem. Two major legislatures were passed in the Legislative Yuan in early 1999 after a long process of deliberation: one, *the Law of Local Government* [*difang zhidu fa*] and the other, *Amendments to the Law of Division of Financial Authorities* [*caizheng shouzhi huafenfa zai xiuzheng an*]. These new laws define a more balanced central-local relationship and gave the democratic structure more substance at local level.

Finally, while the KMT continues to control national government, the DPP strongholds are found more at local level. Driven by move active involvement of the citizens and the growing power of local government, contestation among political parties at local level has also intensified. This could be seen as a consequence of the newly established democratic order, as political parties have to win elections at local level. But there were additional factors in the case of Taiwan.

Dominance of local factions in local, as well as national politics, for instance, was critical in directing political capital to local politics. Politics in Taiwan has never been a 'direct' process. It was mediated and manipulated through factions especially in local politics. This indirect and factionalised politics has been built into the internal party process of both the KMT and the DPP. With the voting power in the hands of the citizens and the whole authority structure leaning 'downwards,' local factions became more important than ever in securing the loyalty of their constituencies and therefore the party's political basis. In a sense, factions played a pivotal role in the democratic redistribution of political power as they created initial cracks in the monolithic part-state system. They also, as I have pointed out, attracted political capital to local politics and therefore effectively helped to reshape the centralised and elitist authority structure (for more on this, see Chao 1996).

The State In Contestation

The formation of the two-party dominated and open competitive party system, reconstruction of the constitutional order, and expansion of local politics and government, constituted the substance of the democratic redistribution of political power. In the redistribution, political parties, branches of national government, and local factions and government have taken much of the political power and resources previously in the hands of the party-state elites. Behind the democratic institutions and values, there were clear and persistent political interests and a reality of balance of power among defining political forces.

All the benefits of the democratic order aside, the new distribution will certainly affect the function of the state, its Policy making and implementation. It is beyond the scope of this chapter to provide a systemic investigation of the quality of state capacity in the new democratic environment. Also, the new democratic structure is not the only factor that may have affected the state capacity. What the following discussion intends is to emphasise, through individual cases, that the new authority structure has indeed had a limiting effect on state capacity.

The first case, the Bayer investment project in Tai-chung, suggests growing constraints on state capacity by local factional politics. Bayer Taiwan, a subsidiary of the German drug manufacturer, planned an NT$50 billion (US$1.7 billion) investment project in the Tai-chung County. Since 1994, the company had spent about US$10 million on planning, design, commercial assessment and two environmental evaluations, with all the support of the Executive Yuan, and was ready for actual ground-breaking. But the project encountered political difficulties after the 1997 local elections when the newly elected DPP Governor of the Tai-chung County requested the project be put to a public referendum before he could issue a land permit and construction licence. After a prolonged period of political wrestling, with no clear sign of permit issuing, Bayer decided to withdraw the project and moved it to the United States (*WJ* 19 December 1997 and *CT* 11 April 1998).

There were many issues involved in this case. The DPP leadership, sandwiched between the local DPP factions and the business community, regarded it as an issue of 'industrial policy' that the Party needed to evaluate, and hoped to solve the problem through an internal Party debate. For the Governor of the Tai-chung County, this was an issue of the rights and responsibility of the local government. For Bayer Taiwan and the business community at large, as well as central government itself, this was an issue of local politicians playing a political game to seek more power and resources from central government. The CEO of Bayer Taiwan, for instance, claimed that the Bayer case exposed the irresponsibility of some politicians and their politicising of a pure economic issue (*WJ* 18 and 19 December 1997).

But more than anything else, we can see in the Bayer case, as well as in many other similar cases such as the No. 4 Nuclear Plant Construction Project, how the new political order effectively limited the state's capacity to pursue a national agenda. The Bayer project had passed standard public hearings, community comments as well as environmental evaluations required for such an investment project. From the viewpoint of the national economy, the Bayer project would bring thousands of employment opportunities, and substantial tax contribution. The Executive Yuan regarded the project as a major stimulus for the sluggish economy and declining foreign investment. The Executive Yuan mobilised all the forces it could to get the project through.

The actual picture was bigger than that. Because of the long suppression under the centralised state, local government was incapable and less experienced in handling national issues. Its interests were often taken less seriously in national deliberations of public policy issues. Politicising of a public policy issue could help the weak local government strengthen its role in national as well as local politics.

The issue had also to do with factional politics in Tai-chung itself. The politics in the port area of Tai-chung County where the Bayer project was to be located was dominated by two major political forces: Red Faction and Black Faction who simply cannot tolerate one another. To compete for the support of the voters in local elections, they all stood against the Bayer project. To overcome the problem, Bayer Taiwan had to use a third force as its local partner to push the project: Ch'ang-I Group which had influence in both Tai-chung and national government. Unfortunately in the 1997 elections, Ch'ang-I Group supported a third-party candidate, rather than those of either Red Faction or Black Faction, which, since then, has spelt political misfortune for Bayer. Local politics, specially factions in battles to win elections, played a critical role in the new political environment. It is only fair to say that in projects such as Bayer's, the government's ability to mobilise, and the long term interests of the society as a whole, could easily become a victim of such politics.

A second case, the increasing competitive relations between the Executive Yuan and the Legislative Yuan, shows the redistribution of power among branches of government and consequently the decline in the capacity of the executive branch in getting its agenda through and its programmes funded. Under the old authoritarian party-state, all major national decisions were made by the KMT central decision making body, *zhongchanghui* [the Central Standing Committee of the KMT], and in most cases, by the paramount leader himself. The government branches were mainly implementing arms of the party-state.

The democratic transition and constitutional reform gave many essential legislative and financial authorities back to the Legislative Yuan. In addition to the constitutional division of labour, the capacity of the executive branch is further limited in several ways. First, legislators, transforming themselves from being responsive to the state to being accountable to the constituencies and financial donors, learnt to use their privileges in allocating national resources for their own electoral interests. Often public policies were to be compromised.

One case at hand was the appropriation decision for the state enterprises in the 1999 budget exercise. The consensus regarding funding for state enterprises was that it should be reduced to further the process of privatisation. On 30 December 1998, both the KMT and the DPP legislators agreed that the funding in the government budget proposal should be withdrawn. One week later, the same legislators overthrew their own agreement and reinstalled and passed the funding of almost NT$ 2 trillion (US$ 65 billion), to satisfy the affected enterprises that the legislators were associated with one way or another (*CT* 31 December 1998 and 6 January 1999). The general direction of the government's policy proposal could not survive the agenda of individual legislators.

The public policy process is also constrained by factional politics in the Legislative Yuan. Like politics in Taiwan in general, the Legislative Yuan is dominated by factions. Factions organised in the form of so-called '*ciji wenzheng tuanti*' [secondary policy group] either among legislators of the same party or those across party lines. Each group has a specific political background and follows a particular policy agenda. Differing slightly from factions in the KMT where political support is a major concern or in local politics where family connection is the founding basis, secondary policy groups are more interested in policy, and function as 'caucuses' in the Legislative Yuan.

The bargaining process among these factions often led to a situation where it took an unreasonably long time for a bill to pass if it passed at all. Thousands of bills piled up waiting for deliberation. Ineffectiveness and inefficiency of the Legislative Yuan seriously hindered the implementation of the government's policy agenda. The same legislative process can also be used to serve political purposes of key players. In the last day of the 3rd Legislative Yuan, for example, the legislators worked overnight to pass five major laws of constitutional reform and the two other laws redefining the central-local relations: the Local Government Law and the Amendments to the Law of Division of Financial Responsibilities between Central and Local Government. According to observers of KMT politics, this was the last-minute efforts by the House Speaker to rescue his bid for reelection against a challenge from the Deputy Speaker of the same KMT (*CT* 21 January 1999).

Finally, partisan politics created conditions that often limited the ability of the government to pursue public policy for the sake of public interests. Reform of the electoral system was an example. It was evident to all major parties that the existing electoral regulations have many areas that are not necessarily serving the emergent democratic order. Taiwan, for example, still uses the system of 'single-non-transferable vote,' or, SNTV, which is found to exist in only a handful of countries around the world. Up until the end of 1998, the law prohibited political campaign promotionals on TV during the official campaign period. The law also prohibited campaign rallies after 10 p.m. the day before the vote. But no candidates seemed to listen and the government did not intend to enforce the laws either.

There was a prolonged debate on whether the current SNTY should be replaced by a new system of proportional representation which would combine smaller districts and party proportional representation (*dan-xuanqu, shuangpiaozhi*).[9] The debate symbolised best the political effect of a particular institutional arrangement on different political parties; how these parties can effectively determine the fate of such an arrangement; and how party manoeuvres could marginalise the role of government in providing a fair and effective playground for competing political forces.

While there is an agreement on the need for proportional representation, disagreement has remained as to whether a German version or a Japanese one should be adopted. The current system is generally considered as benefiting large parties. The KMT and the DPP would prefer keeping the system if possible. But the problems with the existing system are overwhelming and the changeover to the proportional system appeared to be inevitable. If the current system has to be given up, the KMT would prefer the Japanese model which gives fewer party proportional seats and therefore fewer small party challenges (*CT* 5, 6 January 1999).

With both the KMT and the DPP hesitating, the reform of the electoral system never went too far from academic discussion and politicians' pledge. As the chief of the Central Election Commission of the Executive Yuan conceded, it is not too difficult for people to see the necessity of the proposed changeover, and, technically, the change itself is not difficult either. But it is very difficult to actually introduce the change because it would affect the existing power structure among major political parties (*CT* 25 January 1999).

An Active and Engaging State

The democratic redistribution has provided the foundation for the new political order. It is natural to think that the state in a democratically contested political order would be less assertive and less effective. In a way, the previous section was intended to demonstrate just that. The monolithic party-state has dissolved into a structure of power sharing among often competing institutions: the KMT vs. DPP; the Executive Yuan vs. the Legislative Yuan; central vs. local government, etc. Even the Legislative Yuan itself is often split among political parties and influential factions.

It would be difficult for a 'fragmented' state to function as an unitary actor on its own in the name of national interest. It would be particularly so and even 'immoral' for the state to take on the kind of responsibilities that would be otherwise expected in an Asian Model environment. Indeed, as shown earlier, along with the restoration of civil liberties, constitutionalism, and more political participation, the policy process has become much more politicised, and often a victim of partisanship, factional politics, and local interests.

The perceived weakening of state capacity was also accompanied by the expectation of the retreat of the state from the management of national economy. The late 1980s and early 1990s has seen not only the shift in political power from the state, but also restructuring of its functions to embrace the market economy at home and abroad. In Taiwan, such restructuring occurred on several fronts: transferring of state-owned enterprises (SOE) to private ownership; relaxing of the government's macro-control and micro-management of the economy; and rationalising of the government's economy-related actions on the principles of global market and economic individualism.

The government started the privatisation [*minyinghua*] programme in the 1980s and encouraged SOEs to reinvest their assets in private enterprises. In 1987, the government lifted restrictions on foreign capital accounts. The following year, regulatory controls on bank loan rates and deposits were abolished and foreign exchange rates became free floating. In 1989, banking laws were amended to allow new private banks and foreign banks to operate in Taiwan.

In contrast to the fundamental restructuring in the political arena, changes in the above-mentioned areas were moderate, and perhaps insignificant from the point of view of those with higher liberal expectations. As we shall see below, the SOEs remain substantive and influential after a decade of privatisation. The government does not hesitate in combining old practices with new methods to promote, protect, discipline, and manipulate various aspects of the economy. It still has a fairly solid control of the resources and institutional mechanisms necessary for its interventional functions. The public and corporate community are generally willing to support such activism. But before we elaborate further on how the state governed the economy in the new environment, it is necessary to first explain why state activism is still needed under the new conditions in the first place.

'To Be or Not To Be'

The problem of state activism is not new. The state's active engagement and effective manipulation are seen as the 'engine' of the envied and yet controversial experience of economic growth and social development in East Asia (For Taiwan in particular, see Wade 1990). On the other hand, similar state dominance in national economy is believed to have caused the economic failure in the former socialist countries, and increasing difficulties in European and Australasian welfare countries. Even for the AMCs, many believe that the state-centric Asian Model is incapable of generating sustainable growth because of its particular way of gaining competitiveness (Krugman 1994). Such a mode of political economy is not compatible with the new conditions emerging from political liberalisation and global integration of markets (Lingle 1997 and 1998).

A consensus seemed to have emerged in the late 1980s and early 1990s that instead of serving a positive model of economic growth for other parts of the world, the Asian style state activism needed to be limited and eventually eliminated. Institutional restructuring and liberalisation in trade, investment and finance were seen as a fundamental solution to the problems in countries where there are various forms of state involvement and intervention.

The challenge to the statist approach to economic management was also driven by very different beliefs in the fundamental nature of economy. Liberal economists believed that the capitalist economy has within itself the mechanisms for equilibrium-building. The overall beauty of the modern economy could come only after the satisfaction of private interests at the level of business owners and managers. There is no need for organised manipulation beyond that. Many globalists, on the other hand, rested their hope on the prospects of a new global arrangement. They recognised the uneven distribution of global resources and capacities; the national nature of the global economy, and discriminative effects of such an economy on different national units of economic accounting and distribution. Nevertheless they believed the solutions could be found only at the global rather than national or even corporate level.

Then there came the financial crisis. The crisis, among other things, forced many to rethink the old problem of institutional responsibility and accountability when the state was discredited and the global monetary economy grew rapidly and became much 'bigger' than the nation-state in its capacity to influence national economies. At the same time, such rapid expansion carried no clear line of responsibility and few mechanisms for accountability.

The 1997–98 financial crisis allowed many an opportunity to reconsider the utility of economic management at national level. Indeed, the utilitarian[10] return of an assertive state in many East Asian countries in response to the turbulence, compels a second look at the Asian Model; a revisit to the political and economic transition in the region; and rethinking of the process of globalisation. The crisis added more empirical substance to the on-going debate about the Asian Model, political and economic transition in the Asia-Pacific and the impact of globalisation.

In essence, the recent financial crisis could be seen as a manifestation of the fundamental changes in economic conditions that have constantly shaped the Asian economies and, indeed, the Asian Model itself. The Asian Model was a national organised response to a particular set of economic conditions and a set of institutional arrangements with the ability of swift adjustment to the shifting comparative advantage. A strong and effective state has been the primary assurance of such responses and adjustments. The utilitarian return of the active state following the recent financial crisis not only validated the basic spirit of the Asian Model, but, more importantly, the continuing utility of the state under the new conditions of the market economy and democratic politics. On the other hand, under such a new political and economic environment, new methods of state engagement with the national economy have to be found and indeed have emerged in transitional polities such as Taiwan.

The New State Activism

The new state activism in Taiwan is substantive and can be seen in a wide range of economic activities. This section will focus on three of them: state-owned enterprises; industrial promotion programmes; and market-governing measures. While state activism in the first two areas is very much the continuation of the system of the 'miracle' period, measures in the third category reflected many new aspects of the state-market relations continuously shaped by the rapidly changing global and national conditions.

STATE-OWNED ENTERPRISES

SOEs had been the backbone of the government's presence in the economy and the foundation of the party-corporation-state. Ten years after the implementation of the privatisation programme, the SOEs still have total annual retail sales at NT$ 2 trillion (US$65 billion) in 1998 (2.9 per cent of 1997 total GNP), almost 1.6 times the total annual government budget (NT$1.22 trillion, US$42 billion) of the same year. In 1998, almost all the twenty one SOEs were running at a profit, with an average of 8 per cent before tax. They provided NT$128 billion (US$4.3 billion) revenue for the government, 8.9 per cent of total government revenue (*CT* 31 December 1998 and 6 January 1999; and CEPD 1998).

Besides their 'healthy fundamentals', the SOEs' privatisation faced additional challenges. First, the SOEs involve a significant slice of government budget. With the Legislative Yuan becoming a key battlefield for allocation of national resources among various factions of legislators and the corporate and societal interests they represent, the SOEs become something that nobody really wants to give up. Even for those designated for privatisation, there are difficult labour problems to deal with. Employees are more conscious of their own rights and ways of influencing the institutional restructuring, and are better organised than before.

Those SOEs who have actually converted themselves into private corporations, have often 'reinvested' their government holdings in the private sector so their total government holdings are reduced to just below the legal line of 50% share. This essentially is more a transfer of ownership of state assets than a change in the nature of their management, a big dark hole in the privatisation business.

Moreover, the line separating a SOE from a privatised corporation was often intentionally kept simple and easy. In many cases, 1 per cent below or above the 50 per cent makes the qualitative difference. Converted SOEs with government holdings 'below' 50 per cent are not no longer a SOE and therefore not subject to the supervision of the Legislative Yuan. Nevertheless they continued to receive government support for its share. This new form of corporation, with combined private and state ownership and the benefits of both, provided a strong basis for the continued presence of mutual engagement of the business community and the government.

Finally, there is a substantive part of the SOEs that the government did not want to 'privatise.' This part of the SOEs, including the Postal Service, Pension Fund, Postal Savings, Government Employees Fund, state banks, are mainly finance services rather than manufacturing companies. As financial operations, they do not need government regular investment but are as profitable as other SOEs. They generate rather than consume capital. These fund-based state run enterprises became a primary tool with which the government engaged the markets. Of a total NT$ 283 billion

(US$70 billion) the Ministry of Finance (MOF) made available late 1998 for the government's intervention in the financial markets, these funds provided a total of NT$189 billion, or 67% (*CT* 17 November 1998).

INDUSTRIAL PROMOTION PROGRAMME

Industrial policy is a set of financial, monetary and administrative measures that are designed to promote certain industries over others and enhance the overall competitiveness of national industries in the global market. Industrial policy as another key supporting mechanism of the Asian Model has been criticised for adding an institutional component in the exports expansion of the national economies and consequently making the global competition unfair.

While the government is still trying to hold on to its role as the chief export promoter and organiser,[11] there were factors that have rendered East Asia's export-centered industrial policy less attractive, less effective and increasingly difficult. The first was the development of the global market itself and efforts to make it a fair playground on the basis of market principles. Through global (WTO, for example), multinational (APEC) as well as bilateral (US-Taiwan) arrangements, national 'barriers' have been greatly reduced and liberalisation in trade and investment has changed and will continue to change business practices in Asian countries.

Second, the national character of business has been increasingly blurred. Components of a product could originate in different nations, and phases of production and sections of a corporation can be multinationally located. Traditional measures of national industrial promotion, such as control of foreign exchange rates, preferential loan interests and government-funded export insurance, are difficult to implement. One of the factors that led to China's decision not to devalue its currency during the crisis was precisely the complexity in its economy and the fact that a change in exchange rates may not be able to achieve the clear-cut effect it desired.

Third, as international markets are tightening up and becoming increasingly unstable and unpredictable, national economies, from Japan to China and from Taiwan to Korea, are confronted with a strategic challenge to develop potentials in the domestic market for a sustainable growth. Thus the protective role of industrial policy will become less relevant.

But industrial policy still has its well respected function in Taiwan as a convenient and effective way for the government to provide incentives and discipline for the efficient use of national resources and effective steering of industrial growth. New global conditions created new comparative advantage. Industrial policy is to help individual businesses adjust to the shift. For example, Taiwan's *Act of Industrial Upgrading Promotion*, extended for another ten year after its expiration at the end of 1998, 'gives' various tax and financial benefits to 'important high-tech industries' and 'important investment projects,' specifically enterprises of electronic research and manufacturing, and their share-holding investors. The purpose is simply to enhance the competitiveness of those high tech industries, as they are seen as the engine of continual growth and capable of attracting global investment. In contrast to traditional direct subsidies encouraging export expansion, the main concern behind the new industrial policy seems to be in a balanced and sustained growth of the national economy.

Besides targeting the key industries, industrial policy also functions as a credible framework for the market calculation of individual investors. For instance, the Ministry of Economic Affairs (MOEA) implemented a plan in May 1998 for long-term industrial restructuring. This plan declared that the weight of heavy industries in the overall manufacturing sector in the next twenty years would decrease by 50 per cent. Its annual growth rate from 2006 to 2020 will be kept under 1 per cent. To reach that target, the overall economic growth for the same period will have its annual growth rate at 4.35 per cent (*CT* 18 May 1998). This long-term economic plan, with its matching measures of government fiscal and monetary support (or discipline), will inform the investors of the sectoral direction of future economic growth and effectively direct the flows of capital.

In addition to different purpose and methods, industrial policy is now carried out in a more open policy environment, and subject to the public's inputs, parliamentary consent, interest group interference, professional advice, and inter-departmental check and balance. Once again the example of the *Act of Industrial Upgrading Promotion*: the proposal of its extension was not only thoroughly debated in the Legislative Yuan, but also put on the table for professional comments and public inputs. The MOF, more concerned with the plan's consequences on tax revenue; and the MOEA, more interested in sustainable growth, finally worked out a compromise on a balance between economic growth on the one hand, and financial costs and social justice on the other.

While the purpose and methods of the government's engagement in the economy may be different and so is the policy environment for such active engagement, the same philosophy still reigns: use of government-operated mechanisms to direct market forces which is necessary for the market to work but which cannot be an automatic function of the market itself. This was true 30 years ago and is still so now. It is true in Taiwan as much as it is in Singapore, Japan or mainland China.

MARKET-GOVERNING MEASURES

One thing that distinguishes the state activism of the 1990s from, for example, that of the 1960s, is that the market has become *the* dominant force in the management of the national economy. This has turned the state's economic governance into a whole new game. There are several aspects to the development. First, the market has ascended to become the primary target of economic activities and a principal value in social life. As such, the state has to take the market itself as the centre of its economic planning, operation and manipulation. In the final analysis, it is the market that determines the necessity, substance and effectiveness of these activities of economic engagement.

Second, the ascendance of the market has also brought about an increasing separation of the monetary economy from the traditional goods economy. As modern financial products and monetary mechanisms proliferate, the monetary economy has developed its own dynamism that requires a particular system for its management. Third, not only is the monetary economy separated from the traditional goods economy, its often violent and unpredictable movements tend to threaten the secure growth of the traditional goods economy. These factors have forced the government to shift its directing activities from those promoting goods manufacturing and exports to those targeted at the movement of non-manufacturing market forces.

If there was anything that has made the survival of Taiwan in the recent financial crisis possible, it was the conservative economic philosophy in both the government and the business community, which limited the scope of the problems they had to deal with and justified the intervening steps and programmes by the government. Moreover, it was the diagnosis of the government that the solution to the economic difficulties was the stability of, and confidence in, the financial market and the expansion of domestic demands.

It was also the determination of the government and the cooperation of the business community that made feasible the timely, appropriate and sometime selfish measures of government intervention. Finally it was the fundamentally sound economy that absorbed the effects of the crisis and provided the resources needed for the government's rescue plan to work. Behind the government's effort, there were sufficient resources at its disposal. Foreign exchange reserves were at a historical height of US$84.5 billion in June 1998 (Miller and Eegbarth 1998), plus US$70 billion additional funds mobilised by the government from various sources affiliated with the government (*CT* 17 November 1998).

There are, however, different interpretations of how Taiwan related to the recent financial crisis in Asia. Many seemed to believe that Taiwan survived the crisis because of its 'basically healthy fundamentals' and different economic conditions.[12] A step beyond that, there is an argument that an important reason for Taiwan's luck was the liberalisation and internationalisation of its financial and monetary system in the past ten years, particularly its free-floating exchange mechanism (*CT* 14 December 1997).

But towards the end of 1998 and in early 1999, a crisis of a unique type emerged in Taiwan. One started to realise that there were also serious economic difficulties in Taiwan, whether or not they were called a crisis. One could argue that Taiwan was also part of the Asian or perhaps global turbulence. Conditions for a crisis existed in Taiwan as much as in other Asian countries. But as discussed earlier, there were two dimensions to the problems in Taiwan that helped shape the unfolding of the economic difficulties as well as the government's response: one is Taiwan's variation of Asian development and the other the new dynamism of the global financial market.

With regard to the first dimension, Taiwan, an essential part of the Asian Model, was different from countries like South Korea, Japan and Indonesia in growth strategy, method of capital accumulation, corporate culture and industrial structure. Consequently, problems in Taiwan were different in form and substance as well as timing and magnitude. Their receptiveness to non-economic manipulation was different as well. Taiwan's economy, for instance, was built around small and medium-sized enterprises (SME). Foreign capital, particularly short-term loans, was insignificant in the overall capital structure. This type of economy was more stable and easier to adjust in the event of major market disturbances.

On the other hand, the 'bubbling' activities in Taiwan were concentrated in the financial market and real estate industry, unlike South Korea and Japan where they were seen more in the manufacturing sector. This made Taiwan's financial market more vulnerable than its manufacturing sector. The combined effect of the internal and external conditions gave Taiwan a form of the unfolding of its economic difficulties that was gradual and centred on a few but critical areas. It also allowed a greater degree of manageability of the tensions built up in these difficulties.

From mid 1997 through mid 1998 when neighbouring countries experienced waves of financial turbulence, the situation in Taiwan was reasonably calm and the impact was minor. The government focused its attention on the stability of its financial market and possible chain-reactions to the external troubles. In the second half of 1998, problems in the 'fundamentals' emerged, along with an increasingly volatile situation in the financial sector. The real estate industry accumulated masses of new houses waiting for buyers. Bank after bank became unable to pay back their dues on time. Facing signs of a more serious crisis breaking out, the government took emergency steps to reduce market tensions and re-energise the economy.

Export Insurance The effort to re-energise the economy was directed first at securing regular export markets. Collapsed markets in Southeast Asia and their new competitive exchange rates left Taiwan's export-oriented economy in a particularly difficult situation. In October 1997, with the wave of currency devaluations in Southeast Asian countries, the government engineered its own devaluation, though minor, hoping to offset the impact of the devaluations on its exports. In March 1998, the government set up a plan, 'Insurance for Promotion of Exports in Southeast Asia,' with a total of NT$11 billion to insure exports to the crisis-devastated region.

Domestic Demand Expansion The effect of the exchange rate manipulation and exports-support was limited, and often invited criticism. Reflecting on the new thinking in growth strategy among many AMCs in the new global market structure dramatised by the financial crisis, the government moved, in a series of steps under the umbrella programme called 'Domestic Demand Expansion Plan'[*kuoda neixu an*], in search of a long-term solution.

The new strategic thinking believed that an ultimate release of the tensions between over-capacity of the economy and the shrinking and competitive international markets had to be found in the expansion of the domestic market. This was in contrast to the logic behind the rescue package adopted in Korea or Indonesia where over-capacity was tackled by the reduction in inflated demands generated mostly from programmes in the public sector and financial institutions, and a cutback of production capacity by forcing out non-competitive businesses. As in China and Japan, the new strategic thinking resulted in a programme of massive government-led capital investment and tax cuts.

The domestic demand stimulation plan was just a general principle. It consisted of several programmes providing tax breaks and new investment opportunities to release the pressures of over-capacity and over production. For the year of 1998–99, the government set aside a total of US$8 billion for the plan (*CT* November 5, 7 1998). In addition to the extension of the *Industrial Upgrading Promotion Act* which concentrated on tax benefits for high-tech industries, both the Council for Economic Planning and Development (CEPD) and the MOEA organised multi-billion-dollar programmes to give further capital support to various industries and services, particularly the SMEs. While the CEPD plan mostly benefited public infrastructure projects, the MOEA's 'Action Plan for Creating Domestic Manufacturing and Business Opportunities' targeted mainly the non-infrastructure projects, such as education equipment, general use of computers, digital TV, water facilities and energy conservation services.

Business Rescue For many troubled enterprises, the export promotion and domestic demands stimulus programmes were too slow to produce the desired effects. In particular the turmoil in the financial market required timely measures of turbulence prevention, damage control and confidence building. The government was under pressures to resort to various emergency measures for immediate effects. Towards the end of 1998, there were increasing signs of troubles worsening in the financial market and the real estate industry. One financial institution after another experienced difficulties in capital flows and in honouring their financial obligations. On 5 November, the Executive Yuan set up a multi-ministerial ad hoc rescue group led by the MOF to deal with the short-term financial difficulties of many businesses. Banks and other lending institutions were instructed to allow an extension of six months for repayment of unpaid debts.

In December 1998, the Executive Yuan decided to set up a Construction Industry Stimulation Fund with NT$150 billion (US$5 billion) funded by the Postal Savings it controlled. The fund provided through the Central Bank a preferential mortgage interest to anyone who would buy a new house within a year at a 'super low interest rate.' The Prime Minister also 'urged' the real estate industry to lower housing prices. While the mortgage subsidy programme attracted various criticisms from scholars, experts and public policy advocacy groups, the government hoped it would lead the construction industry out of recession and prevent the national economy from sliding into further troubles.

Market Stabilisation The determination and skilfulness of the government in directing the economy was no better demonstrated than in its recent campaign to secure the stability of the financial market. Different from many Southeast Asian countries and Korea where controls on capital accounts were lifted, it was still intact in Taiwan even after years of liberalisation of the financial and monetary system.[13] But even this conservative financial system could hardly sustain the months of tensions building up through the procession of the financial crisis. On 26 August, 1998, days after a dive of the stock market to below the 7000 psychological line in reaction to the problems in Hong Kong, the MOF announced the first series of stabilising measures, which included a raise from 70 per cent to 90 per cent in guaranteeing funds for loans [*rongjuan baozhengjin*] and other safe-guarding measures that would make capital flows in the financial market less easier (*CT* 4 September 1998). These measures were pushed further several days later when the market collapsed by 220.30 points, or 3.4 per cent. The government placed a ceiling on stock selling prices, and raised the lending ratio [*rongzi bilu*] from 50 per cent to 60 per cent (*CT* August 26 1998).

Such restrictions appeared to be insufficient in dealing with troubles of this magnitude. The government took even more dramatic steps as the situation worsened. The first unusual step was to mobilise the so-called *dangzheng jijin* [party-state funds] at the government's disposal, including those from KMT-owned enterprises, state-owned enterprises, various government controlled or affiliated funds, and state and private banks. The government used the funds to buy selected stocks to relieve the selling pressures and prevent the collapse of the market.

Through this manipulation, the government, because of the overwhelming size of the funds it controlled, forced the market to move in the desired direction. The government's Work and Retirement Fund, for example, bought US$4 million stocks in August 1998, adding to its already US$600 million strong stock holdings. On 5 November, with further instability in the market, the Fund entered again and bought another US$7 million. This market manipulative mechanism was first used in recent years by the government in the spring of 1996 when the stock market collapsed by 98.08 point, or 2 per cent, reacting to the missile crisis over the Taiwan Straits. It was also successfully used by the Hong Kong government in August 1998 in battling the manoeuvres of international speculators.

Intervention through moves of individual funds nevertheless appeared to be incapable of controlling the volatility of the financial market, and the government then decided to pool all these funds together to form a Market Stabilisation Fund, or 'MSF,' [*guoshi wending jijin*]. In August 1998, the MOF proposed to set up a 'standing mechanism of crisis management' in the form of an ad hoc 'major event response group,' centralising 'wide-ranging' efforts in market stabilisation. The subsequently established MSF, to become a primary tool for the government in the management of the crisis, consisted of ten state banks, many party-state funds and 23 private banks, with total disposable funds of US$10 billion (*CT* 16 November 1998).

With this Fund in place, the government's intervention in the market became a standing operation. In December, the Fund selected for its members a set of stocks as targets for their intervening purchase and set the stock index's lowest level in ten years (6,300) as the bottom line for members to act. For many members, their claimed supportive purchases perhaps never actually took place, but their actions had an effective impact on the market. This is one key element that distinguishes the state activism of today from that of the past. The state no longer acts in its administrative capacity to *control* or even *substitute for* the market. Rather, like anyone else in the market, the state now acts as *one of* market forces and plays by the market rules.

Moral Persuasion In the new political and legal environment, however, the government could not direct the market beyond the party-state funds under its direct control. The mechanism that the government applied to compel private institutions to follow its market governing guidelines was so-called 'moral persuasion.' The government considered it as the moral responsibility of private enterprises to help the government and other enterprises to overcome the financial and economic difficulties. Much of the government's intervention measures were based on that assumption. For example, one reason for the problem in the real estate industry was the high prices of new houses. While the government provided a mortgage subsidy for new house buyers, it also used 'moral persuasion,' in view of the increasingly sluggish real estate market towards the end of 1998, to press house builders to lower house prices. The government did so by suggesting target prices publicly and negotiating with the house builders association for voluntary compliance.

The government received an expected response from the Construction Investment Society which promised to persuade its members to initiate a price reduction within the reasonable margins of costs (*CT* January 13 1999). As the housing construction industry was no longer administrated by the government and there were no relevant laws to regulate the industry's pricing, moral persuasion was a way to seek the cooperation of the business community. In fact such moral persuasion involved clear consequences of various options for the real estate industry in terms of the government's administrative support and preferential treatment in the future. For example, the government could tighten licence issuance and financial auditing for those who fail to follow government guidelines.

Moral persuasion often sought the support of the business community against economic 'common sense' and the principles of the market economy. In the case of Hongfu Securities, for example, one of a series bad loan cases involving financial institutions in late 1998, the government mobilised US$100 million in just one day from other banks to meet the cash shortage Hongfu had from its due financial obligations. Many financial institutions who participated in the rescue operation disagreed with the government on this, believing that Hongfu's bad and even selfish business practice had created the situation and other banks had no obligation to rescue it and should not do so. To prevent further chain collapses of the Hongfu type, the MOF extended its moral persuasion to 62 financial institutions and asked them to 'join' the government in helping the survival of troubled businesses by postponing their debts for another six months (*CT* 8 November 1998).

The dilemma for the government between the value of market stability and that of free market principles can be better seen in its decision to intervene in the stock market. The MSF's manipulative moves did have the effect of disciplining individual and corporate investors, but when the intervention was administrated as a regular response to the market, its effect diminished as its interventional activities became a pattern of behaviour upon which other market participants could base their calculations. On 29 December, after days of MSF heavy intervening purchases, the market experienced a sharp drop of 201 points. It was estimated that about US$3-4 billion of MSF members' funds were lost. When investors detected the government's intervention pattern, they sold and took advantage of government-engineered purchases while MSF members bought in, following the government's instructions.

From the above analysis, one can argue that the state's active economic engagement in Taiwan is as substantive as it was, though the forms and substance may be different. Such a substantive role facilitates the security and continual growth of the economy under the new global economic conditions. It is hard for the SMEs to battle large-scale market turbulence on their own. It is equally difficult to leave an economy like Taiwan's to the mercy of the global market.

Overall, the state's intervention is as effective as it was. It is the economic and social structure and corporate culture that made the interventionist government much easier to be expected and respected. The public and the business community not only hold the government responsible for the economy, but naturally allow it some leeway in performing such responsibility. Close 'incorporation' among the government bureaucracy, business community and different sectors of the society turned their relationship into a mutually dependent partnership in which the government designs its financial and monetary policies, with the interests of the business community taken into consideration. In return, the business community supports the government when needed, even at the sacrifices of their particular interests. Here, one has the best example of the Asian Model in action.

A Democratic and Effective State

The state's continuing substantive engagement and intervention suggests that the new political structure has not become a confinement to such an active state. This, at least at the factual level, casts doubt on the thesis that a strong state is incompatible with democracy and the market economy. What is interesting is the institutional foundation of this active, strong and effective state in the new political economy, – in other words, why the state is still preferred; how the preference is formed; and how the state is still capable of such an active role.

An answer may be found, in this author's bias, in the problem of institutional selection and indeed the initial conditions under which the state became the primary form of human organisation in a contest with other competing forms centuries ago. Hendrik Spruyt, in examining the historical process from the 14th to 17th century in Europe out of which the state emerged as the winner over city-league, and city-state at the decline of the feudal system, church and multinational empire, argues that the hierarchical state prevailed 'because it proved more effective at preventing defection by it members, reducing internal transaction costs, and making credible commitments to other units' (Spruyt 1994: 527).

Building his theme on a blend of new institutionalism and historical sociology, Spruyt sees the state as an institutional solution to modern market conditions where individuals (and their groups) operate 'in the absence of higher authority to arbitrate disputes and enforce agreements' (Spruyt 1994: 529). The faith in the market is built upon the classical assumption in the chaos theory that 'market arrangements will suffice to achieve efficient solutions.' But 'transactional and informational costs are not zero, and a more hierarchical form of human organization is called for' (Spruyt 1994: 531). 'Individuals engaging in commerce thus will have reasons to prefer more hierarchy when this reduces information and transaction costs and creates more certitude in their environment. Political entrepreneurs will prefer to extend such hierarchy based on a calculation of a variety of factors. This calculation will depend on their responsiveness to the demands of domestic actors and on the costs of attempting such a strategy' (Spruyt 1994, p. 531). The state 'won out' over rival institutions because of its 'competitive institutional efficiency' (Spruyt 1994, p. 554).

Spruyt's thesis is part of the intellectual tradition of Oliver Williamson (1975), Douglass North (1981), Robert Gilpin (1981), Margaret Levi

(1988) and Mancur Olson (1965). Also his focus is on the external side of the state building. But two messages from the notion of the state as a preferred institutional solution to market dynamics are particularly relevant here. First, the market function will ultimately lead to institutional interference and the state is so far the most preferred and effective institution for this.

The case of Taiwan has demonstrated that, in addition to the reduction of transaction and information costs; prevention of defection and free rides; provision of long-term commitments to forces internal as well as external to the state; and dispute arbitration and agreement enforcement, contemporary market conditions give even stronger justification for the 'institutional efficacy' of the state. If the market failed to 'achieve efficient solutions' five hundred years ago and thus paved the way for the institutional solution of the state, it is even more difficult for such market efficiency today. In contrast to conventional wisdom, transaction and information costs are becoming more substantive as the magnitude and speed of the markets increase. Defection and free rides are much easier, and, in fact, become a principal practice in market operations, thanks to the growing number of new forms of economic transactions. Credible commitments are much more difficult to nurture because of increasing fluidity in institutional relations and mobility in economic activities.

Besides the continual relevancy of these founding elements demanding the provision of internal order by the state, there are new conditions that add further weight to the value of the state, particularly for those economies dominated by weaker and/or smaller businesses. Global market competition is no longer among equal individuals, if it were ever five hundred years ago, or in the abstract model of the chaos theory. It takes place among economic entities of different magnitude (consider Macdonald's and a family restaurant business in Beijing), or individuals of different capacities (say, Mr. Soros and a stock market investor in Taipei). Market competition of this kind involves huge 'magnitude costs' often bearing on those of less magnitude. The state not only provides a sense of security but, indeed, through its 'representational' actions, makes up the magnitude deficiency of individual businesses.

The second message, on the other hand, suggests that such an institutional choice by individuals in the market environment is hostile to democratic institutions because of its preference for 'political hierarchy.' This study has shown otherwise. The market, an active and strong state, and the new democratic order seem to work side by side. The problem may lie in these concepts themselves. What the market function would lead to, in Spruyt's model, is a centralised prioritising of economic activities. It is the state's institutional efficacy that matters, not the constitutional nature of the authority structure. An institutionally strong state could be found in a democratic environment or an authoritarian one.

Democracy, on the other hand, as the first part of this study has argued, is an individual-based distribution of political authority and a set of arrangements for the sustenance of such distribution. It is the antithesis of a state-privileged authority structure rather than a state-preferred public mandate. In a democratic polity, the state is the carrier of the public's mandate, shaped by contending political and social forces. This democratic authority structure, in this author's view, can far better ensure that the individuals' market-driven preference is transmitted with the least distortion to the mandate carrier. Democratic institutions and procedures are intended to make sure that the state will continue to act on such a preference. It is possible therefore that an active and engaging state is compatible with the normal function of the market and democratic political order. Under certain conditions, they can be mutually supportive.

Democracy, however, does affect the state's ability, as this study has also shown. It not only authorises the state to act on behalf of the individuals, but also allows individuals (and their groups) to act on their own whenever and wherever possible. More often than not, this affects the contents of the public's mandate through the tempering by effective participants of parochial interests, and circumscribes the ability of the state to perform its designated functions, because of the procedural consequences of the new political structure.

Overall, democratic structure and procedures, at reasonable procedural costs for the fundamental soundness of the political order, facilitate the market-state interaction and consequently reinforce the preference for the state as the institutional solution. This explains the simultaneous growth of democratic politics, market economy, and an active and engaging state in Taiwan over the past decade and perhaps in the years still to come.

Concluding Remarks

What can one draw from the case made so far? First, the state-centric authority structure and the state-preferred economic governance are not necessarily the same thing. While an active and engaging state may not necessarily entail an authoritarian structure, the function of the market and democratic institutions may well lead to such a state.

Second, institutional support, symbolised by an active and engaging state, should be accepted as an important component in modern economic governance. The essence of the Asian Model is perhaps not the rampancy of the authoritarian regime, nor the superiority of some cultural traits, it is simply a skilful and determined utilisation of such an institutional component. Rather than invalidating the principles of the Asian Model, managing the economy in a democratic Taiwan can be seen as an instance of their continuing usefulness.

Third, the market itself is also an institution in a broader sense. One would have to be an institutional fundamentalist to assign the generative power to either the market or the state or, for that matter, to any other institution. But it is human interests that ultimately determine the form of their satisfaction. It is our ever-changing needs and surrounding conditions that make our institutional selection dynamic. And it is this "original substance" to which both the market and the state ought to submit themselves.

Notes

1 Most central figures in the DPP leadership, for instance, were victims themselves of major brutal KMT campaigns against opposition forces in the past 40 years, or members of their legal defence team. All of them are native Taiwanese. The DPP Constitution of 1986 on the other hand, with an amendment in 1991, proclaims a democratic political order and a sovereign independent Taiwan as the two primary objectives of the Party.

2 After a series of internal party clashes between President Lee Teng-hui and his conservative opponents, the KMT leadership of the post-Chiang generation split into three factions around the time of the 14th Party Congress in 1993. The mainstream faction led by Lee Ten-hui managed to control the Party's agenda and established its dominance in the Party. Consequently, those opposing Lee's leadership, generally referred to as 'non-mainstream faction,' were successfully marginalised by the mainstream faction. A third faction was a group of young KMT elite often holding public offices. After years of opposition within the KMT under the umbrella of the New KMT Alliance, the group finally decided to break from the KMT altogether and formed their own New Party. The mainstream faction, among other things, took a more ambiguous position on the issue of national identity.

3 These included the lifting of Marshall Law in 1987; the termination of the Temporary Articles in 1991; a series of national affairs conferences on constitutional reform in the 1990s that led to several rounds of reforms in 1992, 1994, 1996, 1998, and 1999.

4 The 1995 Legislative Yuan election gave the DPP 33.17 per cent of the voters and 32.53 per cent of the seats in the Yuan, against the KMT's 46.07 per cent and 52.40 per cent respectively. The same distribution of power was confirmed again in the 1998 Legislative Yuan election, with the KMT receiving 46.53 per cent of the voters and 54.67 per cent of the seats and the DPP, 29.56 per cent and 31.11 per cent (*CEC* 1998).

5 For the past five years, 45–55 per cent of those surveyed preferred a status quo over either independence (10%) or unification (20%) on the issue of Taiwan's relations with mainland China (*CEC* 1998; Liu 1998).

6 The elections of 1997 and 1998 clearly indicated the effects of the KMT's efforts. Up until the 1997 election, the KMT had been on a decade-long trend of shrinking party membership, weakening party effectiveness; and decline in party influence, all reflected in the number of votes the KMT received in popular elections, seats in the Legislative Yuan and offices at all levels of government the KMT won through the years. The 1998 elections saw for the first time a decisive reversal of that trend. The KMT won back the important office of Taipei's mayor and a solid majority in the Legislative Yuan.

7 In a major campaign speech for a KMT candidate in 1998, President Lee Teng-hui claimed that all who live in Taiwan are Taiwanese, regardless of when they migrated to Taiwan and shall leave behind the sad experiences in their history and work together for a better Taiwan. This so-called '*xin taiwanren zhuyi*' (neo-Taiwanesism) apparently moved away from Lee's long-held controversial position that separated the native Taiwanese from those migrating from the Mainland and saw the KMT government as a 'foreign' one imposing its oppressive rule on the Taiwanese, towards a more inclusive approach to the problem of ethnic and national identity.

8 In the 1947 Constitution, 'local' means the province, county/city and town/village, the so-called four-tiered government structure. With the diminution of Taiwan Province and elections at towns and villages to be suspended, 'local' now refers primarily to counties and cities at the same level.

9 Single seat and dual vote, a system combining single-seat district and party proportional representation where the voter has two votes, one for the district candidate and the other for the party. Of those countries with this electoral system, the German model has a higher allocation (50 per cent) for party proportional seats while Japan's 40 per cent. Also the German model has 5 per cent votes for a party to be qualified for proportional seats while Japan's 2 per cent (*China Times* 6 January 1999).

10 The term 'utilitarian' connotes a narrower definition of the state's role in providing market-conforming guidance and separates it from an 'ideological' one, the one for the more comprehensive role found in the AMCs in their initial economic development during the Cold War.

11 For example, the Ministry of Economy still has a Trade Expansion Promotion Fund that supports business expansion abroad.

12 This is a view certainly held by the government of Taiwan and widely received in local mainstream media. See, for example, Miller and Eegbarth 1997.

13 Taiwan had a plan to lift the control by year 2000 but they now apparently have become more cautious (Wang 1998). In fact, Singapore and China were the two countries that had this mechanism in place and successfully stopped the financial troubles at their door. The survival of China, Taiwan, and Singapore in the financial crisis, plus Malaysia's experience before and after its reinstallation of capital control, suggested, among other things, that institutional mechanisms at the national level did make a difference in the management of the global financial dynamism.

CHAPTER SEVEN

Stephen P. Green

Macroeconomic Dilemmas and Alternative State Strategies: The Post-Developmental State of Taiwan*

The Asian financial crisis forced radical readjustment and painful devaluations for most of East and South East Asia and further destabilised Japan. Taiwan, however, escaped relatively unscathed. Absorbing a devaluation in October 1997 of only 13 per cent, a stock market fall of 16.4 per cent and the prospect of ever-more competitive exporting rivals, Taiwanese business and government seemed quietly confident.[1] With low debt, large foreign exchange reserves, a diversified export profile, a dynamic SME sector, protected financial markets and a world-beating technology industry, Taiwan has remained relatively firm. In fact, the economy seems to have suffered guilt by association in the crisis, rather than attacks aimed at any intrinsic national weakness.

Moreover, the barrage of recent criticism of 'crony-capitalism', inefficient investment strategies and political interference in markets that supposedly characterise Asia's political economies seems largely irrelevant to Taiwan's own experience. While its growth was historically based on a version of the government-focused 'developmental' state which has now been so roundly condemned, something different has since developed. The reasons for Taiwan's success are here traced back to the results of a contest to reconstruct the developmental state.

This chapter will aim to delineate the shape of this 'post-developmental' state, explain how the restructuring of market-government relations have served – intentionally and not – to insulate Taiwan from the winds of crisis and offer clues as to how the social forces present in other former tigers will influence the emergence of a different kind of polity and economy. The state's economic role has mutated and been

* The original version of this chapter was written in early 1998 as part of an MA in International Political Economy at Warwick University, UK. I wish to thank Dr Peter Ferdinand for comments and the Economic and Social Research Council, UK, for financial assistance.

contested, its political authority has been radically questioned while its role as a gatekeeper between the international and domestic spheres has been wholly refined. Yet, significantly, none of these roles of the state have been completely lost or forgotten.

The clear need is not to simply throw out the 'developmental' state paradigm as Asian political economies change, but to understand and map the ways in which the tensions and ambitions of various social forces held within this state-society nexus change and redefine their relationships. The evidence in the case of Taiwan is that two models of a new form of state are present. These states are in competition and potential conflict. The 'intelligent state' is a form of 'strong' state which has drawn back from the direct style of the 'developmental' era but which still actively and effectively pursues competitive advantage. The other form of state has been termed the 'kidnapped state', since this state is controlled and debilitated by internal and exterior interests, and is characterised by a lack of clear policy and failures in supporting development.

Through focusing on five sectors – relations with the PRC, trade, domestic policy, the financial sector and the IT industry – it will be shown that a fundamental struggle over the nature of the relationship between state and business has restructured Taiwan's political economy in the 1990s. While the government has attempted to manage a transition, other actors have competed for rights to governance, disrupting and altering the 'transition' process. While similar tensions have been present in the other tigers, only Taiwan has seemingly negotiated the twin post-developmental impulses effectively. The trend at the end of the 1990s is towards decreased autonomy and 'intelligent' action from the state, yet, on a wider stage, it is far from clear how these social forces will interact in the rest of post-crisis Asia.

The 'old structures' of the 'developmental state', the key mechanisms for Taiwan's relatively smooth development up to the mid-1980s, have been comprehensively examined and debated. A particular form of state has been brought 'back in', one insulated from disruptive social forces yet embedded in commercial and industrial cultures, resistant to the predatory temptations outlined by the neo-utilitarian school through strong bureaucratic structures and incentives (Evans 1992; Johnson 1995; Meier 1991).

In this form of state, politicians reign but bureaucrats rule, and they rule over a political process of capital accumulation and systematic bureaucratic intervention in industrial development (Wade 1990). It is enabled by strict authoritarian rule and a politics of 'survival'. Less direct than in South Korea or Japan, the Taiwanese state allowed the supply of investible resources to be augmented and the risk of long-term investment spread, thus enabling business to operate with lessened risk but with artificially enforced incentives. The state also acted as midwife to emerging industries. Foreign exchange allocation was manipulated to support 'key' industries, Export Processing Zones, or EPZs, promoted and technology transfer and diffusion actively encouraged.[2]

In the late 1980s Taiwan faced a series of serious macroeconomic threats. Labour-supply was tightening, causing debilitating rises in wages and rents. Moreover, the NT$ had appreciated sharply, affecting export competitiveness. The dominant response was relocation of industry off the island, a process which radically intensified between 1988–90.[3] The danger of a 'hollowing out' of industry on the island was a worrying reality. For the Taiwanese companies, however, this was only a partial solution: relocation might cut costs, but it could not solve the lack of R&D nor promote an upgrading to higher quality goods.

To stay competitive in the global market these problems would have to be addressed. Added to this, a speculative bubble developed between 1986–89, fuelled by an economy characterised by extremely high liquidity, low interest rates, and a lack of incentives to invest productively. Many business people and workers opted to '*wan gupiao*' – or play the stock market – and export growth suffered as a result. Actual GDP growth declined from a high of 12.74 per cent in 1987 to 5.39 per cent in 1990(DBAS 1997, pp. 24 and 25; quoted in Tung 1997: 52). Taiwan, it seemed, was having to pay the price of four decades of success. The dilemmas were complex and the old structures could not cope with these new pressures.

As in much of Asia, the developmental tiger began to 'deconstruct.'[4] Macroeconomic dilemmas – positions where one has to chose between equally unfavourable alternatives – were multiple. In the domestic sphere, the strictly controlled financial sector was proving counter-productive. More confident industrial groupings demanded greater autonomy, but both threatened dissolution of the success of the 'governed market'. Democratic pressures and revelations of corruption questioned the utilitarian basis for KMT rule, but worries over social chaos, tensions with the Mainland and crime, spoke to the advantage of an unquestioned single-party state. Dilemmas in the 'foreign' sphere were equally troubling. The cheap, educated and abundant labour of the ASEAN Newly Industrialising Economies (NIEs) had undermined Taiwan's previous competitive advantage.

The imperative was to move up the product ladder, but without experience, R&D facilities or an industrial structure thought to be supportive of this kind of industrial restructuring. Trading partners, especially the United States, were increasingly frustrated by Taiwan's protected markets, but to open them would be economically painful and politically dangerous. And, of course, the shadow of the Mainland loomed large – a perpetual problem, but in the 1990s an increasingly dominant dilemma. Industry on the island desperately needs to relocate to cut costs. However, dependence upon the Mainland as hinterland could entail serious economic risk and is also potentially political suicide.

In summary, domestic and foreign pressures had radically altered the society and market. Chief among the dilemmas, however, was what kind of state would provide the best means for an effective strategic response. This was a challenge across Asia and some responded more successfully than others. South Korea, for example, officially attempted to redefine the state as 'trouble-shooter'; continued to provide subsidised credit; and attempted to limit the strength of the conglomerate class and invigorate small and medium businesses, but the network of financing within the chaebol networks proved unassailable (Koo and Kim 1992; Nan and Lee 1995). The state became dominated by post-military governments which have lacked the authority or the political will to reform the industrial sector.

Bureaucratic intransigence and a conservative bias within the Japanese government have meant an inability to respond to the 1989 stock market crash. Singapore remains relatively vibrant but there are signs of a lack of entrepreneurial activity due to the continued preponderance of government intervention. Constructing the post 'developmental' state is obviously not an easy project to undertake. In the case of Taiwan, two competing forms of state can be seen to be emerging, each promoted by social forces to pursue their own interests. These are presented as useful heuristic devices for understanding the fracture lines and tensions within Taiwan in the 1990s. It needs also to be emphasised that they are not actually completely realised but are models to describe two trends going on in the state at the same time. It will become clear that the *de facto* politico-economic environment is a far messier mix of these ingredients.

Intelligent State and Kidnapped State

The 1990s have seen a new form of government-led Taiwan state trying to emerge. This is the 'intelligent' state, a state where politicians reign, but politicians and business rule in dynamic partnership. It is more flexible and fragile than previous administrations, moulded by conscious planning and readjustment to circumstances outside its control. The 'intelligent state' is characterised as:

- a state which actively and efficiently pursues and creates competitive advantage in partnership with business. While authoritarian mechanisms may have been reformed, the state still maintains economic planning boards, numerous government agencies and business-state groupings which influence policy. The entrepreneurial imperative to aid development remains, embodied in the ambitious Asia Pacific Entrepôt (APE) plan;
- a state which effectively drives at integration within regional and global trading groups;
- a state actively committed to IT not just as a value-added export strategy, but as holding the promise of increased quality of life and 'hyper-modernity';
- a state which intelligently moulds and accommodates various interests and which manages democratic pressures. 'Intelligence' also implies honesty and integrity, guaranteed by institutional checks and balances and democratic accountability and transparency.

C. P. Chang recognises the difficulties of implementing state policy. He states, euphemistically, that 'the increasing complexity of our domestic social and political environment has created numerous disorderly conditions during our period of transition' (Chang 1996). The underlying message seems to be that bureaucratic inefficiency, democratic pressures, business involvement and weak authority have derailed the pre-planned transition from the 'developmental' to the 'intelligent' state.

However, alongside these social and political pressures is the more interesting question of how business itself has set the agenda and pursued its own strategic responses. A contrary form of state has emerged in conflict with the 'intelligent' version. This is the 'kidnapped state,' a dysfunctional bureaucracy that has been 'captured' by business, crippled by electoral competition and corruption and inefficient in planning. In this model politicians may reign, but business rules. It is characterised by the following;

- a state in which with the breakdown of the militarised state large business groups, often with underworld connections, have moved into the power vacuum. Legislature and senior posts are dominated by representatives of big and local business. There has been a hostile takeover bid of all policy relating to industry, trade and, especially, the Mainland matters. Government is seriously worried over its 'increasingly economic dependence on Mainland China' but ineffectual in reversing it (Chang 1996: 63);

- a divided state whose government institutions act and react in conflict with one another;
- an ineffective state – the state's failure in developing automobiles and aircraft are evidence of this, while some even suggest that the IT industry has been more hindered than helped by state intervention;
- a state experiencing major socioeconomic changes – unemployment, increased demand for welfare provision and crime – which it has proved incapable of resolving;

The relationship between these two models of state – the 'intelligent', capable, interest-balancing state versus the 'kidnapped' business – dominated, democratically incapacitated state – defines the political economy of the 1990s. They operate often in symbiosis, sometimes in conflict. Although outside the ambit of this chapter, much of Asia's problems can now be traced to the domination of the 'kidnapped' version of the state over the 'intelligent'. Suharto's Indonesia, for instance, embodied the totalisation of a kidnapped state, where the administrative apparatus was completely deployed to the interests of business.

This chapter intends to outline the broad nature of this continually negotiated relationship in key sectors which impact on macroeconomic health. Its major ambition is simply to begin to identify what is going on in the transition from 'developmental' state to something else, something not yet theorised and seemingly too complex and contradictory to package as a paradigm.

The Mainland Factor

At the centre of Taiwan's political economy of the 1990s is a structural contradiction: the economic logic of further integration with the Mainland and the political gulf that still separates Beijing and Taipei. In the political sphere, Beijing sees economic integration as a means to eventual political reunion. Taipei perceives this as a danger to its political autonomy, and the instinct, therefore, is to limit investment, stall any political negotiations and maintain the *status quo*. Business pushes for 'direct transportation, trade and postal links', but Lee preaches 'be patient, no haste' [*jieji yongreng*] (*FCJ* 3 November 1997). This fundamental dilemma has severely undermined the 'intelligent' state's usual positive 'pro-business' policy stance. Instead, the 'kidnapped' state is very much in evidence – one which fears further integration but which is actually pulled along by the directives of business and is relatively helpless in stemming outbreaks of 'Mainland fever'.

Fujian and Guangdong Provinces offer the complementary resources of the ideal hinterland to Taiwan, – extensive land, cheap and educated labour, geographical proximity and similar business cultures and languages. Industrial relocation before the mid – 1980s mainly headed to Southeast Asia but after 1987 concentrated on the Mainland, much of it without official government approval. Manufacturers estimate that they can produce at 20–40 per cent less cost in the Mainland than in Taiwan and can earn returns in 18–24 months, one year sooner than in ASEAN countries.

However, continued frustration over exact investment policy led to a decline in confidence in the government during 1990. Wang Yung-Ching, the Chairman of Formosa Plastics Group, made a well-reported but unauthorised visit to the Mainland exploring locations for a new Naphtha-cracking plant (*FEER* 8 Feburary 1990: 34). The cheeky theatricality of this move focused attention on both the government's unease and lack of proactive policy-making. The state finally responded with a series of business – sensitive institutional creations in the early 1990s (*MAC* 1990).

Moreover, a radical reformulation of Taipei's policy did come in the potential loosening of the traditional KMT 'Three Nos' policy in Lee's inaugural address (May 1991), which laid down stiff conditions for the revision of this policy, but seems, in hindsight, to have signalled to business that the doors were opening. Reported capital investment in the Mainland leaped from US$1.3 billion in 1991 to US$5.5 billion in 1992 (Chen 1996: 449). In the Mainland, the relaunching of radical Deng style reform, triggered by Deng's Southern Tour of early 1992, marked a qualitative shift in the investment relationship. Before 1992, Taiwanese investment had been characterised by second-hand machinery, low technology products and short-term projects. Informal business policy changed as confidence in reforms increased and longer-term capital and technology-intensive direct investment took off.

By mid-1996, 25 to30 000 ventures had been set up with total investment totalling US$20 – 25 billion. These 'economic' changes were accompanied by more subtle shifts in Taiwan's own state-market relations, especially within the strategic institutions which govern trade and industry policy. The 'developmental state' successfully isolated an economic planning bureaucracy from societal interests – the government was, in effect, an autonomous actor in the distribution of foreign exchange and American aid, developing a patron-client relationship with business. Political legitimacy was partially based on economic success. The 1980s saw the gradual fragmentation of this monologue and new voices and interest groups began to push for a hearing.

With the liberalisation of banking laws in July 1989 (*FEER* 25 January 1990), a boom in the stock and property markets and a trend towards increased linkage, a degree of Keiretsu-like cartelisation of enterprises into large conglomerates occurred in the 1980s.[5] By 1990, the top 100 companies – including President Foods, Formosa Plastics Group and the Hoshin Group – were responsible for 34 per cent of national GNP (Leung 1995: 40). With state policy confused vis-à-vis the Mainland, and under pressure from domestic environmental groups, the new imperative for business was to become involved in politics, to protect its own interests at the heart of the decision – making process.

The state was increasingly seen, not as the tough but efficient nurturer of industry, but the inhibitor of the obvious next step in capital development – the relocation into and opening up of new Chinese markets. In fact, from the viewpoint of business, politics could make the 'intelligent state' stupid, with bureaucracy and self-interest having made it inefficient, and democratic pressures turning it anti-industry.

The state itself ran – and still runs – the risk of becoming the chief macroeconomic problem of the 1990s. The evolving – and highly strategic – response of business, especially the larger enterprise groups, has been to attempt to gain influence, and kidnap policy from within. Political donations from interested business and vote-buying are reported to be widespread (*FEER* 9 December 1993: 21). On a national scale, the 1994 KMT Central Standing Committee election saw four members of large enterprises (including Hoshin Group and President Foods) take senior political offices. Informal influence operates within 'peak' business associations – the National Association of Industry and Commerce and in 1993 the Ministry of Economics formed the Mainland Affairs Committee. Both provide key informal networks which play vital policy-forming roles.

Policy vis-à-vis the Mainland in the1990s is certainly not the autonomous province of the political state. While the government has lacked a strategy of engagement, business has led the moves towards interdependence. Although Lee's calls for limits to investment did cause some of the bigger groups to stall plans, they did little to stem the tide (Tso 1996). Even as foreign direct investment (FDI) into the Mainland stalled in 1997, capital from Taiwan continues to flood in – during January – September 1997 investment surged to US$3.23 billion, compared to US$2.93 billion in 1995.[6] Even Lien Chan, current Vice-President, has predicted that by 2000 Beijing will be Taiwan's largest trading partner, its major investment area and main source of trade source. Yet how do we conceive of the evolving shape of the new political economy? Tse-Kang

Leng summarises this situation thus; 'allocation of resources is not decided by an edict from a strong man but through a conciliation and co-operation process between state and business' (Leung 1995: 57). However, 'co-operation' is too *kind* a word to describe the often conflictual attempts to change state policy. And perhaps 'kidnapping' is too *strong* a word, but importantly it emphasises the fact that the 'intelligent state' has lost its preferred autonomy and its agenda has been effectively captured by business and is, in reality, powerless to prevent further interdependence with the Mainland.

Politically the 1990s have therefore seen the opening up of the public space not only to a voting public, but – and this is perhaps a more significant development – to a well-resourced, influential, well-connected business community. The previous form of state maintained close contacts with this private space, but essentially operated distinctly from it. The post-developmental state includes these new elites through informal funding *guanxi* [connections], formal institutions and policy advisory committees. Tse-Kang Leung proposes that a more corporatist future is likely, but his analysis points to the continuation of informal networks of influence, rather than the open and strict rule-defined institutions more common in European corporatism. In other words, significant 'strategic' responses will be informally decided and usually pro-business.

Trade

Taiwan has also been trying to extend economic links to other regions. The APE Plan attempts to integrate free market ambitions for the 'freest possible movement of goods and services, personnel, capital and information' with the setting up of six operation centres in Manufacturing, Sea and Air transportation, Finance, Telecommunications and Media (Chiang 1997: 1). It is at the heart of the 'intelligent' state's response to the Asian macroeconomic environment of the late 1990s, in attempting to draw multinational headquarters to the island and provide a hub for Asian trade. The project, however, is part myth, part reality, and part unruly ambition.

Simply in geographical terms, Taiwan can never aspire to the status of an Asian 'entrepôt'. It is far better suited for providing transportation links and trading facilities for Mainland-focused business, and in financial terms is years behind Hong Kong, and decades of state monopoly of the telecommunication networks has crippled this sector. There have been limited successes – IBM, Hewlett Packard, MTV and United Parcels have all opened up regional centres since 1996 – but the legislative response has been slow, indicating a loss of co-ordination within the state's institutions.

Much to the chagrin of Beijing, Taiwan has also been active during the crisis. A government party making an official nine-day tour of ASEAN in March 1998 while China Development Corporation, closely linked with the KMT, has pledged a US$300 million investment in Souteast Asia (*Asiaweek* 27 March 1998). This opportunistic state activism echoes the largely failed policy of 'Go South', a government initiative that begun in 1993 to encourage Taiwanese business to 'diversify' their investments into Southeast Asia, rather than the Mainland, It is unclear what diplomatic capital Taipei hopes to gain from any financial aid but Beijing has made its own position adamantly clear.

Otherwise, in the sphere of foreign trade, government and business are aggressively pushing for integration within global markets. Since 48 per cent of exports in 1997 went into Asia, Taiwan's Export–Import Bank is now providing trade finance for countries importing goods made in Taiwan. This provides a rare point of convergence between the two styles of emerging state. Exports in the mid-1990s still proved to be the lifeblood of the economy: 1996 saw domestic consumption shrink, real estate stagnate, and a series of bank runs and Mainland military exercises which triggered massive capital flight. Macroeconomic survival ultimately depended on the strength of exports which rose by 20 per cent in 1994. In contrast, 1998 has seen exports decrease but domestic consumption remain healthy. State and market logics differ, however.

Propelled by the logic that economic interdependence could ensure political independence – or at least recognition – the 'intelligent' state is leading the bid for World Trade Organization (WTO) membership. The government expects that membership would increase export value by 16.7%, and imports by 12% (Chang 1996: 64). Business realises its dependence on external markets and cannot risk isolation. The dilemma is how to restructure and deregulate without alienating support and damaging domestic industries. Tariff barriers have already been cut from 31 per cent of imports to 9 per cent from 1984–92 in a drive that attempted to speed the pace of domestic restructuring, reduce friction with trading partners and integrate Taiwan politically (Howe 1996:1182).

However, WTO conditions – negotiated from a position of international political weakness – will have serious adverse effects. Japanese cars are likely to flood the auto-market. Moreover, dependence upon Japan as the supplier of key machinery, auto-parts and cutting-edge electronic equipment, is a problem for Taiwan and with lessened protection will continue.[7] This quasi-dependency dampens rhetoric over Taiwan as a 'technology island' and casts doubts over the 'intelligence' industry's capacity to guarantee future prosperity.

In the agricultural sector it is estimated that a potential loss of US$1 billion in rural farmers' incomes if rice tariffs were removed. The fear is that cheap Southeast Asian imports would destroy the small-holding rice farming industry in Taiwan and alienate the significant support rural farmers have given the KMT since land reform in the 1950s (Ferdinand 1996). Therefore in the non-Mainland trade sector the signs are that the state is acting proactively and effectively, in concert with private interests. Long-term trade considerations converge with political ambitions, thus allowing a focusing of energies which diverge on Mainland policy. In this sense the state seems focused on long-term objectives and is 'intelligent'.

Social Policy

Macroeconomic restructuring is creating serious dilemmas for the state's social policy. Official unemployment has been steadily increasing in the 1990s – the fallout of labour-intensive industry relocation. An eight year high was reached in 1995 at 1.79 per cent of the labour force, while the trend continued up, approaching 3 per cent in 1996, though this is still far below OECD levels. More significantly perhaps is the worrying trend of a growth in inequality in an economy famed for its equity. The increasing gap between 'the haves and the have nots' will present dilemmas for the future – domestic consumption patterns will be affected, pressures for increased welfare provision will increase and low wages within the service sector may accelerate the emergence of an underclass.

Economic restructuring has created its own social and political dilemmas, credible responses are unclear and the popular conception of what the state can, and should achieve is undergoing transformation. New forms of government legitimacy have to be found in the democratic environment of the 1990s. The state can no longer guarantee protection and well-being or forcefully suppress dissension. The emergence of a welfare state agenda is a partial strategic response to the pressures of the democratic system. In March 1995, the state acted to implement the popular National Health Insurance Programme. After initial concern over increased government spending, there are now signs that the government might even be making a profit on the scheme. However, the 'intelligent state' faces continued pressure for the extension of welfare provision.

It is suggested that public construction works and termination of labour importation should be used to ameliorate unemployment problems (Hung 1996). However, the trends actually point to a government attempting to scale back its infrastructural spending, and many Taiwanese simply refuse to take part in the 'servant' industry. Industry, on the whole, is satisfied that these structural changes are positive – the state is left with the problems of social cohesion and security, and against these inexorable trends, it is hard-pressed. Business will pressurise it not to fund extra welfare schemes through extra taxes. The likelihood is that the previously efficient state will be increasingly seen as ineffectual in popular opinion. Its *de facto* strategy will be simply one of 'bite the bullet'; a slow readjustment in public expectation to more crime, insecurity, and a split society. The popular conception of the state is likely to be anything other than 'intelligent'.

The Financial Sector

The financial sector is one of the most strategic sectors in an economy and is often the last to encounter reform. Robert Wade argues that certain rigidities in the financial system provided a structural support for development in the 1956–1980 period. High interest rates, the lack of welfare support and a strictly controlled banking sector all served to augment national savings rates.[8] Within this period gross domestic capital formation averaged 28.4 per cent GNP while during the 1970s net savings to net national product ratios ran at an average of 30.5 per cent (Wade 1990:107). These world-beating figures allowed rapid growth without foreign borrowing, reduced dangers of inflation and – in coordination with other institutions and mechanisms – supported developmental objectives. They allowed tight state control over the balance of payments, the cost of borrowing, an extension of stable, long-term credit to firms with high debt/equity ratios, and allowed the building of business coalitions around growth objectives (Wade 1990: 116–123).

However, the oligopolistic banking sector did produce dangerous 'inefficiencies'. Neighbourhood loan circles were *the* way to start up a new small business. The unregulated 'curb market' for informal loans, where SMEs sourced an estimated 30–40 per cent of total credit,[9] was unstable and contributed to the speculative mentality of the 1988–9 period. The 1986 relaxation of currency convertibility restrictions and mounting export earnings during the 1980s resulted in an economy awash with cash. In contrast to much of the developing world, Taiwan's main dilemma was how to manage *excess* liquidity. The macroeconomic threat was that the illegal credit operations that had evolved as a lifeblood companion to the rigid formal sector were now destroying stability. The stock market crash in early 1990 prompted a new policy response from the state – credit would be tightened, tight supply-side monetary policy would be adhered to and the financial sector reformed. The 'intelligent state' committed itself to a tactical strategy of selective withdrawal and enhanced regulation.

Reform, however, was not easy. The 'intelligent' state faced a classic dilemma – to achieve the vision of an 'Asian Financial Centre', a vision championed by the Ministry of Finance, innate conservative distrust of 'free-markets', structural interest in the *status quo* and a suspicion that liberalisation could lead to foreign influence, would have to be overcome. With a Central Bank committed to low-inflation and defence against speculative attacks, the site of this reform struggle was, not surprisingly, within the state itself. 'Intelligent' state planning agencies were committed to controlled deregulation – to privatise the three state-owned banks and allow limited free-market competition to modernise the financial sector.[10] Instead, however, in March-April 1991 the Ministry of Finance unilaterally cut its stake in the banks, but the Provincial Assembly (PA) resisted reform. As the primary shareholder, the PA saw the banks as not only offering a source of income but also a lever for patronage (*FEER* 7 May 1992; *FT* 7 November 1997). The banks are, at time of writing, still not privatised.

The once-unified state bureaucracy thus became a site of struggle between liberalising technocrats and rent-seeking (unelected) politicians and conservative economic planners in the Central bank. Moreover, government was forced to issue fifteen new Bank Licenses, instead of the planned six – large businesses were behind moves to extend and radicalise the liberal tendency within government policy. The emasculated 'kidnapped state' emerged to stifle and disrupt the best laid plans of the 'intelligent' reform-oriented bureaucracy. Clearly, already at the start of the decade, the state was no longer a unitary actor or decision-maker and democratic politics have not yet even been instituted. As the decade progressed it was increasingly clear that any strategic response from the state would be stifled in such an environment.

Taiwan's ambitions to rival Hong Kong as Asia's new financial centre have been extremely slow to come to fruition. Relaxation of capital flow and financial instrument restrictions have come in piecemeal measures. The NT$ non-delivery forward market opened to domestic and foreign investors only in July 1995.[11] Commercial banks in 1997 could still hold only 5 per cent of a securities firm and could not invest more than 15 per cent of net worth in listed firms (*FEER* 13 November 1997). Authorities still rigidly insist on Bank of International Settlements (BIS) capital adequacy ratios of 8 per cent for all financial institutions when other countries are more relaxed (*SCMP* 6 July 1998). Moreover, Taipei is currently refusing to issue further licences to banks wanting to set up operation in the Mainland (*FEER* 13 November 1997).

Taiwan aims to deregulate services but in reality the state is painfully unready to liberalise and risk the consequences of these ambitions. In hindsight, this conflictual and partial transition has been rewarded. Far from an 'intelligent state' directing and leading reforms, one senses a hesitant, fractured and conservative state being pushed into market deregulation by macroeconomic exigencies and business pressure, but continually resisting reform with a 'go-slow' attitude. External shocks have also proved to be a potent policy influence, immediate dilemmas focusing the underlying need for constructive strategies. Taiwan's pegged NT$ did not completely escape the maelstrom of speculative attacks on regional currencies in Autumn 1997. 'Black Monday' (20 October 1997) saw the NT$ devalue 2.3 per cent after the Central Bank [*yanghang*] abruptly abandoned an expensive defence. Finance Minister Paul Chiu immediately announced emergency measures in an attempt to broaden defensive tools and extend investor confidence. Ironically, however, the dithering over liberalisation during the 1990s, by limiting the amount of short-term foreign capital entering the markets, did contribute to the defence against speculators. The central bank is resolved to intervene again in the event of further shocks.

Unlike South Korea, Taiwan's banking sector has remained robust – lending even increased by 12 per cent in 1997 (*Asiaweek* 5 December 1997). This health can be traced back to the macroeconomic structure of the economy, with SMEs contributing about 50 per cent of value-added to the economy, employing 62% of the workforce and producing 65 per cent of total export value.[12] In contrast, South Korean chaebols have aggressively sought market-share, neglected short-term returns, and 'benefited' from an interventionist government and the intra-chaebol banking system. In Taiwan, banks often reticent to loan to SMEs, because of lax disclosure and lack of collateral, have been legally required to focus 30 per cent of total lending to this sector, thus spreading the risk of capital investment. Moreover, the state has been strict with directed loans, requiring adherence to export targets.

To reform or not to reform; that is the question, and like Hamlet, the state is bewitched by the disadvantages of both sides of the dilemma. Ironically the sudden change of financial climate makes Taiwan's intransigence appear prudent and further pressure from domestic financial groups, such as the Koo Group, and the WTO, for external access to equity and capital markets, look more easily resisted. The recent banning of Soros-related funds signals a newly legitimised role for the state, to resist the destabilising effects of 'globalisation', which can be effectively defined by each government to serve their own purposes. The Taiwan lesson is apparently not to expand one's financial sector too rapidly. However, this was an unplanned result for Taiwan and certainly not the result of any strategic or 'intelligent' action. There seems clear evidence that a fractured state, under powerful capital influences, is key to the shape of actual financial reform. There have been signs of 'intelligent' behaviour, but the dominant trend is a reactive, lucky and slow to act state – and there have been benefits to this. In contrast, the information technology industry is often cited as the great state-business success story.

Information Technology

At the strategic heart of the 'intelligent state' is a commitment to information technology (IT) as the means to a new development trajectory. Far-sighted economic planning in the 1970s identified IT as both an essential component in the project of economic catch-up and as providing a comprehensive response strategy to deep-rooted problems. Under former President Chiang Ching-Kuo, a popular and industrial computer education programme was envisioned as the key to 'upgrade our industries and enhance our competitiveness' (Chiang quoted in Wang 1997: 556). In addition, Chiang ordered the setting-up of a science-based industrial park, to be organised by the National Science Council.[13] IT has now developed not only into a strategic industry, but a measure of Taiwan's national 'strength' in the 1990s.

Lien Chan's dream of Taiwan as a 'science-and-technology' island does not seem unrealistic when it produces a third to a half of all personal computers.[14] By 1995 Taiwan's 890 hardware firms were responsible for $21.3 billion worth of goods, a 33 per cent increase on 1994 (*Yearbook* 1998). While not only becoming Taiwan's most important source of foreign exchange, competence in IT has become a vital value-added differential with the Mainland and most of Asia. The 'Made in China' labour-intensive manufacturing phase contrasts now with the advanced nature of Taiwan's capital and technology intensive concepts such as 'Innovalue' and 'Its better made in Taiwan'.

In addition, IT is a 'clean' industry, an ideal solution to the dilemmas that industrial pollution has caused. The success is partly due to the industrial structure – SMEs are ideally suited to the short-life span computer products market and the island can provide an 'all-in-one service' with the exception of CPUs; a quality manufacturing and skills base; and an educational system which emphasises technical skills. However, state policy has actively supported high-tech development. As an entrepreneurial agent, the 'intelligent' state identified weaknesses in the industrial structure – SMEs with limited technical resources and little long-term risk protection – and then moved to compensate. The state has been active in providing legal and institutional infrastructure, guiding and sequencing projects and even becoming the producer in some cases of market failure (Wang 1997: 572).

The 'intelligent-state' has spawned multiple institutions, projects and joint cooperative ventures with business.[15] One of the key interventions has been the creation of Hsinchu Science Industrial Park (HSIP), responsible in 1997 for US$14 billion of revenues. Government provided 5 per cent of the initial investment (*FEER* 16 August 1998). Companies in HSIP combine research and production, lease their land and have access to preferential loans, tax breaks and special incentives under the 'Statute for the Encouragement of Investments'. HSIP is also one of the major engines of Taiwan's recent 'brain-gain' of talent back from the United States. The NSC now aims at 2.5 per cent GNP being reinvested in R&D by 2000, in comparison to 1.81 per cent in 1995; more 'Intelligent' industrial parks, and a technology-intensive industrial production of US$300 billion by 2000 (Change 1996: 63). Thus, technology is poised to transform Taiwanese society. Or so the vision goes.

Problems abound. Eighty-five per cent of Taiwan's IT hardware firms are still non R&D investing and technologically dependent – for the government they constitute a 'weak and unstable downstream foundation' (*Yearbook* 1998, 'Industry'). There are reports of 'pork-barrel politics' as politicians struggle to have new parks established in their own constituencies (*FEER* 15 August 1998:15). Some critics, in contrast, do not credit the government with much more than stating the obvious and having little impact on a sector which would have developed without its support. Moreover, Taiwan has yet to develop its own CPU technology and is heavily reliant on Japanese tubes in monitor production. While Taiwan may have succeeded in doing for computer parts and peripherals what Hong Kong did for textiles, the next upgrading stage will be tough. The chief challenge for the 1990s is how to break into the software industry, a culture specific, crowded industry with a small and information-illiterate domestic market.[16] Moreover, the educational system stifles creativity, industry lacks system integration skills and many managers blame the government for its slow, bureaucratic and inefficient IT procurement systems.

The state has responded effectively to the problems facing the hardware industry. It has acted to aid the construction of a new competitive advantage. Now it needs to do different things, as well as the commitment to R&D and APE plans, to create the right environment for excellence in software. More radical, 'intelligent' reforms are demanded to restore flexibility and creativity to a fact-learning, exam-biased school system; to proactively out-source high-tech requirements to private companies; and to aggressively push for hardware and software penetration of the Mainland market. These strategic reforms, however, are not likely to occur in the short-term, and business is likely to suffer from conservative government intransigence. Gradual reform, the state's usual *modus operandi* is, unfortunately, ill-suited to such a fast moving sector as IT.

While IT provides an imperfect success story, the automobile sector badly mars Taiwan's reputation for successful technology transfer and development. Even with a complete import ban on Japanese vehicles, in 1995 over 33 per cent of imported vans from the United States had Japanese brand names and components (*Yearbook* 1998: 46). Taiwan's national car looks incredibly unlikely to challenge Japan's auto-hegemony.[17] The 'developmental' and 'intelligent' states have failed here, unable to catch up with a small domestic market and take advantage of economies of scale. Nevertheless Taiwan has not suffered greatly in macroeconomic terms, though national pride, perhaps the prime motivation behind the project, may have been dented. In overall terms, the IT industry has proven the enduring effectiveness of supportive state activity. As we have seen, it is not perfect and will face severe challenges in the next century, but the 1990s have seen the 'intelligent state' clearly visible in the structure and strategy of an industry which has not only responded to global trends and demand, but now ranks among its IT leaders.

Concluding Remarks

The continually negotiated relationship between public and private social forces defines the nature of Taiwan's political economy. Some of their various interests are conflictual, others harmonious, and these criss-crossing relationships have resulted in a hybrid form of state in which aspects of the 'intelligent' and 'kidnapped' models both appear. The use of the models allows us to focus a critical gaze on a vital, multifaceted relationship and to delineate the terms of conflict and cooperation. There is a delicate balance within Taiwan's current political economy in which the state is, at one and the same time, proactive and reactive, a leader and a victim, effective and dysfunctional. This negotiated state has enabled Taiwan to largely 'sit out' the 1997–8 financial crisis – by chance as well as by design. While Taiwan's specific relationship with the Mainland is, of course, key and unique to its political economy, there are definitive lessons for the burnt-out tigers.

Taiwan proves that even in the 1990s, state involvement in the economy is not intrinsically dysfunctional – *pace* recent pronouncements.

Success depends on an autonomous business sector which is capable of resisting government initiatives which run counter to their interests and taking advantage of constructive policy. It requires a flexible bureaucracy, ready to meet with democratic demands and economic change. In contrast to much of Asia, political suspicion of foreign capital – mostly Mainland-focused – and conservative biases within the state have undermined plans to externally liberalise finance. This lessened vulnerability to foreign portfolio ebbs and flows has proven constructive and may well be a paradigm which other burnt-out tigers will want to learn from.

Yet other factors – the prevalence of SMEs and the refusal to integrate banks within conglomerates – are based on peculiar state-society relations of a KMT ruling party suspicious of a strong local opposition, rather than any goals of economic efficiency. This lack of '*keiretsu*-culture' has contributed to Taiwan's failure in developing an aircraft or car industry, but in hindsight this can be seen to have aided Taiwan's idiosyncratic success. In the final analysis there are only a few prescriptive policy lessons to learn from Taiwan since its own unique political situation has defined so much of its economic success. What Taiwan can teach us, however, is that intelligent and kidnapped states can coexist, and coexist relatively effectively. Post-crisis Asia can take heart from this partial legitimisation of state intervention but needs also to be aware of the particularities of Taiwan's success.

Transition is on-going – democratic demands will increase, export competitiveness will come under pressure and the 'be patient' policy vis-à-vis the Mainland will come under immense strain. Taiwan's hybridised political economy will likely experience greater stress along the intelligent/kidnapped fault-lines in the next decade and Taiwan's political survival will depend on managing the dilemmas these cause. Asia's recovery will also depend, to a large measure, on the nature of the inevitable negotiated compromise between the two faces of the post-developmental state.

Notes

1 By July 1998, the NT$ had dropped 20 per cent year on year. The stock market fall is measured over one year to June 1998. See *Financial Times* 12 October 1998 and 5 November 1997.

2 The notion of state-midwifery is explored in Evans, 1995; Biggs and Levy 1991. For a good overview of the problems with developmental models, see Moon and Prasad 1998: 9–24.

3 Between 1988–90 outward FDI totalled US$16.5 billion – 94 per cent of the total outward FDI of the previous twenty years. (Tung 1997: 55).

4 The internal pressures created by the very success of development are well-explored (Evans 1992; Chowdhury and Islam 1993).

5 This process no doubt benefited from a KMT state undergoing 'Taiwanisation' itself and therefore feeling less threatened by the emergence of large domestic capital groupings.

6 In the first half of 1997 a 'measly' US$20.7 billion entered the Mainland as FDI; a decrease in the growth in funds of around 15 per cent from 1996 (*FEER* 13 November 1997; *FCJ* 7 November 1997).

7 In 1995, 30 per cent of the US$103.6 billion worth of imports were Japanese, while Taiwan's trade deficit with Japan increased to US$17.1 billion (*Yearbook* 1998).

8 At the end of 1979, outstanding non-bank financial claims accounted for only 7 per cent of total claims, while over 75 per cent was based in the banking sector (Wade 1985: 112). Moreover the stock exchange 'remained rudimentary as a source of capital' and firms relied heavily on borrowing rather than equity capital.

9 Data based on a Central Bank survey 1964–90 (Tang 1995, p. 848).

10 An omnibus banking law in July 1989 allowed the privatisation of the state-owned Chang Hwa, First Commercial and Hua Nan Banks, as well as competitors with a minimum of NT$10 billion initial capitalisation, into the market. Central Bank Governor Hsieh Sen-Ching had this 'prescient' prediction: 'that should set the stage for Taipei's emergence as a new international financial centre in time for Hong Kong's 1997 eclipse' (*FEER* 13 November 1997).

11 But now ranks among the most actively-traded currencies in Asia (*DMG* 1997).

12 SMEs are defined for the purpose of the survey as companies with less than 300 employees. Figures refer to 1985. Broadly similar data would be expected for the 1990s (Tang 1995: 848).

13 By the end of 1996, firms located in HSIP employed 54,806 staff, 59 per cent with a junior/technology college education (*NSC* 1997).

14 In 1996, Taiwan controlled 95 per cent of global scanner production, 74 per cent of global motherboard production, 65 per cent of global mouse production and 53 per cent of all monitor production. CPUs are the only PC part Taiwan has been unable to produce and for which it is reliant on Japan (*FCR* 1997).

15 The MOEA oversees the development of industrial technology, directing projects such as the Information Science and Technology Development Ad Hoc Plan, with a budget of US$46.7 million. This allows for joint R&D work involving companies and the Industrial Technology Research Institute (ITRI), a US$20 million fund for private research, and also oversees the Information Infrastructure Initiative. The National Science Council (NSC), the Research, Development and Evaluation Committee (RDEC) (responsible for public information services) and the National Information Infrastructure (NII) Steering Committee are all state 'cyber-players'.

16 In 1996, Taiwan's hardware production amounted to US$3.3 billion, while software only hit US$33.3 million, with only two companies penetrating Japan (*FCR* 1997).

17 The eleven auto-businesses in Taiwan are all joint-ventures with foreign (mostly Japanese) companies. The MOEA has coordinated efforts by China Motor Corporation, San Yang Industrial Company Ltd & Co. to jointly develop a Taiwan engine.

PART IV

The New Global Conditions

CHAPTER EIGHT

Christopher Lingle

Global Dynamics and the Institutional Flaws of East Asian Governance

The economic problems experienced by Asia-Pacific countries in the past decade, particularly the financial crisis that swept much of the region beginning in July 1997, are rooted in the nature of political and corporate governance in the region. While this proposition points to a simple truth, resolution of the problems requires fundamental changes that will be difficult to implement. This is because the financial and currency crises are an outcome of deeply-rooted institutions that reflect cultural conditions peculiar to each nation. In turn, there can be little hope for speedy implementation of the fundamental changes. Indeed, the choice may be made not to effect change that would be too threatening to the political status quo. Consequently, restoration of stability to the region's economies will not come quickly, while recovery may be many years off and will result in a much lower growth trajectory than experienced during their 'miracle' phases.

In essence, the recent turbulence in regional markets sharply contradicts the World Bank's 1993 report on East Asia's 'miracle' economies suggesting that their governments 'got the basics right'. If economic and political fundamentals had indeed been sound in the region, it is unlikely that the discussion of the region would be focusing upon crises. What began as a currency crisis in Thailand spread to other countries where financial crises have sparked recessionary economic conditions.

This chapter consists of an overall examination of the institutional problems of the AMCs in the context of new global market conditions and the cases of China and Japan as a further and more focused empirical exploration of these problems. It will first take a serious look at the mysterious link between interventionist or authoritarian governments and economic growth in the region. It seeks to demystify the notion that interventionist or authoritarian governments were primarily instrumental for the economic growth in the region. It will then demonstrate the incompatibilities of the existing institutional arrangements in East Asia with the new global environment of market economy and democratic politics. The risks and costs of economic activities under the existing political and social environment will be explored. In the second part, the chapter will examine China and Japan as an example of an interventionist or authoritarian government and see how they tried to muddle through the challenges from the failure of their model in the past and from the new global market conditions, and why these efforts would eventually fail if long-term institutional remedies are not urgently pursued.

The presumed successes of an 'Asian Model' provided cover for the dysfunctional democracy of one-party or one-family regimes where electoral success was seldom a function of true endorsement by the masses. Too often, political longevity reflected a grip on power based upon either the carrot of cronyism or wielding the stick of fear and repression. More benign methods involved co-opting key elements of civil society through trade unions dominated by supporters of the regime or filling key university posts with sycophants or concocting laws designed to tame the media.

The thesis offered here is that most governments in the region neglected the necessary infrastructural development for their modernisation. While there were some steps to provide some elements of physical infrastructure (transportation, communications, educational facilities), intangible infrastructure expenditures and human capital investments were too often neglected. What is lacking is the institutional infrastructure where these countries could more readily mesh into a global market that demands increasing transparency as well as the harmonisation of policies, laws and business practices (Lingle 1998).

Authoritarianism, Economic Growth and the Global Market

A Riddle Unravelled

One casualty of the recent economic difficulties is likely to be the myth that interventionist or authoritarian governments can effectively shepherd economic development. Until recently, advocates of 'Asian values' insisted that the rapid growth in the region was evidence of a superior political system that was responsible for their undisputed economic successes (Mahbubani 1995). Another related notion was fatally damaged by the regional turmoil that began with the devaluation of the Thai baht in 1997. In the future, suggestions that political connections can inoculate investments against the vagaries of the market will have little credibility.

Anyone wishing to stake claims for the salubrious effect of authoritarianism for economic growth will find it difficult to explain Indonesia's economic collapse. Likewise, it should be clear that efficient markets eventually punish despotism.

It is contestable whether one can speak about a single 'Asian Model' behind the earlier meteoric rise of East Asia's economies. Nonetheless, a common thread in the political culture in these diverse countries can be identified that offers insights into their recent precipitous demise. More specifically, the economic and political institutions apparent throughout the region are ill-suited for the effective responses required by the demanding climate of the global economy. While the dominant political culture that guided economic and political structures suited the specific agenda of a given ruling party or regime, they also reflected an underlying conservatism inherent to local traditions and culture.

It is difficult to offer a simple categorisation about East Asia, given the wide differences in the national cultures, languages, and historical circumstances. While, admittedly, this task requires generalising the ungeneralisable, there is a commonality in the political arrangements in most of East Asia. This is that politics reflect a deeply rooted collectivist approach to governance. As such, the interests of the greater community, mostly as interpreted by some elite, are placed above individual rights and freedoms. In turn, expressions of individualism are deterred by such admonitions as 'the exposed nail is hammered down.' The sense of the dominance of the collective is seen in assertions that Asian governments and regional institutions operate on a principle of consensus-building and their strong desire to seek harmony. At the same time, success in life or commerce depended upon personal and political connections.

These political and economic arrangements may actually have a venerable history and may have served noble purposes in the past. Like institutions in other parts of the world, they emerged from the process of human interaction, resulting from local conditions that were appropriate for their times. The institutions that allowed communities to survive, and then thrive, were kept, while others would eventually be discarded.

Unfortunately, the current institutional arrangements are in conflict with the requirements of global markets that function best in the presence of individualist-based institutions operating within conditions of greater corporate and political openness. In an advanced market context, reliance upon personal relationships tends to limit the extent of economic exchange and opportunities. As complexities in economic conditions grow, it also becomes more difficult for government policy-makers to pick 'winners' or choose the 'right' policies.

In a modern political context, dependence upon governmental connections invites endemic corruption and may allow for extensive nepotism. At the same time, authoritarian regimes attempt to justify repression on the basis of enforcing cultural traditions of harmony and respect for authority. While East Asia has no monopoly on corruption, surveys of business leaders involved in global commerce by Transparency International indicate that their impressions are that some of the most corrupt regimes are in the region.

While these institutional arrangements might have worked in the past, they are likely to fail to serve well in the future. This is because the most demanding component of the ongoing process of globalising markets is the free and generally unfettered international capital flows. Unfortunately, the political culture in most of East Asia has militated against the development of domestic capital markets that might have allowed their economies to weather competitive storms that have washed over the region. Most governments purposely sought to control credit allocation. In turn, there were restraints on the emergence of free and open capital markets because it suited the domestic political agenda.

Financial markets in most of the region were underdeveloped, inefficient and weak in that the visible hand of government replaced the invisible hand of market forces. Consequently, there was little disclosure and almost no scrutiny of institutions that were under the protection of the ruling governments. In turn, the real cost of non-economic transactions or unsound loans could be more readily concealed.

There were several operational consequences of East Asia's under-developed domestic financial markets. First, much of the internal financing of commercial and development projects was channelled through the domestic banking system. Second, there was greater dependency upon foreign capital to provide liquidity to the domestic banking system. Government-directed investment sent illusory signals to domestic financial institutions that the projects involved low-risk or no-risk commitments of capital since they would bear the imprimatur of ranking officials. A heavy reliance upon bank lending, instead of capital markets, is problematic since bank managers or directors can be more easily swayed by political pressure. In contrast, large numbers of independent private investors in capital markets demand greater access to information and require greater accountability before offering up funds. In essence, financial markets in most of East Asia were politicised so that commercial risks were ignored on the basis of promised protection from political connections. This may have worked while growth rates were high over past decades, but it is now painfully clear that political connections cannot protect investors from downside risk.

At the same time, countries like Japan, Korea and Taiwan continued to apply outdated restrictions on foreign direct investment (Others like Singapore welcomed manufacturing firms but limited the activities of foreign banks). Borrowing from abroad supplanted the participation of foreign companies with greater international experience that could offer balance sheets that made sense to the rest of the world. These outsiders could also have injected a bit of the competitiveness lacking in their coddled domestic economies. It could be argued that cause and effect is blurred here. Perhaps capital markets in these economies were underdeveloped because of the low levels of their overall development. Yet it can hardly be claimed that neither Japan nor Korea would have been unable to open up and modernise their markets.

East Asian's Financial Markets: Opened Too Much Too Soon?

In the aftermath of the financial deluge sweeping across East Asia and other emerging or transition economies, the search for villains and victims has ignored much of this evidence. Indeed, a variety of long-standing critics of globalisation insist that liberalisation went too far, too fast (Greider 1998; Rodrik 1998). A refrain which has gained momentum is for the implementation of limits on capital flows overseen by international watchdogs.

It is unlikely that the end of the Asian 'miracle' was the result of overzealous economic liberalisation and deregulation (Rodrik 1997). Unfortunately, this interpretation has a wide following that may lead to abatement in the process of financial deregulation. Where this message is heeded, markets can be expected to eventually slow down, thus inviting deepening recession. Following the anti-foreigner rhetoric of Prime Minister Mahathir, Malaysia was first out of the blocks. This decision was apparently spurred on by suggestions of the advantages of capital controls offered by Paul Krugman who later issued an apologetic plea that his proposal should only be implemented under extreme limitations (Krugman 1998), limitations that are unlikely to be imposed in an autocratic, single-party state like Malaysia.

Many leaders of emerging economies have no wish to shake up the status quo, and there will be an increasing clamour for more regulation of capital markets, especially to restrain short term flows. However, further liberalisation of capital markets can yield benefits for them if they take steps to strengthen their banking systems by enhancing transparency and competitiveness. These reforms would make capital flows less erratic. By encouraging more efficient use of capital, growth prospects would likely improve.

It is true that the currency and financial crises in Thailand, South Korea and Indonesia resulted from a sharp reversal in capital flows that poured in during the early 1990s. But the stampede was not the result of rapid financial liberalisation. Nor was it the fault of short-term capital flows, *per se*. Short-term capital is compatible with long-term growth as long as there is a balance between inflows and outflows. A mass exodus occurs only when there is a loss of confidence in the overall system. This crisis of confidence arose from government policies that obstructed market adjustments by limiting competition and keeping banks with non- and under-performing loans in business.

East Asian Infrastructural Development Requires Long Term International Capital

There will be numerous opportunities to invest in East Asia over the next decade. In order to facilitate expanding markets, the countries in the region must undertake massive infrastructural development. A World Bank study suggests a need for a total of $1.5 trillion in expenditures, with $600 billion for improving port facilities, roads and other transportation systems. About $500 billion will be spent for expanded power capacity, $250 billion on telecommunication, and about $150 billion for water and sanitation facilities. Prior to the crisis, this would constitute, on average, expenditures of about 7 per cent of average GDP for the region's economies. It would require a substantial increase from 4 per cent that was spent in 1994.

Unfortunately, the underdeveloped capital markets of the emerging economies of East Asia are likely to impose limits upon their capacity to grow due to a shortage of long-term capital lending. Despite high rates of household savings, the region's capital markets remain inefficient and far more under-developed than their trading systems. Emerging Asia-Pacific economies must develop a more efficient means to channel domestic savings and attract international capital to provide funding for infrastructural investments in telecommunications as well as power and transport systems.

Several problems loom large in the provision of domestic or even regional funds for development projects in East Asia. On one hand, family-owned companies that tend to be narrowly concentrated on trade or property development hold a large proportion of the business assets in the region. On the other hand, widespread government ownership requires that a substantial amount of funding for business expansion will involve the issuance of public debt. Eventually, widespread privatisation will allow capital to be raised through the sale of stocks and equities. However, firms based in East Asia will have to shed their preference for secrecy. Potential investors from outside the region will demand greater transparency before lending. Similarly, international investors who wish to participate in East Asia will require increased clarity of risk/return assessments as international transactions extend beyond the range of friends or family contacts.

In sum, despite having domestic saving rates of 30 per cent and higher, East Asian economies do not mobilise their capital efficiently. Historical mistrust of financial institutions leads to high demands for liquidity by savers. In turn, the high stock of savings has not been transformed effectively into long-term investment. Governments and private borrowers in East Asia must develop more transparent and legally reliable investment frameworks. These include improved corporate governance, better clearing and payment systems, acceptable accounting standards, and modernised credit-rating systems.

Economic And Political Risks In East Asian Emerging Markets

Conventional wisdom often declares that emerging markets, especially those in East and Southeast Asia prior to the emergence of the crises, are an investment play not to be missed. This view is not surprising in light of the reported high rates of economic growth in East Asia. The five fastest growing nations in the world in 1996 were in East Asia (Vietnam, China, Malaysia, Singapore and Thailand). From 1990, China has grown 136 per cent, Indonesia 124 per cent, Singapore 99.8 per cent. In the same period Japan grew only 26.8 percent, its worst period since the early 1950s. Eight of the top ten nations in growth since 1990 were in East Asia.

Singapore moved from eighteenth to fourth in per capita GDP since 1990. That meant it overtook its former colonial master (Great Britain) and the United States in this crude measure of standard of living. If it were able to continue on its present course, it would have overtaken Switzerland and Japan by around 2003 to become the world's wealthiest nation. In early 1997, South Korea was awarded membership of the exclusive industrialised club of the OECD. Unfortunately, many of these statistics now look quite hollow.

However, the recent turmoil in East Asian currency and stock markets indicates that considerably more caution should have been exercised before international funds were directed there. In all emerging economy plays, prudent investors should look closely into combined economic and political risks in order to avoid being involved in what might turn out to be a 'crapshoot'. Interestingly, even with the recent well-publicised setbacks, it appears that the greatest fear among many potential investors and business interests was missing out on important opportunities in East Asia.

It is not surprising that emerging markets exhibit relatively high political risks. This type of risk of the disruption of commercial activity arises out of internal conflict like civil wars or power struggles. However, there are also relatively high risks stemming from actions or policies taken by governments that somehow disrupt or destabilise economic activity. These include policies leading to inflation or hyperinflation, increasing budget deficits, or increasing the likelihood of fraud or default on international loans by sovereign governments. Then there are the run-of-the-mill risks that any business venture may simply fail due to lack of commercial viability.

Risks in Equity Purchases in East Asian Emerging Markets

Problems associated with commitments of long-term capital investment also stem from the volatility of East Asia's emerging markets. This volatility undermines the security of international equity investment. Not unlike the experience of other emerging markets, the stock exchanges in East Asia represent a high-risk investment due to their high price volatility. The collapse of the Mexican peso in 1994 led to a simultaneous downturn of most emerging markets, with Latin American markets affected the most. The 'correction' of 1990 was severe and required nearly three years before the markets recovered. A combination of factors, including the Gulf War and the asset freeze in Brazil by President Collor, was behind that sharp market adjustment.

Now, deep currency devaluations in Thailand, the Philippines, Indonesia, Malaysia, and South Korea have been matched by local stock market declines of as much as 50 per cent over the first eighteen months of the crises. Despite so many fingers being burned in similar high-risk emerging-market plays in the past, some of the same players found another bitter pill in Southeast Asian markets. In this instance, it was precipitated by the Thai government's refusal to take steps to ease the financial trauma induced by an abrupt abandonment of the baht's peg with the US dollar in July 1997. As early as June 1996, the International Monetary Fund (IMF) advised Thailand to shift to a flexible exchange rate regime to avoid imminent economic problems. The Thai government blithely ignored this advice and risked further damage to its economy by defending the baht in the forward exchange market. This attempted defence failed, and Thailand's foreign exchange reserves fell dramatically as the baht lost about 40 per cent of its value.

Much of the rest of Southeast Asia experienced similar problems as ASEANs leaders proved themselves incapable of effective crisis management, both jointly and individually. Thailand and Malaysia imposed a variety of capital controls aimed at halting short selling by foreigners. Unfortunately, these measures irreparably harmed investor confidence and were soon scrapped.

Nonetheless, many investment advisers continue to promote portfolio holdings in emerging markets since the stock markets in most of them have out-performed the stock markets in the more developed economies. This is all true, but it means that timing and composition of investments, under highly volatile market conditions, make for a very risky game. A given portfolio of stocks in emerging economies might fall by 20–50 per cent and not recover for several years.

There are numerous reasons behind the volatility of stock markets in East Asia's emerging economies. With their low capitalisation, they are susceptible to quick shifts of 'hot capital.' These flows might be movements away from bad news (coup d'etats, drought, strikes, doubts about succession of leaders, inflation, or structural fiscal deficits) or towards good news (deregulation, privatisation, reduction of trade barriers, or structural reforms). Most of these countries provide little reassurance in terms of minimising political risk, the constancy of real interest rate or stable prices. There are also concerns about the imposition of controls over capital movements, as well as the maintenance of overall economic freedoms. What can be expected is a vicious cycle where market volatility leads to a greater concentration of 'hot capital', which in turn induces greater volatility that frightens off more long-term investment.

In light of these problems, it is almost certain that economic growth in the region will be slow to recover. On the one hand, successful financing of necessary public infrastructure may 'crowd out' other domestic investments by forcing up market rates of interest. On the other hand, if the infrastructural projects are not completed then the capacity of these economies to return to positive rates of growth will be severely limited.

Costs and Benefits of Authoritarianism and Asian Values

The authoritarian nature of regimes both raises and lowers political risks. There is a misleading impression of the contribution of authoritarianism to stability since the various one-party or one-family regimes have been in power long enough to perfect political repression. Such stability is likely to be illusory and can only be counted on for the short run. If despots are too severe, they invite *coup d'etats* or assassination. If they are not strong enough, then the political opposition may sweep them out of office. In all events, the mortality of despots (benevolent or otherwise) ensures that political risks will eventually rise due to uncertainty over the transition of power, as evident in China, Indonesia, and Singapore.

Dynastic succession or one-party regimes are not an uncommon feature in East Asian politics and are often mistakenly associated with stability. Like other forms of nepotism, intra-family political succession is consistent with the culturally-embedded commitment to family that is said to define social relations in much of Asia. Of course the most painful example of this is in Indonesia. In terms of the concerns of international investors, both reflect forms of corruption that arise from leadership whose authority is seldom challenged. Where nepotism is prevalent, there are also a variety of costs to the community that should be considered. Political costs arise in the form of losses of political rights. Nepotism also invites economic inefficiency from the diversion of resources towards a single family or cronies in a dominant political party. By interfering with market transactions, nepotism imposes costs upon the greater community and upon potential investors by reducing returns on gross investment.

Before acquiring political power, the offspring of rulers often develop their own power base, perhaps as grants of national monopolies over certain economic sectors. According to a rating by Transparency International in 1995, Indonesia was considered to then have the world's most corrupt regime. Indeed, six of the ten worst rating were Asian countries. A similar rating for 1996 revealed that Pakistan and Nigeria replaced Indonesia and China as the countries most affected by corruption while five of the ten countries with the worst rating were in Asia (in order, Pakistan, Bangladesh, China, India, and Indonesia). Nepotism and special privileges will distort these markets for insiders as well as for outsiders.

Many Asian countries have leaders who seek to impose secular dynasties upon their citizens. Unilateral transfer of political control to family members is often found where there were anti-colonial movements led by charismatic autocrats. An ill-educated citizenry often faces repression of dissent so Asian autocrats can decide in the best interest of their family, regardless of the impact on the country or foreign investments.

Another problem with authoritarian regimes in the region is that they interfere with the level of transparency in economic dealings demanded by responsible international investors. For example, in addition to tight controls on domestic news reporting, China recently announced its intention to restrict the flow of financial and commercial information from international news services. While the limits placed upon political debate in Singapore are well known, the ruling party has gone to great lengths to punish individuals for leaking economic data. In 1994, several journalists, a private investment adviser, and a civil servant were prosecuted for publishing quarterly GDP estimates before their official release. This sort of obsessive control of data thwarts the independent corroboration required by long-term investors. Similarly, repression of a free press chokes off an independent source of information about events in these countries that might be relevant to foreign investors.

Global Capital and Forces of Economic and Political Modernisation

Successful economic development in the future will depend upon a number of conditions that shape and define the so-called global economy. Perhaps the most important momentum behind the internationalisation of economic activities arises from the high degree of capital mobility. The capacity of capital to migrate and reside more or less at will ensures that the search for the gains from trade arising from comparative advantage is temporary, elusive, and increasingly contested. It will be increasingly important that countries develop greater flexibility and responsiveness in their economic and political institutions. Otherwise the automatic adjustment mechanisms that contribute to stability and aid growth will be obstructed.

Countries wishing to become players in the global marketplace will have to face up to the implications of this simple observation. It will be as important to countries in early stages of development that might more pursue development through the promotion of export-oriented production as it will be to advanced economies that need to tease higher rates of growth to keep living standards high and unemployment low. Aspirants in the global marketplace that wish to remain competitive and enjoy success will be guided toward policy mixes and institutional arrangements that are flexible and responsive. Otherwise, commercial aspirants will find their market shares lost to competitors and national economies will experience an exodus of capital. In the future of a truly global economy, the institutions of every country will be affected by external shocks generated by repetitive waves of competition. Those that are not flexible will simply break down in the face of these challenges.

From the microeconomic side, small and medium-sized enterprises will be well placed with nimble responses to exploit niche opportunities. This will imply that this will work best in situations where there is extensive domestic competition among firms, including allowing foreign producers in to contest local markets. From the macroeconomic side, policies that are market-friendly combined with a liberal trade regime, will increase and enhance linkages with international markets that facilitate trade and capital flows.

There are risks and challenges associated with such arrangements. Not least of these is the upsetting of traditional relationships that may lead to some political instability. However, the political stability associated with the cosy relationships between many Asian governments or politicians and commercial interests has proved to be a recipe for disaster.

China and Japan: AMEs in Response to Global Market Conditions

China: The Drive to Beat The Market

After speculative bubbles burst in erstwhile economic powerhouses in Southeast Asia, the damage spread quickly to Northeast Asia. This should not be surprising since many of the East Asian 'miracle' economies pursued similar paths for development. As suggested above, the systems of governance once acclaimed as the basis for rapid growth in East Asia can be seen as the source of their own economic undoing.

Now that South Korea and Japan find themselves rattled by the chilling winds of economic reality, China's most recent growth spurt is also stumbling. Economic performance is trailing off and export growth is falling just as nearby Tiger economies with weakened currencies are hoping to export their way back to prosperity. Ironically, China may have contributed to its own misery and that of its neighbours. Following its competitive devaluation of the *yuan* by about one-third in 1994, the bitter truth is that China may have contributed to the devaluations that now plague much of East Asia.

Unfortunately, economic advisers and many enterprise managers in China are too ill acquainted with markets to understand that competitive advantage is a moving target. Consequently, China's manufacturers are beginning to confront the realities of growing mountains of unsold inventory. Township and village enterprises (TVEs), a Chinese hybrid of collective ownership where operations follow limited market principles, once served as an important contributor to economic growth. Now they are struggling under excess capacity and increasingly contested markets while they are starved of access to capital that continues to flow from state-run banks to state-owned enterprises (SOEs).

Clearing the growing inventories may require another devaluation of the quasi-floating Chinese currency. However, it will be resisted since it will certainly put strains on the ability of Hong Kong to hold its peg against the US dollar and add to the problems of repayment of China's debt burden. Perhaps the weakest link in China's continued economic progress is caused by the lack of transparency within its financial institutions. In keeping with the development approach in much of the rest of East Asia and its own authoritarian legacy, tight controls over capital markets result in a heavy reliance upon bank lending for industrial and commercial developments.

Avoiding the openness demanded by private investors in bond markets, banks can be obliged to grant loans to meet political ends and so neglect appropriate risk assessment in their lending decisions. Like elsewhere in the region, banks provide a more supple and predictable source of funds. These funds may be for subsidies to support industry policy or to reward political cronies. Additionally, the Bank of China suffers from a complete lack of independence, and it has never carried out the overseeing role of a modern central bank.

Despite announcements of an intent to reduce subsidies or low interest loans to SOEs and to force them to sink or swim, there is no clear plan of action. In light of the regime's gradualist attitude towards economic transition, change will not come soon. Meanwhile, any attempt to clear up the non-performing loans held by the SOEs hangs like the sword of Damocles over the regime's head. Of the nearly 300,000 SOEs, roughly 75 per cent are effectively bankrupt and kept going by loans from state banks. With or without dramatic reform, China's banking sector faces severe problems in dealing with a ratio of 20–30 per cent of bad loans to assets.

However, this figure may mushroom dramatically once property prices and rentals begin to fall in response to the overbuilding in many of China's largest cities. As in Southeast Asia, a property bubble is looming while infrastructural investments in South China, especially in the Pearl River Delta, provide enormous excess capacity. In turn, the cascading effect on Chinese stock markets and the rest of the economy has already been outlined in stark relief in the experiences of their Southeast Asian neighbours.

There is no easy way out of the impending financial crisis. It would be bad enough if banks only had to find a way to unburden themselves from losses arising from lending to property developers and slumping sales by TVEs. However, suggestions to sever the financial lifelines to the SOEs are likely to fall on deaf ears due to the expected social and political costs. All of the solutions require substantial economic pain in the short-run. If SOEs are forced to repay their debts they must privatise, restructure or liquidate. Each option requires massive cost cutting which unavoidably translates into drastic cuts in employment as well as reducing workers' benefits that often include cradle-to-grave services. Estimates of job losses range from 20–50 million workers that will be made redundant through downsizing.

China's hybrid foreign exchange system will not protect it from the pressures of the economic forces that are disciplining countries with more solid fundamentals. Its growing current account deficit will require changes in the real economy or changes in the exchange rate. Governments around the world have suffered from believing that they can defeat market logic. As a first step, it should be made clear that international support for China and other emerging economies will depend upon consistent provision of transparent data in a timely manner. This would allow for more intensive evaluation of their economies and avoid the sort of underestimates of the rot found by the IMF in South Korea's banking sector. As outlined in the new accords, greater foreign competition in the banking systems and formation of an active, aggressive bond market would also provide more external scrutiny.

In comparing China's current economic balance sheet to those in Southeast Asia prior to July, it looks like *deja vu* all over again. However, the result may be worse since China's bubble will burst in the face of over 1 billion people.

Zhu Rongji: Leadership vs. Institutions

As a rising star whose credentials and declarations indicate clear thinking on economic matters, Zhu Rongji's 'election' as China's prime minister is to be applauded. There is a clear consensus that he is a tough taskmaster who can restore discipline among the party faithfuls and act as an able helmsman for the economy. However, it should be remembered that even exceptional cult figures make little real difference when the tide flows against them. Many of Mao's positive achievements were tarnished by the failure to move the economy forward. Similarly, it is likely that Deng's worthy contributions may be seen as too little, too late. Indeed, Chinese authorities must undertake deep reform that goes far beyond fine-tuning or tinkering with economic policy. It remains to be seen whether Zhu will have the authority or the will to direct the necessary thoroughgoing economic restructuring.

Pragmatism, the guiding principal for Chinese modernisation, is headed straight into a minefield of immense proportions. Privatisation is doomed to failure because the SOEs cannot be made profitable without shedding millions of workers. Meanwhile, the drying up of foreign capital will put a damper on growth. In all events, official growth rates are misleading that they do not match with other vital economic data such as energy consumption.

In sum, the obstacles that Zhu will face are a set of realities defined by a highly competitive global capital market. As such, some basic contradictions of China's 'market socialism' may soon become fatal afflictions. The bottom line for China's modernisation is the privatisation of the large number of loss-making SOEs. Political decisions to this end have already been taken. The plan is to scrap those that are loss making – more than half – and reorganise the rest into large, highly diversified and profitable corporations along the lines of the Korean *chaebol*. In the process, the banking system will be transformed so that they are no longer merely agents for distributing government subsidies to cover SOE losses. After reform, the banks are to become profit-making financial institutions to stimulate Chinese growth with an efficient and modern banking system.

So far, so good. But which conditions must be met to make this a policy with any prospect for success? The Chinese capital market is effectively illiquid due to the massive subsidies. Funding for the privatisation programme will have to rely on a variety of sources other than domestic savings. The main techniques are incoming foreign investment, a continuing and substantial trade surplus and international loans. These sources are drying up. Even the trade surplus policy does not look convincing after the rounds of devaluation in other export-oriented Asian economies. Every reasonable conclusion from these observations is then that the privatisation program cannot succeed, for lack of funds. Chinese economic policies will, in the worst case scenario, face a large number of subsidy-demanding firms and half-reformed new corporations that do not generate the expected level of profits. To go from here, it will require some more fundamental policy change in China than we have seen so far – or an aggressive devaluation of the renminbi that looks increasingly likely.

If the economics of the project look bad, the political outcomes might be worse. In many Chinese towns a sole SOE is the principal employer. Closing a number of these companies or moving parts of them to a regional centre will result in a number of industrial 'unemployment islands'. Political unrest is likely to follow the surge of local unemployment. This is especially so, since China has no social insurance safety net in place to avoid such political reactions to policy changes outside of the employment-linked benefits from SOEs. Unlike peasant unrest, industrial unrest does not tend to stay local. It has always a capacity to be transformed into a national political issue. With 20–25 per cent of the Chinese population affected by the planned privatisation project, it is difficult to see how deep political consequences can be avoided.

China and The Globalisation of the Asian Economies

Under Deng Xiaoping, China staked its future on its participation in a new international market order. The forces of the global economy can act as a tidal wave that can easily erase the remarkable gains achieved since the late 1970s. Evidence confirming this contention can be found in the financial crises affecting much of East and Southeast Asia beginning in the late 1990s.

The institutional demands that shadow the new global investment patterns are not often observed or well understood. China is not in a strong position to accommodate these demands. China's economic growth depends upon foreign capital to carry out ambitious infrastructural development or to gain technical expertise. These activities require transparency in commercial operations and accountability for political choices that do not exist in the economic and governmental institutions in China, or elsewhere in the East Asian region.

While the modern globalised capital market builds on centuries of historical development, some recent events have brought about fundamental and perhaps irrevocable changes in its operation. Competitive pressures for investment funds helped stimulate a market for footloose capital. These pressures prompted, and were also aided by, financial and technical innovations to facilitate movement. At the same time there were policy initiatives, like the deregulation of London's financial markets in 1985. Out of this sequence of events and circumstances, capital markets became both more liquid and more efficient. The efficiency is evident in an ever-widening set of financial institutions and innovations in the offering of financial instruments like derivatives and other futures market instruments.

Risk-averse financial actors seek to compensate the inherent risks in the activity of lending money, by being well informed. Whatever the state of evolution of capital markets, they depend, *in extremis*, upon access to reliable and massive amounts of business-related information. With capital having global reach, efficient new information technologies have followed, making the continuing internationalisation of capital markets possible. The endeavour to maximise international information flows had several important political effects.

The most visible among these has been the stronger drive towards democratisation as more countries turned democratic since the 1980s. A democratic community that reflects the influence of individualist-based institutions puts no (or few) restrictions on generation or spreading of information. Authoritarian or 'corporatist' regimes tend to impose greater restrictions as justified by some specified political concern such as social harmony or consensus. A conflict and competition among institutional arrangements will surface in the latter cases, indicating that democratic pressure can easily build up in countries taking active part in the process of globalisation. In an increasingly globalised economy, comparative advantage will be based upon favourable institutional arrangements as much as input costs or resource availability.

There are various problems with China's political development being put in line with these wider requirements for institutional change. The Tiananmen massacre in 1989 indicated that Chinese politics, under communist supervision, fails to meet the standards of the global community or can contribute to the constantly ongoing institutional development demanded by globalisation. Yet, China is basing decisive parts of its long-term financial policy on attracting large commitments of future foreign investments into its economy. This marks a deep conflict in its own internal policy, as well as an unresolved conflict between its rigid and slow-changing economy institutions that contrast sharply with the demands of advanced information markets arising out of the globalisation process.

China's institutional contradictions also arise from requirements of international investors for greater accountability and transparency and who also require a mechanism for settling contract disputes. All these conditions are influenced by the policy settings among economies throughout the world. Consequently, global capital markets inspire a competition among countries to offer the institutional basis that attracts capital. Countries like China, with a political structure that does not accommodate the demands of borderless capital, will not attract the amount of foreign investment needed for its development plans. Instead, it will suffer a net outflow as capital is attracted to better terms elsewhere.

So China will be facing a number of internal contradictions so that changing personalities in leadership positions will be no more effective than rearranging deckchairs on the Titanic. Even if Zhu is able to get the economy right, China will face political pressures that may be overwhelming.

Japan's Big Bang Promises: Rhetoric or Reality?

Former Prime Minister Ryutaro Hashimoto complained that currency devaluations in Southeast Asia were behind devaluation pressures that were forcing down the value of the yen against the dollar. Soon afterwards, Japan's Ministry of Finance (MOF) officials announced plans to minimise short-selling of the yen, including the closer screening of market details to seek out 'irregular' transactions which might represent manipulation of market prices.

Perhaps the promises to liberalise Japan's financial markets and open its economy to competition deflected any sort of criticism when leaders in Southeast Asian countries tried to blame others for their woes. Nonetheless, the excoriation made by Malaysian Prime Minister Mahathir against George Soros and other speculators was different only in tone, not in substance. With these attitudes firmly entrenched among Japan's hierarchy, it shows how difficult it is for its 'Big Bang' financial market deregulation to be fully implemented.

Japan's model for modernising its banking and financial sector was inspired by Margaret Thatcher's reform of the British securities industry in the late 1980s. Beginning in December 1997, Japanese banks and securities firms were able to jointly market investment trust funds. These are essentially mutual funds and are not yet widely used by individual investors. Most Japanese savers hold accounts in low-interest deposits in the postal savings system. While 140 trillion yen goes into securities, only about two per cent of total invested assets go into investment trust funds.

In April 1998, foreign currency exchange laws were liberalised, allowing any individual or business to make foreign currency transactions without prior approval from the Ministry of Finance. Prior to this change, such transactions could only be made to officially designated banks. Businesses can now negotiate for foreign exchange from Japanese or foreign banks or can make arrangements internally with their own finance departments. Most importantly, individuals are allowed to invest personal assets at higher rates overseas or in foreign currencies through foreign banks in Japan.

Other deregulations include securities trades of more than 50 million yen that will allow securities firms to set their own commissions. It is expected that increased competition will lead to an improvement in service and lower trading costs offered by securities firms. If all goes well, it may breathe new life into Japan's sagging equities market. Modernisation of corporate structures will allow new holding companies to be formed for the first time in the post-WWII period. New securities firms will not need to apply for government licensing, banks and securities companies will be able to enter each other's businesses without restrictions, and banks and securities firms will be allowed to sell insurance.

The crises in the rest of the region require even more urgent action to avert widening problems in Japan. The slide of the Thai baht and subsequent assaults on the currencies of Indonesia and Malaysia prompted

Japan's MOF to propose an Asia-based currency fund. This would have replaced the conventional tough austerity measures required by IMF interventions. Most affected countries in Southeast Asia responded favourably to these overtures, but Western governments and their respective banking community were negative.

Japanese banks felt the pinch of the crisis affecting South Korea since they were holding about $20 billion of the $100 billion in short-term debt owed by Korean banks in 1998. In total, Japanese banks lent about $123 billion to various enterprises in Southeast Asia. The looming crises with their overseas exposure added to the woes of Japanese banks that were struggling to cope with $580 billion (76.7 trillion yen) in domestic loans that were bad or questionable.

Despite serious problems threatening Japan's banking system since the beginning of the 1990s, supervisory authorities avoided taking strong remedial actions. Strikingly, the MOF did not require reporting on non-performing loans until 1993. In this regulatory setting, it is no surprise that there were neither requirements to liquidate collateral (property or stocks) held against the bad loans, nor were banks directed to increase their capital to offset losses.

Japan's population is rapidly ageing, due largely to changing demographics and this is also driving reform. Japan has a fertility rate of 1.5 children per woman. That is well below replacement level and considerably lower than in the United States (2.1). According to trends, Japan's 'elderly dependency ratio' (proportion of the population aged 65 and over relative to the population aged 15 to 64) will mean that there will be a decrease in the number of the work force relative to an increasing number of retirees. Such a prospect has focused minds since it directly threatens their social and economic stability. These stark realities require that Japan's capital markets must become more efficient in order to resolve the persistent slump in its domestic economy.

In light of the banking crises sweeping through East Asia, it will be important that capital-adequacy ratios be enforced. Banks with operations limited to domestic activities must meet a 4 per cent ratio requirement within a year while banks with international operations must follow the 8 per cent ratio required by the Bank for International Settlements. However, Japanese banks have used different benchmarks for those assets included as capital than their counterparts in other industrialised countries. After April, Japan's banks must reduce the proportion of their capital-adequacy ratio derived from unrealised gains on stock market holdings. There are signs of continued dithering in the enactment of these necessary reforms. However, containment of the crises sweeping East Asia makes Japan the final line of defence. As such, there is an increasing urgency for the rest of the world that Japan implement global financial standards and modernise procedures for corporate accounting and financial reporting.

Japan's Bleak Future

Japan's economy accounts for two-thirds of Asia's economy and occupies a fifteen per cent share of the world economy. Unfortunately, this powerhouse has experienced a decline of 0.7 per cent in fiscal 1997 with a further decline of 1.8 per cent expected in 1998. Japan's role as linchpin in the global economy is in real danger of crumbling under the combined weight of its own looming domestic and foreign crises (Katz 1998). While various policies have been announced to deal with Japan's long-suffering economy, there is little evidence that there will be the fundamental changes that will be necessary before Japan will experience a restoration of positive growth.

A mountain of nonperforming loans obstructs Japan's economic recovery. Until these bad loans are disposed of, the economy cannot be stabilised and without stabilisation it cannot be revitalised. Along with establishing the political will to accept the bankruptcy of financial institutions, public money will be injected into insolvent banks. The extent of Japan's banking problem and the associated numbers is staggering. Estimates of the value of non-performing or under-performing loans are between US$500 billion to US$1 trillion. The latest accord of October 1998 commits a vast amount of public funds, about 60 trillion yen. From this fund, 25 trillion yen will be made available for bank recapitalisation, 18 trillion yen will be committed to nationalise weak banks with the remaining 17 trillion yen used for protection of depositors.

A shaky alliance was formed when the small Liberal Party and a smaller Buddhist bloc joined with LDP in the upper house to enact a bill forming a 'financial resuscitation committee' that would be empowered to buy bad loans from failed or failing banks. There are three basic options in dealing with problem banks. The first would involve temporary state control through government purchase of common shares while a restructuring plan was implemented for eventual sale to a private buyer. A second option is for liquidation under bankruptcy laws. Finally, struggling institutions could be placed under control of bridge banks.

Unfortunately, these proposals contain no silver bullet to solve Japan's problem and have set off a familiar cycle so often observed in response to impending policy announcements from Tokyo. Bullish market sentiment in anticipation of the package can turn rapidly bearish when the details are announced that send world markets soaring skyward one day, then to plunge the next day as reality sets in. An important element driving market sentiments is voiced by the Democratic Party whose refusal to support the LDP plan reflects worries about lax controls over cash injections administered by the same old-boy network. Similarly, there is no clear timetable for the process or enough specifics to provide a sense of confidence in the package.

There is also the question as to how far the liberalisation of Japan's financial system will go. In particular, will foreign banks be allowed to take full control over any of the banks that might be temporarily under government control? If this is not allowed, there will be a continuing lag in services and efficiency for Japan's domestic banks that are unaccustomed to competition. This situation borders on the tragic. Until the banking crisis is resolved, Japan will be doomed to a prolonged recession. No amount of additional Keynesian pump-priming or reflation will induce Japanese consumers to spend their way out of the current slump. The additional tax burden of the current proposal, combined with increased job insecurity and shaky pension plans, has frightened the Japanese away from being a country with a high propensity to save into a nation of currency hoarders.

As policy leaders in Tokyo stumble in seeking their way, advice from foreign friends offers little clarity or consistency. In Washington, the Clinton administration offers advice based upon unreconstructed Keynesian nostrums. Proposals for pump-priming, reflation and temporary tax cuts offer little hope for a recovery in Japan's economic prospects.

Japan domestic problems include a slow-growth or no-growth recession since the late 1980s after the collapse of its 'bubble economy'. During this time, growth had to be supplied by the international sector that cannot continue to keep the rest of the economy afloat. In the early 1990s, while real estate and stock market values plummeted, the yen experienced a sharp appreciation that prompted production and jobs to move offshore. More recently, the imposition of a consumption tax in April 1996 caused a slump in retail sales. Meanwhile, consumer and business confidence is at an all time low over the failure of the government's attempts to revive the economy. In seeking to minimise domestic political resistance, the government is likely to pin its hopes on an export-led growth strategy to revive its flagging economy. Unfortunately, regional financial turmoil will make it unlikely that trading partners in Southeast Asia will be able to continue absorbing 40 per cent of Japan's exports. Changing realities of increased competition in the global economy will thwart any significant increase in Western demand.

Like other countries that have tied their future to international trade, Japan's future will be moulded by the constantly changing nature of the global economy. As waves of competition sweep the globe, they will spark new imperatives for domestic policies to be in sync with free and open market economies. In particular, the return of Japan as an important player in global capital markets will require an extensive deregulation of the banking industry.

Japan's financial services sector is burdened by a ceaseless bad debt problem while half-heartedly approaching 'Big Bang' financial deregulation to remove anti-competitive practices. After years of being cosseted from foreign competition while serving the government's programme of directed development, 'Big Bang' will require Japanese banks to respond to competitive conditions. They will have to measure performance in terms of return on equity instead of concentrating on maximising asset size. To this end, Japan's banks will have to restructure their balance sheets to reduce non-performing loans through write-offs or securitisation.

Japan's banking sector which has extensive exposure to the rest of Asia is enormous as creditor and equity investor. With an estimated loan exposure of about US$300 billion, Japanese banks are the region's largest creditor with about one-third of these loans in Hong Kong and its increasingly precarious property market. Another US$24.3 billion is in Korea, which is an economic domino that fell in the wake of Asia's financial contagion. Compounding Japan's bad debt problem is the drastic fall in the market value of their Asian equity portfolios. Without these 'hidden' reserves to provide the financial cushion needed to absorb loan losses, domestic bank failures will inevitably rise.

While some consolidation in Japan's financial sector is overdue, there is a real risk of system-wide implosion owing to government inertia and mismanagement. The Ministry of Finance has still not addressed the pressing issue of reforming the mammoth postal-savings system, which accounts for as much as one-third of Japanese individuals' deposits. Regulators still have no legal responsibility to shut down unsalvageable banks as part of their mandate to take 'prompt, corrective action.' Leaving such discretion in the hands of the regulatory bureaucracy ensures that resolution of these problems will not be easy or swift. The government's failed attempt to stave off the recent bankruptcy of Sanyo Securities through an arranged merger, attests to the tenacity of the government in applying anachronistic remedies in the face of impending deregulation.

Despite the conspicuous pattern of problems in the present, the vacillation for Keynesian fine-tuning does not bode well for the future. A demographic Damocles sword is hanging over their head. A misstep today will impose an increasing burden on a shrinking workforce that will also find fewer job opportunities. Perhaps the greatest tragedy will be that young Japanese will choose to migrate to countries that offer better opportunities.

Conclusion

As suggested, inhibitions of domestic capital markets in East Asia were consistent with the political culture of the region. Authoritarian interventionist governments sought to exercise of tight control over the flow of economic information either by dictate or appeal to tradition. Most other countries also followed or enforced traditions of collectivist institutions guided by governance by consensus that often created an illusion of harmony. In these settings, criticisms of economic conditions or policies tend to be suppressed while independent corroboration of government supplied data is unlikely or impossible. Unfortunately, by limiting access by investors and traders to information, markets are prone to greater volatility arising from rumours and misinformation.

Faced with deep and perhaps intractable problems in putting their economic and financial houses in order, economies in East Asian face a difficult uphill battle. Most will seek to cut prices to export their way out of their predicament, but other countries both in and outside of the region will increasingly challenge them in their traditional markets. Meanwhile, foreign investors will impose higher standards in assessing commercial and political risk before committing funds to East Asia. With hindsight, the high performance of the economies in the region which came more easily than expected will even lower growth rates in the future.

In essence, shared aspects of East Asia's political culture reproduced flaws in the institutional infrastructure of the 'miracle' economies. Consequently, they were ill prepared to sustain external shocks generated by inevitable global capital flows. As such the rigidity of conservative political institutions led to policies that interfered with the self-adjusting mechanisms in their economies. While restoration of stability in East Asian economies will be a difficult road, the slow pace of institutional changes will make recovery an even longer one. Indeed, it may require a generation before some East Asian economies can replicate the required institutional infrastructure for sustainable economic growth that will be required by the increasingly efficient global capital market.

CHAPTER NINE

Harry D. Shutt

Global Capitalism in Crisis: The East Asian Problem in a Wider Context

Much of the analysis in this book has been concerned with seeking an explanation for the problems in the AMCs experiencing dramatic political and economic transition after the economic boom over most of the previous two decades or longer. In particular, the focus of many chapters has been on possible weaknesses in the systems of governance of these countries, which may have permitted undue lapses of proper control of the behaviour and performance of both government agencies and private companies or individuals. The present chapter casts doubt on whether there is, in fact, any *prima facie* evidence from the East Asian experience of any correlation between economic dynamism and systems of political governance.

It further demonstrates that such failings are now in fact endemic (to a greater or lesser extent) in the global market economy as a whole, including those Western industrial market economies which mostly have a much longer history of democratic government than those of Asia. Hence any suggestion that the East should look to the West as a model to help it attain economic salvation is misplaced – as will soon become more apparent as the West itself succumbs to spreading economic depression. An explanation for the emergence of these flaws in Western democracy is offered in terms of the long-term evolutionary trends of global capitalism – which are themselves to be seen as the true cause of economic failure in Asia and elsewhere.

Finally, some implications are identified for the type of change in systems of governance (both political and corporate) that will be needed as part of a broader restructuring of the world economy designed to restore it to health on a sustainable basis.

The Hyping of the Asian 'Miracle'

Over many years, up to 1997, a powerful mythology had developed in the world's media concerning the exceptional dynamism of East Asian nations and their supposedly formidable economic potential. The origin of this notion may be traced to the extraordinary rise of Japan over three decades from the late 1950s from being a relatively backward, war-shattered country, to the position of the second largest economy in the world. Such was the scale of its growth and apparently unstoppable conquest of world markets for one product after another that there was even talk of it becoming the world's largest economy by the end of the twentieth century.

More recently, a similar mystique came to surround other nations in the region – notably South Korea, Taiwan, Hong Kong and Singapore (the original 'Asian Tigers') – as they industrialised rapidly in the 1970s and 1980s on the basis of capturing large shares of world markets for manufactures. Finally by the early 1990s a number of Southeast Asian countries – including Malaysia, Thailand and Indonesia – were identified as having successfully embarked on a similar path of rapid export-oriented expansion, while the People's Republic of China, having adopted an 'open door' policy in the late 1970s, achieved the highest growth rates of all during this period. Indeed some even began to predict that China would become the world's largest economy by as early as 2010, apparently heedless of the fact that Japan – the subject of earlier such predictions – had by the 1990s sunk into chronic stagnation which made even Western industrialised economies look dynamic by comparison.

In fact, long before this regional phenomenon dissolved in the Asian crisis of 1997 it was apparent to the dispassionate observer that both its extent and its durability had been much exaggerated. Nevertheless the bare statistics of sustained high growth in Gross Domestic Product – generally in the range 7–10 per cent a year for each of the countries concerned during the 1980s and (except for Japan) much of the 90s – were superficially very impressive and in sharp contrast both to the rest of the developing world and to the nations of the industrialised West, where 2–3 per cent annual growth (on average) was the best that could be achieved.

As long as this statistically dazzling performance continued it naturally held the rest of the world in awe. Just as naturally, explanations were sought for such seemingly unique dynamism. Yet as with so many historical phenomena, real or imagined, most analysts were more concerned to prove a preconceived ideological point by being shamelessly selective rather than to cast an objective eye on the phenomenon as a whole.

Thus it was common to find that those who professed to believe the East Asian 'miracle' was a demonstration of the benefits of free trade and market liberalisation pointed to Hong Kong to illustrate this point, even though its status as a free port (without a rural hinterland) meant that it had many advantages which were not present in other countries in the region and could not readily be replicated elsewhere, while in no sense could it have been described as a democracy.

Still more bizarre, perhaps, was the attempt to portray South Korea as a model of economic liberalism despite its obviously dirigiste approach to economic as well as political management throughout the period of its most rapid economic expansion (Lal 1983). Moreover, this author's claim that Korea's trade regime (combining strong protection against imports with heavy subsidisation of exports) could be defined as 'virtual free trade' – on the grounds that one can be said to cancel out the effects of the other – represents an extraordinary perversion of economic theory, one which none the less was sanctified by the World Bank in its 1987 World Development Report.

A scarcely less crude attempt to explain the apparently exceptional economic achievements of East Asia in the 1970s and 1980s was that it was a demonstration of the peculiar strength of 'Asian values', often rather glibly identified with Confucianism. The central features of this culture were, it was suggested, a traditional propensity to work hard and respect elders – in contrast to the self-indulgent individualism which was thought to have become typical of Western societies.

The collapse of the Asian 'miracle' since mid-1997 has obviously exposed the superficiality and opportunism of this kind of analysis. Indeed almost overnight, as it seems, the rhetoric of adulation for Asian values has been turned on its head. Thus the 'Confucian' virtue of respect for elders is now seen as fostering the vice of too ready acceptance of 'cronyism' and the corrupt relationships between businessmen and politicians which are widely viewed as a major factor behind the corporate and economic meltdown that has occurred in the region.

With equally shameless inconsistency, leaders of opinion in the Western media and elsewhere who a few years ago were disparaging Western decadence and predicting that it would be overwhelmed by Asian dynamism as the world moved into the 'Pacific century', have suddenly rediscovered Western virtues they had previously overlooked. Chief among these is seen to be the strength of the West's democratic tradition – based on the rule of law, freedom of speech and respect for human rights – which is somehow believed to have saved it from the corruption and economic collapse that has overtaken so much of East Asia.

However, this new attempt to offer a simple explanation for complex phenomena is likely to be exposed very rapidly as an even more baseless myth than the earlier one of emerging Asian supremacy. Perhaps the most obvious reason for doubting its durability is that the economic crisis which began in 1997, which most Western commentators have affected to believe will be confined to Asia and other 'emerging' markets, will inevitably be shown to be a global catastrophe to which the East Asian collapse was merely the precursor.

As this becomes ever more apparent over the coming years, any pretence that the West's more solid democratic institutions might help to protect Europe or North America from the worst ravages of the economic typhoon gathering strength around the world, seems bound to be swept away. Furthermore, this spreading upheaval seems certain to reveal that the supposed robustness of Western democratic institutions – while it may be rooted in a longer tradition than in the case of East Asia – has been found all too vulnerable to the corrupting forces of unbridled corporate power unleashed by economic globalisation and the associated process of liberalisation which has been undertaken with such missionary zeal over the past twenty years.

However, even if we ignore the probable globalisation of economic disaster, it would be difficult to sustain the argument that the revealed failure to sustain the economic transformation of East Asia has been associated to any meaningful degree with the weakness of political institutions in the countries concerned. For the obvious problem with such a hypothesis is that it fails to account for the case of Japan. This is because the latter has quite clearly adopted and maintained, ever since the end of World War II, a democratic system of government based on Western models.

It is true that it has also retained many social attitudes and relationships based on older, quasi-feudal norms. Yet it would be hard to claim these were fundamentally different from the kind of social ties which characterise many West European economies and have formed the basis of 'corporatist' relationships linking government, large corporations and other 'mafias' such as the *énarques* of France based on the Ecole Normale d'Administration and other 'grandes écoles' founded by Napoleon, or the Oxbridge elite which at least until very recently so dominated positions of power in Britain.

Clearly Japan's commitment to democracy, freedom of expression and human rights – although much greater and more long-standing than in any other East Asian country – has not prevented it from falling into economic decline. Indeed the reversal of fortune it has suffered since the

1980s preceded that of the rest of East Asia by several years and if anything now shows signs of intensifying rather than abating. Indeed many economists have quite plausibly maintained that Japan's chronic weakness in the 1990s has been a major factor, if not *the* major factor, behind the collapse in the regional economy as a whole.

It is of course possible to point to numerous weaknesses and rigidities in the pattern of governance in Japan, not least in respect of large corporations – where, for example, the influence of organised crime in the conduct of affairs is all too commonplace, as is the use of shareholders' funds to bribe politicians. Yet, as will be argued later, such deficiencies do not necessarily distinguish Japanese corporations from Western ones in any fundamental way. The immediate point to note, however, is that despite conforming to Western norms of political control and economic management much more closely than any other East Asian state, Japan was the first in the region to experience a dramatic fall from the heights of economic success and has since been conspicuously unable to redress the position.

At the same time, it should be recorded that the achievements of other countries in East Asia in sustaining uniquely high rates of economic growth over many years has been scarcely less remarkable than Japan's. Yet perhaps the most notable instance of successful imitation of the Japanese economic model, South Korea, could hardly have differed from it more completely in terms of political governance.

Thus, while Japan not only adopted a Western-style democratic constitution after 1945 and renounced militarism totally, Korea was a de facto military dictatorship throughout most of the period of its economic transformation, from the mid-1960s to the late 1980s. One could even point out to anyone determined to try and prove a positive correlation between democratic, law-based political systems and economic success that the country's recent slide into relative stagnation and financial crisis has coincided with the introduction of more democratic structures.

In fact, however, to make a balanced assessment of the relationship, if any, between patterns of governance (both political and corporate) on the one hand, and durable economic strength on the other, it is necessary to look at a far wider picture than that of East Asia alone. The appropriateness of doing so is underlined by the recognition that the process of economic globalisation has made all countries and regions of the world far more sensitive to economic developments and behaviour in other parts, and that therefore, as already noted, we can hardly expect that the current crisis will be confined to East Asia.

It is scarcely deniable that abuses of governance, in terms of failure of accountability on the part of those entrusted with administering either state power or corporations, have been evident in both Japan and Korea – notwithstanding the very different political systems they have adopted for most of the post-1945 period – as well as in all the other Tiger economies of East Asia. What is more questionable is whether these failings should be regarded as causes of their eventual economic downfall or mainly as symptoms of an economic system which, by its very nature, created both the opportunity and the incentive for abuse of power. To shed more light on the question we must examine global economic trends of the last few decades, particularly in the industrial market economies of the OECD, and consider their relationship to the steadily mounting concern at abuses of corporate power and their effect on political governance.

The Rise and Fall of Keynesian Corporatism

Put simply, the essence of the post-war economic order in the non-Communist world was that the private corporate sector could, and should, be enabled to deliver sustained growth and prosperity with the benefit of appropriate state support and policies of intervention. This 'mixed economy' model, traditionally identified with the economic theories of Keynes, was for long seen as the only way of maintaining a basically capitalist economic system while ensuring that the mass of the population would be protected against a politically unacceptable degree of insecurity resulting from the fluctuations of the business cycle. As such, it could be said to have incorporated an implicit bargain, namely that the taxpayer, through the state, would maintain necessary backing for private enterprise in return for the latter assuring sustained levels of investment, output and employment.

In truth this 'corporatist' model of economic management was by no means a new phenomenon in the history of the capitalist world, having been at the heart of the process of industrialisation from the nineteenth century in much of continental Europe as well as Japan, involving the state to a greater or lesser extent in the promotion or even extensive ownership of enterprise. What was new was that by 1945 it was explicitly recognised – even in the Anglo-Saxon countries which had traditionally been the most ardent apostles of *laissez faire* – that the state had an obligation to intervene in the economy to try and sustain the level of activity and employment.

Yet even though now, for the first time, there was a clear political assumption that such state support for the private sector was justified on the basis that it would ensure general prosperity, there was no explicit guarantee of this, nor any suggestion that the private corporate sector would, or could, be held formally accountable for failing to deliver its half of the bargain. Ironically, East Asian countries such as Korea were for long much more rigorous in demanding a specific *quid pro quo* from corporate beneficiaries of state support (Chang 1993), notwithstanding their lack of political democracy.

As long as the experiment was successful in sustaining growth, this lack of accountability scarcely seemed to matter. In the 1950s and 60s – a period of sustained rapid growth without precedent since the Industrial Revolution – few doubted that this mixed economy approach was a major factor behind the boom and that it represented a durable remedy for the traditional instability of market capitalism. Not surprisingly, few were inclined to worry about the dangers of undue cronyism and corruption in the relationship between business and government under a system which was manifestly delivering such remarkable prosperity for so many. Thus, claims such as that 'what's good for General Motors is good for America' did not strike many as particularly shocking.

However, once the model began to fail from around the early 1970s it was inevitable that the dangers which such corporatism posed to democratic governance would become more conspicuous. Critics of big corporations and of their ability to manipulate the political system to their own ends, without necessarily responding to the needs of the public, began to be taken more seriously.[1] Likewise it was widely observed that 'transnational' corporations had become so large that in many cases their revenues exceeded the Gross Domestic Product of some of the developing countries in which they operated, and that they found it correspondingly easy to subvert their governments, many of which made little pretence of being democracies in any event.

But although criticism of corporate power became more vociferous in the 1970s, it was not strong enough to threaten that power, which had by then become strongly entrenched in the political structures (and parties) of all the major OECD countries. The result was that, as the mixed economy model was rapidly discredited after 1973 and governments were forced to come to terms with a world of lower growth, higher unemployment and recurrent inflation, even supposedly left-wing political parties could easily be co-opted to oppose radical change – i.e. any reforms which might threaten the ability of private sector corporations to manage their businesses autonomously, while continuing to benefit from the support of the state and the largesse of taxpayers.

Such lack of radicalism in the industrial market economies can of course be partly explained by the normal conservative instincts of the public, especially in a climate where most people were still enjoying considerable prosperity. Yet it was further reinforced by a relentless propaganda barrage from the mass media – control of which was naturally dominated by big business interests – which drummed home the message that the failure of corporatist model demonstrated the damaging consequences of excessive state involvement in the economy. Hence so far from there being a need for even greater government intervention, it was argued by the apostles of the new consensus, the central goal must be to 'roll back the frontiers of the state'.

By a stroke of good fortune (from the point of view of the dominant corporate interest) the crisis of the industrial market economies in the 1970s coincided with a far more serious one in the Soviet bloc. This served to discredit the 'socialist' economic model just at the time when the corporatist one was manifestly failing in the West. This naturally made it even harder to argue for a stronger dose of interventionism in the industrial market economies – even had there been any political group on the Left with a coherent alternative strategy to offer. Thus economic circumstances both within and outside the industrialised West combined with the overwhelming financial power of big business to ensure a political reaction in favour of the latter.

The Sham of Neo-liberalism

Hence by the start of the 1980s the stage appeared to be set for an emphatic shift away from the mixed economy model which had predominated since World War II. Indeed what occurred in Britain and the United States under the Thatcher and Reagan administrations was frequently referred to as a revolution. According to the newly ascendant theory, cutting taxes and public expenditure would unleash the forces of enterprise and enable the newly liberated private sector to assure growth and prosperity.

Whether its proponents ever seriously believed it could do so in such a way as to restore anything like full employment is not clear, although the huge boost to unemployment in Britain which was the immediate consequence of the Thatcher government's policies clearly indicates a perception that this was a price worth paying – at least in the short-run – for stabilising the economy and boosting corporate profitability (by helping to hold down wage costs). In fact it seems more likely that they recognised the inherent impossibility of ever reconciling the goal of full employment with assuring the level of profits needed to satisfy the financial markets, and that consequently they hoped this long-standing policy commitment – which, as we have noted, was central to the implicit post-war pact between government and the private corporate sector – could be quietly abandoned.

If it was also the hope of the corporate interest groups who backed this neo-liberal strategy that it would be consistent with a significant cut in the level of state expenditure, they were guilty of a serious degree of self-deception – or at least a remarkable lack of realism. For it implies that they reckoned without the need for extra public spending to meet the enormous addition to the social welfare bill which inevitably arose from this sharp increase in joblessness.

This error was all the more harmful in that it compounded the fiscal damage resulting from the substantial cuts in corporate and personal taxation which were also, of course, essential features of the New Right's agenda (and which were never offset, as promised by the 'Supply Side' school of economists, by a corresponding stimulus to economic growth). Against this background efforts to square the circle by making significant cuts in welfare entitlement only succeeded in exacerbating social divisions without preventing a sharp rise in the public sector borrowing requirement in OECD countries – from around 40 per cent to nearly 60 per cent of GDP – in the course of the 1980s.

This tearing up of the unwritten social contract of the post-1945 era may have been seen by some as a necessary acceptance of reality in a world where it was simply a self-indulgent fantasy to suppose that either full employment or a welfare state offering a decent level of security for all could be sustained. This was precisely the message that many politicians and business leaders have sought to project with increasing stridency in the West during the 1980s and 1990s.

Strikingly, indeed, the 'Asian Model' was for a time cited in support of this argument, as it was suggested that the absence of a social safety net in the Tiger economies was a key factor behind their apparent dynamism.[2] To what extent it is, or ever could be made politically acceptable, is perhaps a matter of individual judgement, although the final collapse of Soviet Communism in 1989–91 clearly convinced many leaders of Western opinion that it could be in view of what they claimed was the final historic triumph of *laissez-faire* capitalism (Fukuyama 1992).

Whether or not in the long-run such a socially divisive model could prove politically sustainable in Western industrialised democracies which have so decisively rejected it in the past may be debatable. What seems much harder to dispute is that its advocates in the corporate sector have been on very weak ground in arguing for it, when they themselves have become such large-scale recipients of state benefits. As already noted, the access of private sector corporations to state support, both financial and regulatory, had been a central element of the post-war corporatist model of economic management – and indeed has, to some extent, been a feature of all economic systems, both before and since the Industrial Revolution.

In the brave new world of reduced dependence on the state promoted by the Thatcher-Reagan doctrine it might have been supposed that the benefits of cutting state support to the economy – in terms of the stimulus to greater competitiveness and the reduced burden on the public finances – would have applied as much to the corporate sector as to the mass of unemployed and other recipients of social welfare.

In reality, however, while benefit entitlements to the latter have been substantially cut in real terms over the past twenty years in all Western market economies, the scope and cost of 'corporate welfare' has, if anything, been increased, encompassing such phenomena as tax-breaks and direct subsidies for investment, subsidies to wage bills and, most significant and costly of all, the bail-out of failing financial institutions through the state's 'lender of last resort' function.

Quite strenuous official efforts have been made to conceal the nature and scale of this largesse – as in Britain, where the government has frequently refused to disclose how much taxpayers' money it is committing to subsidise certain investment projects on grounds of 'commercial confidentiality' and where the New Labour government (in power since 1997) has sought to disguise a massive new programme of subsidies to wages (and hence to corporate profits) as a 'Welfare to Work' scheme designed to help the unemployed. Yet all the evidence suggests that few members of the public are still fooled by such subterfuge, as even mainstream organs of the corporate establishment such as *Business Week* are now moved to protest (*Business Week* 14 July 1997).

The Fragility of Western Democracy

The exposure of this hypocrisy at the heart of the New Right's agenda has inevitably been a serious blow to their continuing attempts to impose greater austerity on the mass of the public through cuts in social welfare benefits and public services. Yet the evident failure to make this application of double standards acceptable has had further consequences beyond the undermining of official economic strategy. For it has also served to focus greater attention on two related phenomena that are tending to undermine democracy in Western countries which have long prided themselves on being its leading exponents, namely the enormously privileged position enjoyed by private sector corporations, whereby they not only have access to very valuable support from the state but can exercise great power over whole communities without the restraint of any legal accountability to the society which accords them such privileges; the increasingly corrupt nature of the political process resulting from the mounting pressures which drive the unaccountable corporate sector to ever more indiscriminate pursuit of profit maximisation.

It has of course been all too common in human history to find that those commanding great material wealth seek to use it to advance their own narrow political interests – even at heavy cost to the wider public interest. Claims that modern Western societies exhibit a robust form of democracy and the rule of law in which the ability of the wealthy to infiltrate and suborn governments has been largely controlled reflect a widespread perception in the West that their systems of governance have indeed progressed beyond the cruder buying and selling of political favours which so obviously disfigured the political process in earlier epochs – and continues to do so in many less developed countries.

In the light of many recent scandals, however, it is sobering to reflect that Western political processes may be scarcely less susceptible to the influence of big money than they were in the days of Britain's 'rotten boroughs' before the Reform Act of 1832, when almost anyone with enough wealth could simply buy themselves a seat in Parliament – often without even having to visit the constituency they were supposed to be representing.

It is perhaps surprising that the right of elected legislators to represent the interests of particular 'lobbies' has long been accepted as normal in Western parliamentary democracies, since it is all too probable that on occasions support for the interests of a particular lobby would run counter to the interests or wishes of the majority of electors to whom the legislators are theoretically accountable.

Supporters of this approach perhaps feel able to justify it on the grounds that no serious conflict of interest is necessarily involved – and that the useful purpose of informing debate is served – as long as the lobbying is confined mainly to ensuring that the point of view of a particular sectional interest (such as a trade union or professional group) is brought to the attention of the legislature – and provided that the lobbying relationship is transparent (between interest groups and legislators) and any associated payment is nominal. This doubtless explains why, in the British House of Commons, MPs are simply required to register or declare any such 'interests' rather than abstain altogether from accepting favours from such lobbies.

Yet it is striking that in recent years the scale and intensity of lobbying of governments by business interests has gone far beyond the relatively innocent process of providing information. Evidence abounds in all Western countries of the spreading tendency of corporations to pay substantial sums of money both to individual legislators or other officials as well as to political parties in order to secure government decisions favouring their interests. Of the many examples from every Western country that could be cited, one of the best known in Europe was the payment of large sums to the Belgian Socialist Party which resulted in the award of a military helicopter contract to an Italian manufacturer, which led to the criminal conviction of Willy Claes, former party leader and Secretary General of NATO.

A high-profile case in Britain was the strange coincidence of a decision by the New Labour government (contrary to an electoral commitment) to exempt motor racing from the ban on tobacco sponsorship in sport soon after a £1 million contribution to party funds had been received from the owner of the Formula One company that controlled the sport (where a major scandal was only averted by the return of the contribution).

A more graphic measure of the growth of this tendency is the aggregate growth in political donations – most strikingly in the United States, where expenditure on congressional election campaigns alone rose more than sixfold in real terms between 1978 and 1996 (to around $600 million). At the same time the tendency of corporations, which clearly account for the vast bulk of this increase, to demand specific favours in return for their contributions is becoming more blatant.

A case in point is the recent insistence of Chiquita Brands (a well known contributor to Democratic Party funds) that the Clinton administration pursue its demand to have European markets fully opened to its exports of bananas from Central America – even at the cost of considerable damage to the economies of small Caribbean states and to US-EU relations.

There has, not surprisingly, been growing public unease at the scale of corporate corruption, most notably expressed in the *mani pulite* (clean hands) campaign in Italy in the early 1990s. At the same time even some business leaders have felt the need to form pressure groups against corruption, such as Transparency International (if only because of its destabilising effect on competition) and to pressurise OECD government to enact laws against corrupt practices in international business transactions. Yet there has seemingly been little attempt to understand the phenomenon or to discover why it has suddenly become so much more prevalent in societies where it has been widely supposed that the rule of law is well established.

The popular notion that Western societies can be considered advanced democracies has led many people to ignore the fact that there are in reality few restraints to the ability of corporations to exercise influence over government policy in ways which could easily be, and often are, at variance with the public interest. This kind of complacency was also of course fostered by the Keynesian/corporatist ideology of the post-war era which, as already noted, led many too readily to assume an identity of interest between big business and the community as a whole, and therefore to accept the benefits of state support for the former, largely without question.

Arguably, therefore, this 'mixed economy' culture paved the way for the explosion of influence peddling that has been such a feature of all the industrial market economies over the past twenty years. Yet equally there can be little doubt that this phenomenon has been fuelled by the combination of intensifying market pressures to raise profits and the related trend towards liberalisation, encouraging companies to believe that almost any action to enhance 'shareholder value' would be seen as acceptable. It is far from clear that the political will exists to purge (or even substantially diminish) such corrupt tendencies.

One obvious reason for this is that virtually all political parties are themselves dominated by groups or individuals who have themselves benefited from the culture of corporatist corruption that now permeates the whole system. Hence the Blair administration in Britain is receiving the tacit support of the other major political parties in resisting calls for the introduction of state funding for political parties – for the obvious, though naturally unspoken, reason that it would tend to undermine the justification for corporate (and indeed trade union) funding of political parties and thereby threaten the ability of these interest groups to determine the political agenda. Similarly, in the United States, the perennial public demands for reform of the scandal-ridden political funding system are just as regularly kicked into touch by the powerful groups within Congress (and their corporate backers) who have so much to gain by preserving the status quo.

Corporate Governance

Another area of governance where popular disquiet is growing, but where resistance to change appears even stronger, is that affecting the running of corporations themselves, where the actions of management are often seen to be anti-social and irresponsible. Among the general public such concern relates to decisions such as those resulting in damage to the environment, plant closures (and associated job losses) and massive remuneration packages for directors, typically awarded by themselves.

Yet all too often discussion of the subject among experts focuses on how to make companies more accountable to their shareholders – the legal owners in whose interests they are supposed to be run but who are routinely ignored in favour of the directors' tendency to pursue their personal self-advancement. In the case of some specialist commentators there often appears to be a rather casuistic assumption that more effective shareholder 'activism' would solve the problem (Monks and Minow 1996).

However, such a view fails to recognise the obvious likelihood that the interests of shareholders are all too likely to conflict with those of other 'stakeholders' (employees, suppliers and consumers) or of the public at large represented by the taxpayer. Thus, for example, a proposed takeover of the company could be greatly to the advantage of shareholders but lead to substantial job losses among employees. Hence even if it were possible to enact laws that would enhance the ability of shareholders to exercise control over the corporations they collectively own – which is in any case doubtful – this would scarcely resolve the problem of how to oblige companies to fulfil their obligations to society as a whole.

We are thus brought back to the still unresolved question which has lain at the heart of the study of political economy since before the Industrial Revolution: what should be the limits to the right of property? In general, of course, it may be said that the question must and will be answered in different ways at different times and places. However, in an era when private corporations not only enjoy such immense power but are accorded such extensive privilege, protection and subsidy from the state the view that the state (acting on behalf of the community as a whole) should also have a say in how they are run is increasingly hard to resist.

As we have seen, this issue was essentially fudged or ignored in Western countries during the post-war era of corporatism – at a time when economic success ensured that conflicts between the collective interest and that of privately owned corporations could be glossed over. What future historians may find surprising is that, once that comfortable era came to an end in the 1970s and differences of interest became harder to conceal, society did not insist on making the private corporate sector more publicly accountable.

As long as it was possible to pretend that the new consensus (embodied by the Thatcher-Reagan 'revolution') really involved a withdrawal of the state from running or subsidising private corporations the dominant political forces representing the interests of the latter might plausibly claim the right to be free of public interference. Once, however, it becomes apparent that the corporate sector is in fact increasingly dependent on public subsidy it is hard to see how it can avoid being brought to account.

The True Sources of Global Calamity

On the basis of this necessarily brief examination of the evidence, it is apparent that any attempt to explain the collapse of the East Asian economic 'miracle' in terms of a failure to apply Western norms of democratic governance and accountability must be dismissed for two reasons. First, within the East Asian region itself the pattern of governance has been far from uniform, and the country which has most closely adhered to Western standards of democracy – Japan – has been the first to sink into economic decline since the 1980s. Second, while the Western industrialised countries undoubtedly have a longer and better established tradition of democratic accountability and the rule of law than those of East Asia, their governments have long been susceptible to the undue influence of big private corporations – an influence that has arguably become stronger and more corrupt in recent decades.

In retrospect it seems quite bizarre that any Western observer with significant first-hand knowledge of East Asia and its economy could have arrived at such a simplistic explanation for the dramatic reversal of fortune that has befallen the region since 1997. For many Western organisations which had invested in the region during the boom years had done so in the full knowledge that standards of governance and respect for legality were often far below what was regarded as acceptable in the West.

Indeed certain countries, notably China and Indonesia, had long been among the most notorious in the world for corruption, abuse of human rights and minimal commitment to the rule of law. To suggest that most Western investors – or indeed officials of the International Monetary Fund – were somehow ignorant of this is even less plausible than their claim that they were caught unawares by the outbreak of the crisis in 1997.

The implication of such an obviously disingenuous analysis is that it is really an attempt to distract attention from more disturbing explanations of the crisis – or rather ones less palatable to the dominant Western interest groups (which are also the leaders of global opinion) and, at the same time, less flattering to the reputation of Western financiers and investors. For the attempt to suggest that foreign investors in East Asia were somehow misled into believing that they were dealing with respectable and soundly regulated markets could reasonably be interpreted as begging the question of why, from the 1980s, there had been such a sudden craze among Western (and Japanese) investors to put money into emerging markets which had for so long been regarded as highly risky.

In truth, a more realistic analysis would have to conclude that this Gadarene rush by foreign investors was a) driven more by the desperate search for high-risk / high return investments in a world awash with surplus capital; and b) that this process, involving the indiscriminate hyping of investments on the basis of little or no knowledge, was itself a major factor in destabilising markets. Had such investment inflows been based on a more realistic appraisal of market prospects – which would have indicated obvious limits to the scope for rapid growth of manufactured exports from East Asia – they would undoubtedly have occurred on a much smaller scale than they did.

As it was, Western fund managers and their abettors in the financial press systematically promoted the idea that almost any investment in East Asia or other emerging markets was bound to be profitable and indeed likely to outperform more stagnant markets in the West. In short, it turned into yet another of the speculative bubbles such as litter the history of capitalism (from the Dutch tulip mania of the Seventeenth century onwards).

Hence we may reasonably suspect that those who seek to blame the demise of the East Asian boom on failings of governance, whether political or corporate, within the region were all too aware that responsibility might more properly be laid at the door of irresponsible international speculators who, in encouraging investment in excess capacity, had provoked the destabilisation of industries which might otherwise have been able to grow on a viable and sustainable basis, albeit at a slower pace. Such a conclusion has indeed been authenticated by the growing chorus of opinion – led by none other than the arch-speculator George Soros (Soros 1998) – that the principal lesson of the crisis is the need to find a way of limiting such destabilising flows. This view, moreover, is reinforced by the undeniable indications of a rising world-wide excess supply of capital (Shutt 1998).

Despite this mounting body of evidence of more fundamental flaws in the global economy order, the international financial establishment continues to insist on the primary need to improve different aspects of governance. A bizarre example of this obsession recently encountered by the author is the orchestrated attempt by the IMF and World Bank to suggest that the main reason for the chronic lack of productive investment and decline in output in many republics of the former Soviet Union is the absence of proper corporate governance legislation and institutions enforcing the rights of shareholders, despite the fact that in all these ex-Communist economies – where few people understand the role of shareholders in any case – the cripplingly high cost of borrowing (necessitated by the removal of all exchange controls), collapsing infrastructure and lack of law enforcement (particularly in respect of customs duties) are obviously more immediate deterrents to investment.

Yet clearly the IMF and the bank, representing interests in the West which are desperate to avert any moves to curb the freedom of investors to speculate, prefer to avert their gaze from such problems even at the cost of the prolonged suffering of millions. This wilful refusal at the highest level to contemplate the need for any reversal of the trend to liberalisation which has been so universally imposed since the 1980s – even where its effects have been manifestly damaging – would seem to indicate a hidden agenda.

The most plausible inference is that what is really driving the strategy of the global corporate establishment and the governments that are so much beholden to it, is a fear of two closely related menaces: the prospect that the perception of continued economic weakness and the associated intensification of social problems – not to mention the breakdown of civil order in an increasing number of countries – will fatally undermine public confidence in the liberalised capitalist economic order; and the strong possibility, now bordering on overwhelming certainty, that there will be a world-wide collapse in the value of financial securities (stocks and shares) such as to destroy much of the wealth of both companies and individuals, with obvious consequences for the economic well-being of the entire world.

Clearly to the extent that the first of these fears is realised it will make it increasingly impossible to resist demands to restrict the financial benefits accorded to corporations by the state as well as to limit their freedom of action in such a way that they will be compelled to behave more in accordance with the collective need of the community. Whatever form such restrictions might take it is likewise obvious that the effect will be to curtail their profitability, thus making more inevitable the fulfilment of the second fear – a large-scale market sell-off. Furthermore it is easily imaginable that this twin threat could turn into a vicious circle of intensifying decline in living standards and irresistible calls for fundamental changes to the economic system.

Conclusions

It is thus entirely understandable that the global elite of big business and government, which has such enormous power to influence public opinion through the mass media, should be prepared to resort to any distortion of the truth to preserve its interests in what is an increasingly hostile climate. In this context, the attempt to put the blame for the Asian crisis on weaknesses of governance – that is to say on deficient institutions at national level – is both plausible and highly convenient.

It is plausible in that such flaws in institutions of governance are undoubtedly very real in most countries in East Asia (not to mention the rest of the world) and call for drastic measures to enhance democratic accountability at both governmental and corporate levels. At the same time it is obviously convenient in that it offers a scapegoat for the disaster other than the real culprit of systemic failure.

On the other hand, the effort to concentrate scrutiny on the issue of governance will tend ultimately to force more people to address the highly pertinent question of what is the proper aim of economic management in a democracy and what should be the framework of institutions and obligations needed to secure adequate accountability. This likelihood seems all the greater in that there is increasingly widespread awareness that in the complex world of today many key issues relating to economic management – such as employment rights and the environment – cannot be left to the mercy of competitive market forces, and certainly not to corporations which are driven solely by the motive of short-term maximisation of their own profits.

If a debate on this issue is openly conducted it seems almost certain to lead more and more people to recognise that the untrammelled exercise of corporate power according to the classic *laissez-faire* Western model is in fact a negation of democratic accountability. Indeed, as already noted, the belief that corporations which benefit from state protection and support (i.e. given in the name of the whole community) must be required to give something back to that community – and in any event must not behave in anti-social ways – is more or less explicitly recognised in the practice of a number of countries in both East and West.

Even in Britain, the cradle of *laissez-faire* ideology, this principle was implicit in the pre-industrial era when companies with limited liability could only be formed by charter of the Crown (sanctioned by Parliament) for specific purposes approved by the latter. The notion that anyone had an automatic right to form a company with limited liability for any purpose within the law was only adopted with the first Companies Act of the 1850s – at a time when this was felt necessary in order to meet the need at that time to mobilise large amounts of capital without undue delay for investment in railways and other rapidly expanding industries.

Defenders of this model might reasonably argue that it made possible the rapid economic development of many countries as well as Britain – although it is also true that the Soviet Union showed it was possible to industrialise rapidly without depending on private capital at all. Perhaps, however, the intensifying global glut of capital – in an age when technology has rendered capital far more productive (relative to output) than in the past – means it is no longer a public necessity to give such indiscriminate encouragement to investors.

At the same time it should be pointed out that the right to ultra-free exercise of property rights, which is implicit in the privilege of limited liability, was granted before the age of universal suffrage – at a time when in Britain the right to vote was still subject to a property qualification. In the present age of mass democracy it may well be wondered whether such a strong legal bias in favour of private property rights is still appropriate. In the light of such doubts it is particularly ironic that the New Labour government which came to power in Britain in 1997 has adopted the slogan of 'modernisation' as a code for giving even more privileges to big business.

If we are thus to conclude that the essentially Nineteenth Century model of economic governance which still dominates the world is no longer compatible with the needs and democratic aspirations of a more complex global society at the dawn of the Twenty-first Century, it is appropriate to consider what should be the essential features of a more functional model for today. Based on the above critique it seems clear that the minimum requirements must include community representation on the board of directors of all enterprises in receipt of explicit state subsidies or guarantees; the grant of limited liability only on condition that beneficiary enterprises are subject to supervision by a regulator appointed by and accountable to the community; and effective restrictions on the level of profits to be retained by enterprises subject to community[3] support and supervision.

It is not possible here fully to explore the far-reaching implications of adopting such an approach to regulation of the corporate sector. It is clear, however, that it would tend to reduce the potential rewards to investors relative to the risks, in so far as state supervision of an enterprise would not necessarily mean a pledge to bail out shareholders in the event of company failure.

For this reason it is likely that investment in equities would become less attractive to private individuals and institutions – not to mention speculators – than it has been hitherto. By the same token the state (whether at local or national level) would probably need to assume a larger role as shareholder. Based on past experience the prospect of a significant revival of collective ownership of enterprises might well be viewed with alarm even by those not opposed to it out of ideological bigotry.

It must therefore be stressed that it would be essential to require all state-controlled enterprises to be subject both to performance targets related to attainable standards of efficiency and to independent scrutiny and democratic accountability for their actions.

It will be immediately apparent that the application of such principles raises considerable problems in the context of a global economy which is organised on the basis of sovereign nation states but where many companies are transnational in their reach. It is for this reason that such a model could only be implemented in the context of regional blocs of states prepared to accept similar norms in respect of corporate regulation and taxation and on the basis that they would limit, if not totally exclude, capital flows and imports from regions not subscribing to the same standards. Ideally – and indeed logically in view of the desirability of not creating undue grounds for inter-regional conflict – the long-term aspiration should be to achieve a large measure of regulatory harmonisation and economic integration on a global basis.

It is because corporate interest groups are aware of the difficulties posed by any proposal to achieve international economic harmonisation, while also perceiving the benefit to themselves of the continued fragmentation of the world into nation states, that they often tend to oppose moves towards greater integration. This helps to perpetuate a global order in which corporations can and do exploit the tendency of different countries to compete with each other for investment by lowering taxes and to join in a 'race to the bottom' in respect of standards for the treatment of labour and the environment.

Yet there are grounds for believing that senior representatives of many major corporations are not happy with the status quo and the instability which global liberalisation and deregulation has brought. Hence, while many business leaders in Europe and elsewhere react with horror to the prospect of harmonisation of taxes and other regulations within an integrating European Union, an increasing number also favour it – perhaps precisely because it offers some prospect of escape from the anarchic environment of the global 'free market'.

Whether it can be envisaged that a sufficient mass of corporate opinion will soon come to support a significant re-regulation of global business for political parties in OECD countries to be induced to change their attitude may well seem doubtful. Yet in view of the virtual certainty that the present upheaval in the world economy – and the collateral damage to society in so many countries – will cause more and more sections of the community to question the neo-liberal consensus, the demands for drastic moves toward a more stable order seem bound to grow.

Notes

1 The best known was Professor J. K. Galbraith, who had been a trenchant critic of what he called the 'planning system' operated by big corporations at least since the 1960s.

2 This claim has arguably posed something of a problem for enthusiasts for 'Asian values', since it evidently turns on its head the argument that one of the strengths of the Asian Model is greater social solidarity in contrast to Western individualism.

3 The term 'community' is used here as indicating the possibility, indeed the desirability, that public accountability should be devolved to the local level as much as possible, provided that all concerned should remain constitutionally answerable to those providing public funds or support.

Conclusion

CHAPTER TEN

Xiaoming Huang

Beyond the State and the Market: The Primacy of Human Interest

It has always been unclear, ever since the term was coined, whether *political economy*[1] is about economics or about politics, that it, whether political institutions and processes have the privilege over those economic ones in their interrelationship, or the other way around. The problem can be traced back to the era of early capitalism when new capitalist entrepreneurs were convinced that pre-capitalist political institutions and social structure severely hindered the ideal function of the new economic dynamics and argued for an intervention-free environment for their best performance.

On the other hand, Marxists and mercantilists called our attention to the inadequateness and often destructive and discriminative nature of the new capitalist forces and to the fact that a specific economic order is rather the effect of political institutions and processes. Hence these institutions and processes carry much of the original substance and generative power of the political economic nexus.

The debate has never reached a decisive conclusion and both sides have since been able to build considerable theoretical and empirical support. Asian development over the past half century has dramatically intensified the debate. From one perspective, the pattern of Asian development is an 'anomaly' in the globally celebrated experience of modern development. Among the indicators of such an anomaly, the particular state-market relationship is often singled out as *the* defining element. More specifically, Asian development is regarded as relying on the kind of relationship where the state and its associated institutions have privilege over the market. The working of the market itself would primarily serve the interests of the state and its associates.

The provocative mode of Asian development forced both sides to focus their attention on the relationship between the market and state which are considered to be the primary agents of modern economic dynamics and the managing institutions respectively. The notion that the developmental state in East Asia proved to be the real 'hidden hand' behind the growth raised many difficult questions. The whole debate about the Asian Model is to ascertain whether and/or how the Asian experience can shed new light on the relationship. It is in this sense that directions of the transition over the past decade and the nature of the emergent political economy are issues of particular significance: they provide evidence as to whether the anomalous developmental state is merely a transitional phenomenon, or is in fact a permanent option.

But it is unlikely that the state-market debate will take us too far, as we have been debating this issue for at least the past 20 years since Chalmers Johnson's MITI study in the late 1970s and early 1980s (Johnson 1982), and are still unable to fit the Asian puzzle into the dichotomy. In fact, framing the East Asian experience and its further evolution along the lines of the state-market relationship is increasingly limiting our ability to understand the entrepreneurial and pragmatic spirit of Asian political economy. What is missing in the state-market debate is really the human actors themselves whom the market and state are to serve and who are their ultimate movers and shapers.

Built on this point, this concluding chapter will first examine the findings reached in the chapters and see if we can identify a pattern in the latest developments; and if so, how well this pattern fits into the expectations of the state-market antagonism. Anticipating a substantial gap, we will then seek an explanation of the 'Asian problem' in a redefined framework in which the state and market, rather than being our ultimate values or purpose, are essentially the effect of the constant interactions between human interests and their surrounding conditions. How much the state is involved in the working of the market, and where the balancing point is located between the state and market, depends on how well it would satisfy these interests, particularly those of the essential shapers and movers.

Subsequently, we will also reframe the Asian Model debate in a context of the ever intensifying tension between two dominant intellectual traditions: one which sees the world increasingly becoming one on a set of core institutions and values; and the other which perceives the world as consisting of different experiences or 'civilisations' with their own sets of 'incommensurable' core institutions and values. We will see whether the Asian phenomenon is a mere temporary anomaly – in which case, eventual adaptation of these countries to the global institutions and values shall be expected. Or it is an instance of a separate human experience and more sophisticated interactions with other experiences are to be encouraged. Finally, as the new political economy is still in the making, we will suggest some areas worth further inquiry.

Findings

The political and economic transition has not only been responding to new conditions but has already brought about new dynamics and arrangements. These new conditions are new in at least three significant senses. First, the economic conditions are constantly renewing themselves. Professor Kim and Professor Zheng identified the more sophisticated markets China and South Korea are facing, with issues ranging from currency stabilisation to investment promotion and control; and from banking system reform to domestic demand stimulation; from debt control to capital efficiency. Together with the two chapters on global conditions, they also demonstrated a significant erosion of the separation of domestic and international markets. These new economic conditions have been further complicated dramatically by the integration of the global monetary economy through instant electronic transactions in stocks and other innovative financial instruments.

In a significant way, the new economic conditions have reinforced many of the premises underlying reform and institutional restructuring in East Asia and modified many others. The need for insulated bureaucracy to be more responsive and for growth alliance to be more economically rational, for example, has become stronger and more urgent. The benefits for market-driven efficiency and productivity are clearer. Moves have been taken, after a long hesitation, to tackle the issue of corporate structure in Korea and Japan, and the new democratic order is reshaping the function of the bureaucracy and economic management. Even in China where democratic order is still a remote expectation, decentralisation and the rise of the private sector have forced the bureaucracy to reorganise and re-engage itself.

On the other hand, a shift in comparative advantage has continued to demand the constant 'beyond-profit' sensitivity and organisational effectiveness of the public sector in steering and supporting individual enterprises in their adjustment to the changing conditions. As clearly demonstrated in Chapter 3 and 7, for example, expansion of the domestic market has become the new growth strategy for Taiwan, China and Japan, as the international markets continue to shrink in the face of their increased competitiveness and a lack of stability and predictability. In each of these countries, the new expansion programmes required a huge amount of the government's capital inputs and sophisticated financial, monetary and administrative manoeuvres. Moreover, the dramatised market fluctuations forced the government to take more active steps to ensure the survival and competitiveness of the private sector.

Overall, the new economic conditions, as assessed in this collection, have not led to the emergence of a clear form of economic governance along the lines of either market primacy or state centralism. We have not seen convincing evidence that the conditions there have overwhelmingly demanded an unconditional embrace of the market or preservation of the engaging state at any price. What is emerging is an attempt to search for a delicate point of balance between the need of respect for the market and of effective state support and organisation.

Political conditions are new as well. The chapters by Professor Harris and Professor Endo focus on the state itself as the most defining aspect of the political conditions. Professor Harris depicts a state in China that is increasingly losing its purpose as the changing society and populace has deprived it of its defining substance. Professor Endo on the other hand sees a state in Japan weakened by the new global political economy that is eroding the national structure Japan's developmental state has been built upon. Consequently, while the overall pattern of the government's involving, engaging and intervening in the economy remains in these countries, there is increasingly a problem of leadership and purposefulness in economic governance, demanded by the more sophisticated and aggressive market conditions and by the urgent need for directions and priorities in reform, restructuring and sustainable development. Both chapters suggest that even though there are forces in these countries wanting aspects of the developmental state to continue and even though a strong and effective state is demanded to meet the challenges of the new conditions, whether the changing state is capable of living up to such expectations seems to be questionable.

With the new economic and political conditions as such, it would be logical to argue, as Professor Harris and Professor Endo have shown in their chapters, that the government would be more reluctant and less effective in performing 'market-governing' functions. The chapters by Professor Huang and Mr. Green, both focusing on Taiwan, suggest, however, a more complicated picture. Professor Huang, investigating whether a more contested democratic state is still willing and capable of economic activism, found a still willing and effective, perhaps more engaging state, in the new democratic environment. The study examined various new interventionist methods by the government in market stabilisation, domestic demand stimulation, moral persuasion, and rescue of failing enterprises. On the other hand, Mr. Green's study has identified both the trends of the state's intelligent activism and capacity kidnappedness in Taiwan. In terms of intelligent activism, the state still actively and effectively pursues competitive advantage in the old style of the developmental state. As for capacity kidnappedness, the state is controlled and debilitated by internal and external interests and is characterised by a lack of clear policy and failures in supporting development. Overall, both studies have shown that the new political conditions and their consequences on the political economy have also failed to produce conclusive evidence to the interpretation of the transition and new political economy along the lines of state-market dichotomy. More respect for a pluralist political order and for the market has not led to less respect for the state, nor to less willingness and effectiveness of state involvement, at least not in Taiwan.

Finally, the new political economy no doubt is a product of, and has an effect on, global conditions, particularly economic ones. As the Asian Model flourished, primarily on the unique structural relationship between the domestic and international market, changes in global market conditions have profoundly affected the AMCs. Professor Lingle and Mr. Shutt in their chapters have clearly demonstrated this fundamental impact. However, they differ considerably in their interpretation of the impact and how AMCs should respond to the global challenge. Professor Lingle points out the inevitability of global market expansion and integration, and the need for institutional restructuring and cultural 'recultivation' in AMCs to meet the challenge. Mr. Shutt, on the other hand, sees the incompatibility between the global dynamics and local structure not merely as an Asian problem, but rather as a problem of the global capitalist system itself. Again, from their studies, evidence is conflicting and views differ as to whether it is an imperative of the global system that national economies should submit themselves to the global market.

On the Ladder of Generalisation

What does all of this add up to? First, there is a clear change of mood on the part of the AMCs in terms of the purpose, strategy and target institutions in their reform and restructuring, from the idealistic enthusiasm in the early years of the transition to more sophisticated thinking and pragmatic policy decisions as the reform and restructuring went further and deeper. From China to Japan, and from Korea to Taiwan, policy-makers and opinion-shapers have taken a more model-free and problem-centred approach to various controversial issues, such as state-enterprise reform, intervention in the stock market, market liberalisation, restructuring of corporate organisation, banking reform, and market re-targeting.

Across the countries of diverse conditions, there is one thing that seems to be shared: the sense of national economy is stronger than ever. The purpose of reform and restructuring was not simply to match a model, however ideal it may sound in theory, but to make the economy more competitive and more profitable. This is true in Taiwan and China, as well as in Korea and Japan. Opening to the global market, for example – if it is indeed happening – is only a means to that purpose. Based on this basic premise, the problem of how much of the state is too much becomes more a dependent variable than an independent one. When reduction in state involvement in the working of the economy helps raise efficiency and productivity, this would happen sooner or later, even with resistance from the 'embedded' interests. This happened in China twenty years ago and is still an on-going process. It happened in Korea and Taiwan, and to lesser extent and at a slower pace, in Japan over the past several years.

But under certain circumstances, particularly those of the AMCs, opening to the global market could also weaken competitiveness and perhaps productivity of the national economy, temporarily or permanently, because of operational costs in open competition, impact of market fluctuations on less sustainable corporations, and the weakened manipulative capacity of a less insulated national bureaucracy. In this case a protective and manipulative state with necessary public mandate and institutional support is still a convenient option. That is what we have seen in the handling of the 1997–98 financial crisis in Hong Kong, Taiwan and China and in the strategic hesitation of the AMCs in comprehensive trade, investment and service liberalisation.

Further along the lines of the national economy argument, the increasing exposure of the AMEs to global market conditions has reinforced the very external condition upon which the Asian Model has been built: the formation of the global market in the nation-state system of property arrangements and wealth distribution. While the global market can be seen as evolving into a single one in manufacturing, distribution and marketing, the ownership of its elements is nationally privileged, managed and protected. This is a condition for the continual relevance and persistent power of the national economy. If the national economy is ultimately measured by property holdings, wealth possession, and product consumption and service use, then *their* national promotion is only natural. The economy is not just about productivity, but also about the control and management of products and services. Competitivity is not just about how cheap one can sell, but also how much profit from the sales it can keep.

An essential element in the success of the AMCs in moving up in the global structure of wealth and power[2] is the fact that the state in these countries put in motion a set of institutional arrangements to turn their relatively weak economy into a competitive one and sustain a long term economic growth and large-scale wealth accumulation. All this was possible mainly with the separation of the domestic and international market and the state's control of transactions and flows across the borders. Increasing interactions with the global market have further exposed the weakness of these economies as well as the effects of the Darwinian law in the global market. The state can only be a convenient and unfortunately most effective institutional defence.

Finally, the state is not just a part in a machine that can be reduced, removed or replaced when deemed necessary. In addition to its purposeful functions, it is also a set of reflective arrangements forged among various interests (Migdal, Kohli and Shue 1994). The tendency of the state in East Asia to intervene is more than just an effect of the developmental purpose as envisaged in the developmental state model (Johnson 1982). Its actions are also, often in a subtle fashion, an effect of the collective preferences of the movers and shapers in society. These movers and shapers under the Asian Model provided in substantial part the motivation for the state's intervention which the inclusionary nature of elite governance in these countries allows (McCargo 1998). Reform may have reshaped the way these movers and shapers operate, but the evolving state-society interaction will continue to produce movers and shapers of different kinds who will keep the state engaged in accommodating their interests and carrying out policies reflecting their preferences.

The last point leads us to a more fundamental issue. In fact, this collection has shown that while the transition and resultant new political economy in East Asia still recognises the values of both the market and the state, it seems to reject either of them as the ultimate purpose. The ambiguity in state-market relationship in the new political economy, like that in the Asian Model of the past, suggests that the engine of growth is perhaps located somewhere else.[3] If neither the market nor the state is the ultimate driving force, a fact we have tried to ascertain in this collection, what is the original substance behind a particular set of market conditions or state functions? Or what is the ultimate purpose of our activities in political economy?

The Ambiguity in State–Market Relations

It is widely assumed that the Asian Model represents a state-centric model while the so-called neoliberal economy a market-driven one. The transition in East Asia, therefore, was conceived as a process in which AMCs adopt the neoliberal model. In the state-centric Asian Model, the state was conceived as the primary value or purpose. Logically, the market should replace it in the grand transition. Judged by the findings discussed in the previous section, evidence for a sole-value driven transition along the lines of state-market antagonism is inconclusive, if not contradictory. There are signs that the AMCs are adapting to market principles. On the other hand, evidence is plenty that they are hesitating to move away from many of the state centric principles and arrangements that have brought them to where they are.

One might attribute the ambiguity to the unsettledness in the shifting balance of power between state and market forces in the AMCs. But if we look deeper and further, it is perhaps the defining categories perceived essential for understanding political economy that are to share the blame. Despite all the differences they have on various critical issues, defenders and challengers of the Asian Model seem to share one thing with regard to the state-market relationship: either the state or the market is the real shaper of the relationship and its consequent development. The defenders demand our attention to the indispensable role of the state's vision, strategy and capacity; while the challengers emphasise the market's neutral role, generative power and guiding functions.

In broader terms, the state represents the function of institutions while the market represents natural conditions. Institutionalists generally have a faith in the power of social engineering and the necessity of collective and organised intervention in the reshaping of natural order. On the other hand, natural order believers, often referred to as realists, normally have doubts on the collective effects of human intentions. In one way or another, they all seem to believe that either institutions or natural conditions could function independent of human interests and activities. Institutionalists claim, for example, that societal conditions can be improved with the aid of institutional arrangements that redefine the relations among elements in society, reallocate resources in support of the redefined relations, and therefore increase their effectiveness in the pursuit of a particular set of social purposes. One could argue that the Asian Model is an example of the working of such an institutionalist logic. What is 'Asian' about the Asian Model, therefore, is the institutional component in the organisation of national economic growth.

Realists on the other hand urge people to conform to, and survive in, the natural condition. Natural order has its built-in mechanisms of self-generation as well as self-correction that will eventually bring things to their ideal state of existence, function and interaction. Human interventions, while capable of producing temporary effects in favour of 'parochial' interests, will over the long run distort the process of, or even prevent, the materialisation of the ideal state. The neoliberal expectations of the transition in East Asia reflects such a fundamental belief.

This is perhaps how the ambiguity regarding the state-market relationship in the transitional AMCs could be better explained. In the battle between the market and state, or between economic conditions and their organising institutions, it is the interests and activities of those movers and shapers in society that ultimately determine the direction of their interaction and location of the point of balance. It is these interests and activities that lead to the formation of institutional arrangements and changes in economic conditions. The strengthened market forces in the AMCs are a recognition of the market as a primary source of competitiveness, productivity and profitability. The statist elements on the other hand indicate the weakness and inadequacy of these market forces and perhaps their undesirability from the viewpoint of some dominant interests in society.

How much statist elements and market forces develop depends, indeed, on the nature and structure of dominant interests in society and their ability to be incorporated in the restructuring of political economy. The state or the market can be strong and effective only when it serves the interests of those movers and shapers. If not, alternative forms will be called for. Growth alliance, autonomous bureaucracy, military developers are examples of the logic in the past, and the intelligent state, illiberal democracy, a dependent middle class, and the state as an economic agent, are samples in the emergent political economy.

In sum, if there is something 'new' in East Asian political economy after the decade of transition, it is the ambiguity in its relationship to the state and market. More than reflecting the inability of the AMCs to live up to our expectations, this ambiguity is perhaps rather an indication of the inadequacy of our expectations in the first place. It should force us to rethink the problem of the state-market relationship for a better and more realistic understanding of the Asian phenomenon, and to see how the original substance in these political economies has shaped and will continue to shape the existing conditions and methods of their betterment at various levels of human collectivity.

In other words, a convincing explanation of the transition and emergent political economy in East Asia – perhaps its further evolution as well – must go beyond the state-market relationship and look at those more fundamental forces that not only move political and economic activities in a particular social environment, but also shape the state-market relationship itself.

What Lies Ahead for East Asian Debaters?

As demonstrated in the chapters, the transition continues as an on-going process, and the new political economy is still in the making. Many areas require further observation and investigation. First, the growth of the world political economy is increasingly caught up in the dilemma between the benefits of an integrated global market and the convenience, and even necessity, of the nation-state system. While the nation-state system appears to be one which will stay, the question is how should we manage the line between the national economy and the global market, particularly in the AMCs?

Second, assuming the nation-state will continue to be the primary unit of global organisation, and at the same time, national authority will be further dispersed across levels of the national political system as political liberalisation goes further, do national responsibilities and capacities move with them? If not, how can effective governance be possible where interests and authority are increasingly separated from responsibilities and capabilities?

Third, the tension between competitive ideal institutional models and local conditions has been intensified, particularly in the case of those economically successful but socially and politically divergent AMCs. If the tension persists, for whatever reasons, and if cases are strong for either the model side and the local condition side, which side should have the privilege? Or is the privilege necessary?

Contributors in this collection have touched upon these issues and formed diverse views. But we are all confident that developments in East Asia will continue to provide further and, hopefully, more convincing evidence.

Notes

1 Karl Marx and Friedrich List are said to be among the first to use the term (Marx 1857; List 1885).

2 One could see this ascendance as a challenge to much of what Wallerstein argues in his theory of the world capitalist system (Wallerstein 1974).
3 For arguments for the state or market as the engine of growth, see Chowdhury and Islam 1993: 42–56.

Appendices

Appendix I South Korea's Financial Market Indicators

	3-year Corporate Bond Yields % (average)	*Ratio of Overnight Call Rates % (average)*	*Ratio of Dishonored Bills to the Total*	*Korea Stock Price Index Jan. 4, 1980=100*
October 1997	12.5	13.6	0.56	584.1
November	14.1	14	0.48	494.1
December	24.3	21.3	2.09	390.3
January 1998	23.4	25.3	0.72	475.2
February	19.8	23.4	0.83	525.2
March	18.9	22.5	0.62	523
April	18.1	21.3	0.57	444.2
May	17.9	18.6	0.62	356.3
June	16.6	16.3	0.58	313.3
July	13.7	12.7	0.69	327.8
August	12.4	9.5	0.55	312.8
September	12.5	8.5	0.42	312.2
October	10	7.3	0.28	358.8
November	9.6	7.3	0.26	429.2
December	8.3	7	0.17	524.7
January 1999	7.9	6.4	0.12	597.6

Source: Ministry of Finance and Economy, Republic of Korea.1999.

Appendix II Trends in Price, Industrial Output and Industrial Sales in South Korea

	CPI	*Industrial Output*	*Sales*
1997 average	4.5	6.9	3.2
January 1998	8.3	−9.4	−9.4
February	9.5	−10.4	−12.8
March	9	−9. 1	−11.6
April	8.8	−22.5	−15.5
May	8.2	−11.1	−16.5
June	7.5	−14	−15.9
July	7.3	−14	−17.5
August	6.9	−12.8	−16.3
September	6.9	−1.7	−11.6
October	7.2	−9.3	− 13.2
November	6.8	0.3	−8.1
December	4	4.8	−3.6
January 1999	1.5	14.7	2.8

Sources: Ministry of Finance and Economy and Korean Development Institute.

Appendix III Trends in Unemployment Rates and Year-on-Year Real Wage Changes in South Korea

	Real wage in all industries (%)	*Real wage in manufacturing (%)*	*Unemployment (%)*
October 1997	2.3	1.3	2.1
November	0.4	−1.9	2.6
December	−12.3	−19.2	3.1
January 98	2.7	−0.5	4.5
February	−20.1	−23.2	5.9
March	−8.3	−9.7	6.5
April	−6.7	−13.5	6.7
May	−6.9	−9.5	6.9
June	−13.4	−12.7	7.0
July	−13.2	−16.4	7.6
August	−12.9	−17.5	7.4
September	−18.9	−17.5	7.3
October	−8.6	−8.0	7.1
November	−8.3	−7.8	7.3
December			7.9
January 1999			8.5

Source: Calculated from Ministry of Finance and Economy data.

Appendix IV Foreign Exchange Rates and Useable Reserves in South Korea

	Gross Foreign Debts *US$ Billion*	*Useable Foreign Reserves* *US$ Billion*	*Exchange Rate (Average)* *Won/$*
October 1997	–	22.3	921.9
November	161.8	7.3	1025.6
December	158.0	8.9	1,484.3
Yearly	158.0	8.9	949.9
January 1998	155.1	12.4	1706.8
February	154.0	18.5	1623.1
March	153.8	24.2	1505.3
April	157.6	30.8	1392.0
May	157.3	34.4	1394.6
June	154.9	37.0	1397.2
July	153.7	39.3	1 300.8
August	153.6	41.4	1303.2
September	153.6	43.4	1370.8
October	153.5	45.3	1,338.7
November	152.4	46.5	1294.1
December	151.5	48.5	1213.7
Yearly	151.5	48.5	1403.2

Source. Ministry of Finance and Economy, Republic of Korea.

Bibliography

Amsden, Alice H. (1989) *Asia's Next Giant: South Korea and Late Industrialisation,* New York: Oxford University Press.

Arogyaswamy, Bernard. (1998) *The Asian Miracle, Myth, and Mirage: The Economic Slowdown Is Here to Stay,* London: Greenwood Press.

ASRC. Asian Studies Research Centre. (1998) *From Miracle to Meltdown: The End of Asian Capitalism,* Conference Proceedings, Perth: Murdoch University.

Barmé, Geremie. (1999) *In the Red: Contemporary Chinese Culture,* New York: Columbia University Press.

Baum, Richard. (1988) 'The Fifteenth National Party Congress: Jiang Takes Command' *The China Quarterly,* 153: 141–58.

——, and Alexei Shevchenko. (1996) 'The "State of the State" in Post-Reform China', Conference paper, Cambridge: Harvard University.

Berger, Peter, and Hsin-huang Michael Hsiao. (1988) *In Search of an East Asian Development Model,* New Brunswick: Transaction Books.

Bernal, Martin. (1976) *Chinese Socialism to 1907,* Ithaca: Cornell University Press.

Bernard, Mitchell, and John Ravenhill. (1995) 'Beyond Product Cycles and Flying Geese: Regionalization, Hierarchy, and the Industrialization of East Asia,' *World Politics,* 47 (2): 171–209.

Biggs, T. S., and Brian Levy. (1991) 'Strategic Interventions & the Political Economy of Industrial Policy in Developing Countries,' pp. 365–401 in Dwight Perkins and Michael Roemer. eds. *Reforming Economic Systems in Developing Countries,* Cambridge: Harvard University Press.

Bol, Peter. (1993) 'Government, Society and State: On the Political Visions of Ssu-ma Kuang and Wang An-shih,' in Robert Hymes and Conrad Schirokauer, (eds.), *Ordering the World: Approaches to State and Society in Sung Dynasty China.* Berkeley: University of California Press.

Borthwick, Mark. (1992) *Pacific Century: The Emergence of Modern Pacific Asia,* Boulder: Westview Press.

Bowen, J. Ray II and David C. Rose. (1998) 'On the Absence of Privately Owned, Publicly Traded Corporations in China: The Kirby Puzzle,' *The Journal of Asian Studies,* 57(2): 442–52.

Brook, Timothy. (1998) *The Confusions of Pleasure: Commerce and Culture,* Berkeley: University of California Press.

CASS. (1959) Research Group on the History of Philosophy in the Philosophy Institute, Chinese Academy of Social Sciences. *Zhongguo datong sixiang ziliao [Materials on the Datong Idea in China]*, Beijing: Zhonghua shuju chuban she.

CEC Central Election Commission and Election Study Centre. (1998) *Election Information Databank*, Taipei: National Chengchi University.

CEPD Council for Economic Planning and Development. (1998) *Major Economic Indicators*, Taipei: The Executive Yuan.

Chamberlain, Heath. (1998) 'Civil Society with Chinese Characteristics?' *The China Journal* 39(1): 69–81.

Chan, Hok-lam. (1984) *Legitimation in Imperial China: Discussions under the Jurchen-Chin Dynasty 1115–1234*, London: University of Washington Press.

Chang Hao, (1971) *Liang Ch'i-ch'ao and Intellectual Transition in China, 1890–1907*, Cambridge: Harvard University Press.

Chang, C. P. (1996) 'ROC Economic Development: Retrospect & Prospect.' *Industry of Free China*, 86(6).

Chang, Ha-Joon. (1993) 'The Political Economy of Industrial Policy in Korea,' *Cambridge Journal of Economics*, 17: 131–157.

Chao, Yung-mau. (1996) 'Taiwan difang paixide fazhan yu zhengzhi minzhuhuade guanxi' [Relations between local factions and political democratization in Taiwan], *Zhengzhi kexue lunchong* [*Political Science Review*], 7: 39–56.

Chen, Min-tung. (1995) *Paixi zhengzhi yu taiwan zhengzhi bianqian* [*Factional Politics and Political Transition in Taiwan*], Taipei: Yueh-tan Press.

Cheng, Anne. (1997) 'Nationalism, Citizenship and the New Text/Old Text Controversy in Late Nineteenth China' in Joshua Fogel and Peter Zarrow. eds. *Imagining the People: Chinese Intellectuals and the Concept of Citizenship.* Armonk: M.E. Sharpe.

Cheng, Tun-jen. (1989) 'Democratizing the quasi-Leninist regime in Taiwan,' *World Politics*, 42(4): 471–499.

Chiang, Pin Kung. (1997) 'Toward a More Liberalised Economy – Taiwan's Actions,' *Industry of Free China*, 87(7): 41–46.

China Quarterly. (1998) 'Quarterly Chronicle and Documentation,' 154 (2): 443–476.

——. (1988) 'Quarterly Chronicle and Documentation,' 113 (1): 143–173.

Cho, Dongchul. (1999) 'A Year after the Korean Economic Crisis: What Next?' conference paper, New York: ASSA meeting. January 6.

Choate, Allen. (1997)'Local Governance in China' *Focus on China*, New York: The Asia Foundation.

Chowdhury, Anis, and Iyanatul Islam. (1993) *The Newly Industrialising Economies of Asia*, London: Routledge.

Chu, Yun-han. (1989) 'State structure and economic adjustment of the East Asian newly industrializing countries,' *International Organization*, 43(4): 647–69.

Claessens, Stijn, Swati Ghosh, and David Scott. (1999) 'Korea's Financial Sector Reforms,' pp. 83–110 in *Korea and the Asian Economic Crisis: One Year Later*, Washington, D.C.: Korea Economic Institute of America.

Corsetti, Giancarlo, Paolo Pesenti, and Nouriel Roubini, 'What Caused the Asian Currency and Financial Crisis?' Internet publication: http://www.stern.nyu.edu/~nroubini/asia.

Cumings, Bruce. (1984) 'The Origins and Development of the Northeast Asian Political Economy: Industrial Sectors, Product Cycles, and Political Consequences,' *International Organization*, 38(1): 1–40.

Deyo, Frederic. (1987) *The Political Economy of the New Asian Industrialism,* Ithaca: Cornel University Press.

DBAS. Directorate of Budget, Accounting and Statistics. (1997) *Quarterly National Economic Trends,* Taipei: The Executive Yuan.

Dickson, Bruce J. (1997) *Democratization in China and Taiwan: the Adaptability of Leninist Parties,* Oxford: Clarendon Press.

DMG. Deutsche Morgan Grenfell (1997) *Guide to Emerging Currencies 1997.*

Duara, Prasenjit. (1996) 'De-Constructing the Chinese Nation,' in Jonathan Unger. ed. *Chinese Nationalism,* Armonk: M.E. Sharpe.

Endo, Seiji. (1995) 'East Asian Security Issues in the Post-Cold War Era,' pp. 31–71 in Toshihiko Kawagoe and Sueo Sekiguchi. eds. *East Asian Economies: Transformation and Challenges.* Tokyo: Seikei University/Singapore: Institute of Southeast Asian Studies.

Evan, Peter. (1992) 'The State as Problem and Solution: Predation, Embedded Autonomy & Structural Change,' pp. 139–81 in Stephan. Haggard and Robert Kaufman. eds. *The Politics of Economic Adjustment.* Princeton: Princeton University Press.

——. (1995) *Embedded Autonomy: States and Industrial Transformation.* Princeton: Princeton University Press.

——. (1998) 'State Structures, Government-Business Relations, and Economic Transformation,' pp. 63–87 in S. Maxfield and B. R. Schneider. eds. *Business and the State in Developing Countries,* Ithaca: Cornell University Press.

——. and Dietrich Rueschemeyer. (1985) *Bringing the State Back In,* Cambridge: Cambridge University Press.

Fan, Gang. (1998) 'Shichangzhong de zhengfu [Government in the Market],' pp. 133–150 in Liu Zhifeng, ed. *Di Qici Geming* [*The Seventh Revolution*], Beijing: Jingji ribao chuban she.

FCJ (1997a) 'Inbound investment surges 97% to a record high total,' *Free China Journal,* 7(1).

——. (1997b) 'ROC calls for exchange pacts,' *Free China Journal,* 7 (11).

FCR. (1997) 'Sci-Tech Development,' *Free China Review,* 47 (12).

Feldstein, Martin. (1998) 'Refocusing the IMF,' *Foreign Affairs.* March/April.

Ferdinand, Peter. (1996) *Take-Off for Taiwan?* London: Royal Institute of International Affairs.

Fogel, Joshua and Zarrow, Peter, eds. (1997) *Imagining the People: Chinese Intellectuals and the Concept of Citizenship,* Armonk, New York: M.E. Sharpe.

Foo Choy Peng and Cheung Lai-Kuen. (1997) 'Privatisation looms over the state sector,' *The South China Morning Post,* 11 September.

Frankel, Jeffrey A. and Andrew K. Rose. (1996) 'Currency Crashes in Emerging markets: An Empirical Treatment?' *Journal of International Economics,* 41: 351–66.

Friedman, Edward. (1994a) *The Politics of Democratization: Generalizing East Asian Experiences,* Boulder: Westview Press.

——. (1994b)'Reconstructing China's National Identity: A Southern Alternative to Mao-Era Anti-Imperialist Nationalism' *The Journal of Asian Studies,* 53(1): 67–91.

Fujiwara, Kiichi, (1992) 'Ajia Reisen no Kokusai Seiji Kozo: Chushin, Zensho, Shuhen [International Political Structure of the Cold War in Asia: Center, Front, Periphery]' in *Gendai Nihon Shakai* [*Modern Japanese Society*] 7: 327–61.

Fukuyama, Francis. (1989). 'The end of history?' *The National Interest* 16: 3–18.
——. (1992) *The End of History and the Last Man.* London: Penguin.
——. (1995) *Trust: the Social Virtues and the Creation of Prosperity.* New York: Free Press.
Garrett, Geoffrey and Deborah Mitchell. (1996) 'Globalization and the Welfare State: Income Transfers in the Industrial Democracies,1966–1990,' Unpublished paper. University of Pennsylvania: The Wharton School.
Gellner, Ernest. (1994) *Conditions of Liberty: Civil Society and Its Rivals,* London: Hamish Hamilton.
Gerffi, Gary, and Donald L. Wyman. (1990) *Manufacturing Miracles: Paths of Industrilization in Latin America and East Asia,* Princeton: Princeton University Press.
Gerschenkron, Alexander. (1962) *Economic Backwardness in Historical Perspective,* Cambridge: Harvard University Press.
Gilpin, Robert. (1981) *War and Change in World Politics,* Cambridge: Cambridge University Press.
Godement, Francois. (1997) *The New Asian Renaissance: From Colonialism to the Post-Cold War,* London: Routledge.
Graham, A. C. (1989) *Disputers of the Tao,* Lasalle: Open Court Publishing Co.
Graham, Edward. (1999) 'Restructuring the Chaebol in Korea,' pp. 32–38 in *Korea's Economy 1999.* Washington, DC: Korea Institute of America.
Greider, William. (1998) *One World, Ready or Not: The Manic Logic of Global Capitalism.* London: Touchstone Books.
Habermas, Jurgen, (1991) *The Structural Transformation of the Public Sphere: An Inquiry into a Category of Bourgeois Society.* Cambridge: MIT Press.
Haggard, Stephan. (1986) 'The newly industrializing countries in the international system,' *World Politics,* 39(2): 343–70.
Harris, Peter. (1998) *The Reforms in China and their Implications for Governance, Rights and Civil Society,* Stockholm: Ministry for Foreign Affairs.
Hecht, Jonathan. (1996) *Opening to Reform? An Analysis of China's Revised Criminal Procedure Law,* New York: Lawyers Committee for Human Rights.
Henderson, Callum. (1998) *Asia Falling: Making Sense of the Asian Currency Crisis and Its Aftermath,* New York: McGraw-Hill.
Herman, Kahn. (1973) *The Emerging Japanese Superstate: Challenge and Response.* Harmondsworth: Penguin.
Hirst, Paul and Grahame Thompson. (1996) *Globalization in Question – the International Economy and the Possibilities of Governance,* Cambridge: Polity Press.
HKTDC. (1998) *Market Profile on Mainland China,* Hong Kong: Trade Development Council.
Hobson, John M. (1997) *The Wealth of States: A Comparative Sociology of International Economic and Political Change,* Cambridge: Cambridge University Press.
Hoston, Germaine. (1994) *The State, Identity and the National Question in China and Japan.* Princeton: Princeton University Press.
Howe, Christopher. (1996) 'The Taiwan Economy,' *The China Quarterly* 148: 1171–95.
Hsiao, Kung-chuan. (1975). *A Modern China and a New World: K'ang Yu-wei, Reformer and Utopian, 1858–1927.* Seattle: University of Washington Press.

Huang, Philip C. (1993) ed. 'Symposium: "Public Sphere"/"Civil Society" in China? Paradigmatic Issues in Chinese Studies, III' *Modern China.* 19(2).

Hung, Rudy. (1996) 'The Great U-turn in Taiwan: Economic Restructuring and a Surge in Inequality.' *Journal of Contemporary Asia,* 26(2): 151–63.

Huntington, Samuel S. (1996) 'Western, but not universal,' *Foreign Affairs* 75(6): 28–46.

IMF. (1993) *World Economic Outlook,* Washington, DC: International Monetary Fund.

Jiang Zemin. (1997) 'Gao ju Deng Xiaoping lilun weida qizhi . . .' ['Raise high the great banner of Deng Xiaoping Theory . . .'], *Da Gong Bao,* 13 September.

Johnson, Chalmers. (1982) *MITI and the Japanese Miracle: The Growth of Industrial Policy, 1925–1975,* Stanford: Stanford University Press.

——. (1995) *Japan: Who Governs?. The Rise of the Developmental State,* London: Norton.

Jones, David M. (1997) *Political Development in Pacific Asia*, Cambridge: Polity Press.

Kamikawa, Takao, and Eietsu Imamatsu. (1997) eds. *Yen no Seiji-Keizai-gaku: Ajia to Sekai Sisutemu* [*The Political Economy of the Yen: Asia and the World System*]. Tokyo: Dobunkan.

Katz, Richard. (1998) *Japan, the System That Soured: The Rise and Fall of the Japanese Economic Miracle,* Armonk: M.E. Sharpe.

Katzenstein, Peter. (1985) *Small States in World Markets: Industrial Policy in Europe,* Ithaca: Cornell University Press.

KEIA. (1994) *Korea's Economy 1994.* Vol. 10, Seoul: Korea Economic Institute of America.

Kelliher, Daniel. (1997) 'The Chinese debate over village self-government' *The China Journal* 37(1): 63–86.

Kim, Dae-jung. (1999) *Gnomes – A New Foundation for the Korean Economy,* Seoul: Development Institute.

Kim, Duk-choong, and Dong-suk Suh. (1998) 'Financial Liberalization and Korean Corporations' Financing Policy for Globalization,' *Journal of Asian Economics.* 9(1).

Kim, Kwan S. (1985) *Politica Industrial y Desarrollo en Corea del Sur.* Mexico City: Nacional Financiera and UNIDO.

——. (1995) 'The Korean Miracle (1962–80) Revisited: Myths and Realities in Strategies and Development,' pp. 87–143 in H. Stein, ed. *Asian Industrialization and Africa – Studies in Policy Alternatives to Structural Adjustment.* New York: St Martin's Press.

——. (1997a) 'From Neo-Mercantilism to Globalism: the Changing Role of the State and South Korea's Economic Prowess,' pp. 83–105 in M. T. Berger and D. A.Borer, eds. *The Rise of East Asia: Critical Visions of the Pacific Century,* London: Routledge.

——. (1997b) 'Income Distribution and Poverty: An Interregional comparison,' *World Development,* 25(11): 1909–24.

Kim, Youn-Suk. (1998) 'The Korean Financial and Industrial Crisis: Causes and Implications,' *Korea Observer,* 29(3): 511–34.

——, and Hyeng- Keun Koo. (1998) 'the International Monetary Fund Policy and its Impact on Korean Chaebol.' Conference Paper, New York: the ASSA meeting.

Koo, Hyeng-Keun and Youn-Suk Kim. (1992) 'The Developmental State and Capital Accumulation in South Korea,' in R. Appelbaum and J. Henderson, eds. *States and Development in the Asian Pacific Rim*. Newbury Park: Sage.

Krugman, Paul. (1994) 'The myth of Asia's miracle,' *Foreign Affairs*. 73(6): 62–78.

——. (1998) 'Saving Asia: It's Time to Get Radical.' *Fortune* 7 September.

Lal, Deepak. (1983) *The Poverty of Development Economics*, London: Institute of Economic Affairs.

Lardy, Nicholas. (1998) *China's Unfinished Economic Revolution* Washington: Brookings.

Lawrence, Susan. (1998) 'Unfinished business – President Jiang puts his own stamp on reforms' *The Far Eastern Economic Review*, 17 December.

Lee, Jong-won. (1993) 'Higashi Ajia ni okeru Reisen to Chiiki Shugi: Amerika no Seisaku wo Chuusin ni [The Cold War and Regionalism in East Asia in American Policies],' pp.185–239 in Takehiko Kamo ed. *Koza Seiki Kan no Sekai Seiji* Vol. 3: *Ajia no Kokusai Chitsujo, Datsu Reisen no Eikyo* [World Politics at the Turn of the Century Vol. 3: Regional Order in Asia: The Effects of the End of the Cold War]. Tokyo: Nihon Hyoron-sha.

Lee, Peter Nan-shong. (1991)'The Chinese industrial state in historical perspective: from totalitarianism to corporatism,' pp. 153–79 in Brantly Womack, ed. *Contemporary Chinese Politics in Historical Perspective*, Cambridge: Cambridge University Press.

Leung, Tse-Kang. (1995) 'State, Business & Economic Interaction Across the Taiwan Strait,' *Issues & Studies* 31(11): 40–58.

Levi, Margaret. (1988) *Of Rule and Revenue*, Berkeley: University of California Press.

Leys, Simon. (1979) Mao Tse-tung and Chinese History' in *Broken Images: Essays on Chinese Culture and Politics*, London: Allison & Busby.

Li, Shenzhi. (1998) 'Ye yao tuidong zhengzhi gaige [We also need to promote political reform]', pp. 39–48 in Liu Zhifeng. ed. *Di qici geming* [*The Seventh Revolution*], Beijing: Jingji Ribao Chubanshe.

Liang, Qichao. (1989) 'Xin min shuo' ['On Renewing the People'] in *Yin bing shi he ji: zhuan ji*, vol. 6 book 4 [1902]. Beijing: Zhonghua shuju chuban she.

——. (1989) 'Xin shi xue' ['A New Historiography'] in *Yin bing shi he ji: wen ji*, vol. 1 book 9. [1902], Beijing: Zhonghua shuju chuban she.

Lieberthal, Kenneth. (1995) *Governing China: from Revolution Through Reform*, New York: Norton.

Lindauer, David, and Michael Roamer. (1994) *Asia and Africa: Legacies and Opportunities in Development*, San Francisco: Institute for Contemporary Studies.

Lingle, Christopher. (1996) *Singapore's Authoritarian Capitalism: Asian Values, Free Market Illusions, and Political Dependency*, Fairfax: The Locke Institute.

——. (1998) *The Rise and Decline of the 'Asian Century': False Starts on the Road to the 'Global Millennium,'* Hong Kong: Asia 2000.

Link, Perry. (1992) *Evening Chats in Beijing*. New York: Norton.

List, Friedrich, (1885) *The National System of Political Economy*, London: Longman.

Liu, Binyan, (1999) 'Climbing a Tree to Look for Fish,' *China Focus* 7(1).

Liu, I-chou. (1998) 'The Democratisation of Taiwan: Changing Political Structure and Diversified Mass Behavior,' unpublished manuscript, Taipei: National Chengchi University.

Liu, Ji. (1997) *Shehuizhuyi gaige lun* [*On socialist reform*], Shanghai: Shanghai renmin chuban she.

——. (1998) 'False dawn,' *The Far Eastern Economic Review* 1 October.

Liu, Zhifeng. ed. (1998) *Di qici geming: 1998 Zhongguo zhengfu jigou gaige luewanglu* [*The Seventh Revolution: a Memorandum on the Chinese Government's 1998 Administrative Reform*]. Beijing: Jingji ribao chuban she.

Ma, Shu-Yun. (1994) 'The Chinese Discourse on Civil Society' *The China Quarterly*, 137 (1): 180–93.

MAC. (1994) *Taihai liangan guanxi shuoming shu [On The Relations Cross the Taiwan Strait*, Taipei: Mainland Affairs Council.

MacFarquhar, Roderick. 1998. 'Reports from the Field: Provincial People's Congresses,' *The China Quarterly*, 155 (3): 656–67.

Mahbubani, Kishore. (1995) 'The Pacific Way,' *Foreign Affairs*. 74(1): 100–11.

Mao, Tsetung. (1977) [tr. Moss Roberts], *A Critique of Soviet Economics*, New York: Monthly Review Press.

Mao, Zedong. (1974) 'Talks at Three Meetings with Comrades Chang Ch'un-ch'iao and Yao Wen-yuan, February 1967,' in Stuart Schram, ed. *Mao Tse-Tung Unrehearsed – Talks and Letters: 1956–1971*, Harmondsworth, England: Penguin Books.

——. (1975) *Selected Works of Mao Tse-tung*, vol. 4, Beijing: Foreign Languages Press.

——. (1975) 'On the People's Democratic Dictatorship – In Commemoration of the Twenty-Eighth Anniversary of the Communist Party of China, June 30, 1949' in *Selected Works of Mao Tse-tung*, vol. 4, Beijing: Foreign Languages Press.

Marx, Karl. (1918) *Introduction To A Contribution To A Critique Of Political Economy* [1857], Chicago: Kerr.

MCA. (1993) *Zhongguo nongcun cunmin weiyuanhui huanjie xuanju zhidu* [*Study on the Election of Villagers Committees in Rural China*], Beijing: Ministry of Civil Affairs.

——. (1996) *Village Elections: Democracy in Rural China – Commentaries [by George Mathew, Frank Gibney and others]*, Beijing: Ministry of Civil Affairs.

——. (1994) *Zhongguo nongcun cunmin daibiao huiyi zhidu* [The Report on the Villagers Representative Assemblies in China]. Beijing: Ministry of Civil Affairs.

McCargo, Duncan. (1998) 'Elite governance: business, bureaucrats and the military,' pp. 126–149 in Richard Maidment, David Goldblatt and Jeremy Mitchell, eds. *Governance in the Asia-Pacific*, London: Routledge.

Meier, G. ed. (1991) *Politics and Policy Making in Developing Countries: Perspectives on the New Political Economy*. San Francisco: International Centre for Economic Growth.

Meisner, Maurice. (1996) *The Deng Xiaoping Era: An Inquiry into the Fate of Chinese Socialism, 1978–1994*, New York: Hill & Wang.

Migdal, Joel S., Atul Kohli and Vivienne Shue. (1994) *State Power and Social Forces*. Cambridge: Cambridge University Press.

Miller, Matthew and Dennis Eegbarth. (1998) 'Interview with the Finance Minister,' *South China Morning Post*, 9 July.

Miyazaki, Yoshikazu. (1992) Fukugo Fukyo: Posuto Baburu no Shoho-sen wo Motomete [*Depression Complex: In Search of Prescription for the Post-Bubble Economy*], Tokyo: Chuokoron-sha.

MOF. (1998) *Questions and Answers about the Internationalization of the Yen,* Tokyo: Ministry of Finance.

MOFA. (1993) Waijiao hengce baipishu [Foreign Policy White Paper], Taipei: Ministry of Foreign Affairs.

MOFE. (1998) *Challenge and Chance: Korea's Response to the New Economic Reality,* Seoul: Ministry of Finance and Economy.

MOFE. (1999) *The Road to Recovery in 1999,* Seoul: Ministry of Finance and Economy.

Monks, Robert and Nell Minow. (1996) *Corporate Governance,* Oxford: Blackwell.

Moon, Chung-in. and Rashemi Prasad. (1998) 'Networks, Politics and Institutions,' pp. 9–24 in Steve Chan, Cal Clark and Danny Lam, *Beyond the Developmental State: East Asia's Political Economics Reconsidered,* Basingstoke: Macmillan.

Murakami, Yasusuke. (1984) *Shin-chukan Taishu no Jidai: Sengo Nihon no Kaibo-gaku* [*The Era of New Middle Mass: Anatomy of Post-War Japan*], Tokyo: Chuokoron-sha.

Murakami, Yasusuke. (1992) *Shin-Koten no Seiji-Kiezai-gaku* [*Anti-Classical Political Economy*], Tokyo: Chuokoron-sha.

Nan, S. W., and C. H. Lee. (1995) 'Korea,' pp. 31–55 in S. Haggard and C. H. Lee, *Financial Systems and Economic Policy in Developing Countries,* Ithaca: Cornell University Press.

North, Douglass. (1981) *Structure and Change in Economic History,* New York: Norton.

NPS, (1998) *A Brief Introduction to China's Efforts to Improve its Legal System,* Beijing: National People's Congress.

NSC. (1997) *Hsinchu Industrial Science Park,* Taipei: National Science Council.

Oakeshott, Michael. (1975) *On Human Conduct,* Oxford: Oxford University Press.

Oi, Jean. (1995) 'The Role of the Local State in China's Transitional Economy,' *The China Quarterly* 144 (4):1132–49.

Olson, Mancur. (1965) *The Logic of Collective Action,* Cambridge: Cambridge University Press.

Park, Se-il. (1999) 'Labor Market Reform and the Social Safety Net in Korea,' pp. 202–20 in *Korea and the Asian Economic Crisis: One Year Later* Vol. 9. Seoul: Korea Economic Institute of America.

Pei, Minxin. 1997. 'Citizens vs. Mandarins: Administrative Litigation in China' in *The China Quarterly* 152 (4): 832–62.

——. (1998) 'Constructing the political foundations of an economic miracle,' pp. 39–58 in Henry S. Rowen, *Behind East Asian Growth: The Political and Social Foundations of Prosperity,* London: Routledge.

Peng, Foo Choy, and Cheung Lai-kuen. (1997) 'Privatisation looms over the state sector,' *The South China Morning Post* 11 September.

Pérez-Díaz, Victor. (1998) "State and Public Sphere in Spain during the Ancient Regime' *Ddalus* 127(3): 251–52.

Potter, Pitman B. (1995) 'Foreign Investment Law in the People's Republic of China: Dilemmas of State Control,' *The China Quarterly* 141(1): 168–70.

——. (1994) "Riding the Tiger: Legitimacy and Legal Culture in Post-Mao China,' *The China Quarterly* 138 (2): 325–358.

Pu, Xingzu, Ding Rongsheng, Sun Guanhong and Hu Jinxing. (1995) *Zhonghua renmin gongheguo zhengzhi zhidu* [*The Political System of the People's Republic of China*], Hong Kong: San lian shudian.

Pye, Lucian W. (1985) *Asian Power and Politics: The Cultural Dimensions of Authority,* Cambridge: Harvard University Press.

Radet, Steven and Jeffrey Sachs. (1998) *The Onset of the East Asian Financial Crisis,* National Bureau of Economic Research Working Paper 6680.

——. and Jong-Wha Lee. (1997) *Economic Growth in Asia,* Cambridge: Harvard Institute for International Development.

Rodrik, Dani. (1997) *Has Globalization Gone Too Far?* Washington, DC: Institute for International Economics.

Root, Hilton L. (1998) 'Distinctive institutions in the rise of industrial Asia,' pp. 59–77 in Henry S. Rowen, *Behind East Asian Growth: The Political and Social Foundations of Prosperity,* London: Routledge.

——. (1999) *The New Korea – Crisis Brings Opportunities,* Santa Monica: Milken Institute.

Rowen, Henry S. (1998*) Behind East Asian Growth: The Political and Social Foundations of Prosperity,* London: Routledge.

Sachs, Jeffrey. (1997) 'The wrong medicine for Asia,' *The New York Times,* 3 November.

Sanger, David E. (1998) 'Clinton Appeals for Joint Attack in Economic Crisis,' *The New York Times,* 6 October.

Schmidt, Helmut. (1989) *Men and Powers: A Political Retrospective,* New York: Random House.

Schmitter, Philippe. (1993) 'Corporatism,' pp. 195–198 in Joel Krieger, ed. *The Oxford Companion to Politics of the World,* Oxford: Oxford University Press.

Schram, Stuart. (1966) *Mao Tse-tung.* Harmondsworth: Penguin Books.

——. ed. (1974) *Mao Tse-tung Unrehearsed – Talks and Letters, 1956–1971,* Harmondsworth: Penguin Books.

Schwartz, Benjamin. (1985) *The World of Thought in Ancient China,* Cambridge: Harvard University Press.

Shutt, Harry D. (1998) *The Trouble with Capitalism: An Enquiry into the Causes of Global Economic Failure,* London: Zed Books.

Skocpol, Theda, Peter Evans and et. al. (1985) *Bringing the State Back In,* Cambridge: Cambridge University Press.

Soros, George. (1998) *The Crisis of Global Capitalism,* London: Little, and Brown.

Spruyt, Hendrik. (1994) 'Institutional selection in international relations: state anarchy as order,' *International Organization,* 48(4): 527–57.

SSB (1999) The State Statistical Bureau. *China Statistical Yearbook 1998,* Beijing: The State Statistical Bureau.

Stevenson, Richard W. (1998) 'Europeans Challenge U.S. in Economic Crisis,' *The New York Times,* 7 October.

Stiglitz, Joseph E. (1998) 'More Instruments and Broader Goals: Moving Toward the Post-Washington Consensus,' UNU/ WIDER Annual Lectures 2.

Strange, Susan. (1995) 'The defective state,' *Daelalus* 124(2): 55–74.

——. (1996) *Power Diffused: State and Non-state Authority in the World Economy.* Cambridge: Cambridge University Press.

Sun, Liping, Li Qiang and Shen Yuan. (1998) 'Zhongguo shehui jiegou zhuanxingde zhongjinqi qushi yu yinhuan [Trends and Problems in the Transition of Social Structure in China],' *Zhangliu yu guanli* [Strategy and Management], 30(5): 1–17.

Tai, Hung-chao. (1989) *Confucianism and Economic Development: An Oriental Alternative?* Washington, DC: Washington Institute Press.

Tang, S. Y. (1995) 'Informal Credit Markets and Economic Development in Taiwan.' *World Development* 23 (5): 845–55.

Tien, Hung-mao. (1989) *The Great Transition: Political and Social Change in the Republic of China*, Stanford: Hoover Institution Press.

——. and Yun-han Chu. (1996) 'Building Democracy in Taiwan,' *China Quarterly* 148(4): 1151–54.

——. and Tun-jen Cheng. (1997) 'Crafting Democratic Institutions in Taiwan,' *The China Journal*, 37: 1–31.

Tso, Wuhan. A. (1996) 'Developments in the Cross-Straits Economic Relationship.' *Issues & Studies* 32 (9):131–33.

Tung C., (1997) 'Deindustrialisation and the Decline of the Labor Movement in Taiwan,' *Industry of Free China*, 87(2).

Unger, Jonathan. (1989) 'State and Peasant in Post-Revolution China,' *Journal of Peasant Studies* 17(1): 114–136.

——. and Anita Chan. (1996) 'Corporatism in China: A Developmental State in an East Asian Context,' pp. 95–129 in Barrett McCormick and Jonathan Unger, eds. *China after Socialism: in the Footsteps of Eastern Europe or East Asia?* Armonk: M.E. Sharpe,

USCBC. (1998a) *Forecast '98: China's Economy*, New York: United States-China Business Council, 29 January.

——. USCBC. (1998b) *China Trade 1998*, New York: United States-China Business Council. 5 April.

——. 1998c) *Forecast '98: China's Foreign Trade*, New York: United States-China Business Council. 29 January.

——. USCBC. (1998d) *Forecast '98: Foreign Direct Investment*, New York: United States-China Business Council. 29 January.

——. USCBC. (1999a) *FDI in China, 1979–1998*, New York: United States-China Business Council. 12 March.

——. USCBC. (1999b) *China's Economic and Financial Indicators, 1994–1998*, New York: United States-China Business Council. 2 July.

Wade, Robert. (1985) 'East Asian Financial Systems as a Challenge to Economics: Lessons from Taiwan,' *California Management Review* 27 (4): 106–25.

——. (1990) *Governing the Market: Economic Theory and the Role of Government in East Asian Industrialisation*, Princeton: Princeton University Press.

——. (1995) 'Resolving the state-Market Dilemma in East Asia,' pp. 114–36 in Ha-Joon Chang and R. Rowthorn, eds. *The Role of the State in Economic Change*. Oxford: Clarendon Press.

Wakeman, Frederick, Jr. (1973) *History and Will: Philosophical Perspectives of Mao Tse-tung's Thought*, Berkeley: University of California Press.

——. (1998) 'Boundaries of the Public Sphere in Ming and Qing China,' *Daedalus* 127(3):167–90.

——. (1997) 'Civil Society in Late Imperial and Modern China,' pp. 325–51 in Frederick Wakeman and Wang Xi, eds. *China's Quest for Modernisation: A Historical Perspective*, Berkeley: University of California Press.

Walker, Tony. (1997) 'Li rallies behind flag of reform,' *The Financial Times* 15 September.

Wallerstein, Immanuel. (1974) *The Modern World-System I: Capitalist Agriculture and the Origins of the European World-Economy in the sixteenth Century*, New York: Academic Press.

Wang, V. Weicheng. (1997) 'Developing the Information Industry in Taiwan: Entrepreneurial State, Guerrilla Capitalists and Accommodative Technologists,' *Pacific Affairs* 68 (4): 551–78.

Weiss, Linda, and John Hobson. (1995) *States and Economic Development*, Cambridge: Polity Press.

——. (1998) 'Phoenix Rising? The Vulnerability of Neo-liberal Capitalism.' Conference Paper, August 20–22, Perth: Mordoch University.

Weiss, Linda. (1997) 'The myth of the powerless state,' *New Left Review* 225: 3–27.

——. (1998) *The Myth of the Powerless State: Governing the Economy in a Global Era*, Cambridge: Polity Press.

Westphal, L. E. (1990) 'Industrial Policy in an Export-Propelled Economy: Lessons from South Korea's Experience,' *Journal of Economic Perspective*, Summer: 41–59.

White, Gordon. (1988) *Developmental States in East Asia*, London: Macmillan.

——. Jude Howell and Shang Xiaoyuan. (1996) *In Search of Civil Society: Market Reform and Social Change in Contemporary China*, Oxford: Clarendon Press.

Williamson, Oliver. (1975) *Markets and Hierarchies*, New York: New York University Press.

World Bank. (1987) *World Development Report 1987*, Washington DC: World Bank.

——. (1992) 'Rethinking the state,' pp. 128–47 in *World Development Report 1991*. Washington, D.C: World Bank.

——. (1993) *The East Asian Miracle: Economic Growth and Public Policy*, New York: Oxford University Press.

——. (1995) *Policy Options for Reform of Chinese State-Owned Enterprises*, World Bank discussion paper no. 335. Washington DC: World Bank.

——. (1999) 'The World Bank and China,' Washington DC: World Bank.

Xia, Yong. ed. (1995) *Zou xiang quanlide shidai: zhongguo gongmin quanli fazhan yanjiu* [Towards an Era of Rights: Research into the Development of Civil Rights in China]. Beijing: Zhongguo zhengfa daxue chubanshe.

Xiao, Zhengqin. (1998) *Zhu neige zhiguo xin luxian* [*The New Administrative Strategy of Zhu Rongji's Cabinet*], Hong Kong: Pacific Century Press.

Xin, Xiangyang and Ni Jianzhong. (1995) eds. *Nan bei chun qiu: zhongguo hui buhui zou xiang fenlie* [North and south, Spring and autumn: Could China be heading towards a Split?]. Beijing: Zhongguo shehui chuban she.

Xinhua. (1998) 'Social Organization Registration and Management Regulations', *Xinhua News Agency*, 3 November.

Xiong, Yuezhi. (1987) *Zhongguo jindai minzhu sixiang shi* [*A History of Modern Chinese Democracy*], Shanghai: Shanghai renmin chuban she.

Xu, Bodong. (1998) 'Minjindang zhuanxin si you buke nizhuan zhi shi [The Inevitability of the DPP's Transition],' *Zhongguo shibao* [*China Times*], Feb. 12.

Yamazaki, Masakazu. (1996) 'Asia, a civilizationin the making,' *Foreign Affairs* 75(4): 106–18.

Yan, Shoucheng. (1997) 'Zhuangzi and Wang Fuzhi's Political Philosophy,' unpublished paper.

Yang, Tuan. (1998) 'A Study of NPOs [non-profit organisations] in China,' unpublished paper.

Yearbook. (1998) *ROC Yearbook 1997*, Taipei: The Executive Yuan.

Yoo, Seong Min. (1998) 'Democracy, Equity and Chaebol Reform,' *Korea Focus*. July/August: 1–15.

Index

For Product Safety Concerns and Information please contact our EU representative GPSR@taylorandfrancis.com Taylor & Francis Verlag GmbH, Kaufingerstraße 24, 80331 München, Germany